SCIENCE AND THE CHRISTIAN
EXPERIMENT

SCIENCE
AND THE
CHRISTIAN
EXPERIMENT

A. R. PEACOCKE
Fellow of St. Peter's College, Oxford

LONDON
OXFORD UNIVERSITY PRESS
NEW YORK   TORONTO
1971

Oxford University Press, Ely House, London W. 1

GLASGOW NEW YORK TORONTO MELBOURNE WELLINGTON
CAPE TOWN SALISBURY IBADAN NAIROBI DAR ES SALAAM LUSAKA ADDIS ABABA
BOMBAY CALCUTTA MADRAS KARACHI LAHORE DACCA
KUALA LUMPUR SINGAPORE HONG KONG TOKYO

Cloth bound edition: ISBN: 0 19 213953 3
Paper bound edition: ISBN: 0 19 213956 8

215
P356s

Made in Great Britain at the Pitman Press, Bath

Preface

The interaction between man's scientific analysis of the world around him and his innermost ideals and aspirations, often and unhappily denoted by the adjective 'religious', have generated an immense, if only rarely distinguished, literature. Adding another volume to this over-burdened shelf of the libraries can be justified only by my conviction that any hope of seeing man and his world steadily and seeing them whole must take seriously the perspectives which are afforded by the two great human enterprises of scientific and theological investigation— each with their interplay of, on the one hand, observation, experiment and experience and, on the other, reflection and rationalization. The radical developments in physics at the beginning of this century have only been equalled in their significance in the last 100 years of science by the new vistas opened up in recent years in cosmology by astrophysicists and in biology by molecular biologists. As a result there has developed a scientific perspective of the cosmos and of man within it which must now both constitute the inevitable framework for all our reflections and evoke a renewed sense of wonder at the world in which we find ourselves.

In the introductory chapter of this essay in synthesis of the scientific and theological enterprises, I have tried to delineate their dominant and characteristic features as experienced human activities. The logical and general philosophical status of their respective statements and methodologies is, of course, the concern of professional philosophers of science and of religion; the introduction to this essay is offered, rather, as a contribution to understanding how scientific activity appears from the standpoint of one involved in its practice. To this extent it is a personal view but one, I hope, which reveals the style and mood of the scientific approach to the world, even if it has not been possible to elaborate it in current philosophical terms. In this introduction a parallel account of the theological enterprise, also described from the standpoint of one committed to it, is attempted and brought into juxtaposition and so comparison with that of science. From these two stances, certain

v

similarities are seen to emerge which seem to the author not to have been adequately stressed elsewhere and which are usually concealed by differences in the social milieu and *mise en scène* of the two activities and by the dissimilarities between the two language 'games' and their respective rules of discourse.

The two major parts (I and II) of the essay then move on from this account of the *experience* of the scientific and theological enterprises to survey the respective contents of their *thinking*. The initial aim, in Part I, is to set out as impartially as possible the vista which the sciences now depict of the interconnectedness and development of the world from matter to man and to discern its dominant features and characteristics. These are then, in Part II, set alongside some traditional Christian affirmations, the broad basis of which has been sketched in an introductory chapter (4). Any degree of congruence, required changes in emphasis, and needs for radical revision in the theological affirmations are sought: this is, however, subsidiary to the attempt to discern if these two enterprises, these two directions of exploration, can be seen to be moving at all in the same direction—even if, like parallel lines, they can only meet at infinity. The insights and attitudes engendered by each should then be in harmony or, at least, mutually enriching, even if a common conceptual scheme may still elude us. From the experiential 'within' stance of the Introduction (Chap. 1), such a harmony and enrichment can be said to be a living reality for many who are both scientists and Christians, but Part II explores the extent to which the two kinds of talk, which result from their two kinds of experiment and experience, are in fact congruous.

This venture may well be judged to have foundered—earning only the disdain of the scientists, the disregard of the theologians and the scorn and contempt of the philosophers. Nevertheless, it must be attempted: firstly in order to elicit the dialogue which would compensate for the very real deficiencies in the intellectual equipment of a single author; secondly, because men are individually and corporately dissolving into mere assemblies of disparate and conflicting centres of activity and attitudes and are losing that sense of meaning in existence which is the ground both of personal integration and of social cohesion and community. A postscript takes up this theme in relation to man's wider activities: his control over nature, his work and his hopes. The divorce between the critical scientific approach to the world and the deeply enriching awareness of man-in-the-sight-of-God in our Western civilization has now become one of the major causes, in the author's view, of that neurosis in their mutual progeny and heir, modern Western man, which is most manifest in his characteristic loss of hope. It is an awareness of this increasingly critical situation and a glimpse of the possibility of an enriching and mutual harmonization between these two vital human concerns and activities which prompts the offering of this essay.

An attempt of this kind cannot hope to deal at all fairly and comprehensively with the many issues on which there should be at least a dialogue between those involved in the scientific and theological enterprises. These have been most magisterially surveyed by I. G. Barbour in his *Issues in Science and Religion* (London, 1966) and I willingly refer the reader to that work for a systematic and documented account. My aim has been to indicate a style of approach, to point a direction for mutual exploration, with no attempt to make comparison with other similarly intended probings. More particularly, there is little mention of the reflections of Teilhard de Chardin, or of the work of the process theologians or of the philosophy of A. N. Whitehead, which they find so fruitful. My own thinking has developed quite independently of both Chardin and the process theologians, some of whose works I have only recently read, though a longstanding, but incomplete, acquaintance with Whitehead's writings cannot have been without influence. I can only hope that readers will weigh my own approach in the light of these others and so contribute to the ongoing task of synthesis.

Scientifically oriented readers will note the omission of any adequate account of the impact of relativity theory on the concepts of matter,[1] energy,[1] space and time and of any detailed examination of the chances of finding living organisms elsewhere than on the Earth. Both have important implications for the discussion in Parts I and II; however, the first has long been the theme of authors much better-equipped in this respect and

[1] There appears to be no suitable English word for what can only be called the 'stuff of the world' (matter $\rightleftharpoons$ energy)—a word which will not implicitly exclude those forms of it which are living and/or conscious and/or self-conscious.

the latter still lacks definitive observations which would allow detailed assessment. Theologically oriented readers will note only a tentative account of one approach to the problem of evil, in the context of man seen as an evolving and evolved creature, and an entirely inadequate reference to the insights of religions other than Christianity. These omissions stem, I trust, from no insensitivity to, on the one hand, man's degradation and tragedies or, on the other, to his attainments in non-Christian societies. But they do provide a spur to widen the scope of the approach outlined and an invitation to others to complement these present deficiencies.

I would like to think that this essay is written in the spirit of that catholic and universal approach to science and man which characterized two very different men to whom I am much indebted, Canon Charles Raven and Sir Cyril Hinshelwood, the former by his writings and the latter both by his works and his conversation and guidance as tutor and mentor in research. Hinshelwood's sceptical clarity and broad vision is well brought out in the references to human consciousness in his Anniversary Address to the Royal Society as President in 1959.

I am, it is true, not certain that other people have consciousness. Neither indeed am I certain that the atomic nucleus exists. But I regard its existence as in the highest degree probable. I regard consciousness in other people as equally probable and for similar reasons. The atomic nucleus is not directly observed. It is inferred by elaborate reasoning from many complex experiments, any one of which could probably be given alternative interpretations. What carries conviction is the fact that a coherent body of doctrine emerges from large numbers of varied tests.

We are all the time trying experiments on our relations with other people, informing, asking, ordering, obeying, resisting with varying emotions which are correlated with our actions. Human evolution has developed an elaborate and sensitive communication system, brought into play in innumerable ways. The hypothesis that other people have an interior life not unlike my own enables me to register correspondences at point after point in so intricate a way that I accept the hypothesis, if not as absolute truth, then as something nearly as good. And with most of the basic conclusions of science I am in no position to demand more.[1]

[1] *Proc. Roy. Soc.*, **253A**, 446 (1959).

I would suggest, and here Raven would also have concurred, that theology, too, like other human studies, equally attempts to 'register correspondences at point after point' between the experiences of men of the ways of God with them and to form these into a coherent framework or model as a basis for future action and new experiences.

I owe much to Professor J. G. Davies and Mr. J. H. Eaton, of the Department of Theology of the University of Birmingham (at that time under Professor G. W. H. Lampe), who first initiated me into theology as an intellectual discipline. My more immediate indebtedness is to various colleagues and friends who have attempted to save me from the pitfalls that await anyone who trespasses outside his professional reserve. More particularly, the comments on the whole original draft by Mr. John Howes of the Philosophy Department of Melbourne University and by Canon David Jenkins, the Director of Humanum Studies of the World Council of Churches (both formerly at Oxford), were invaluable—though they bear no responsibility for, and certainly do not necessarily agree with, the positions adopted. The community of an Oxford college allows personal contact with scholars of many disciplines and I have been much helped by the willing advice of my colleagues at St. Peter's, Mansfield, and other colleges. The kind criticisms of my wife and son, with their own particular expertise and awarenesses, were as salutary as they are too often taken for granted: so also, and too often, are the advice and labours of the officers of the Oxford University Press, in particular Mr. G. N. S. Hunt, whose advice I found invaluable and who largely shaped the first appendix on orders of magnitude.

Acknowledgements

For permission to include extracts from the under-mentioned works acknowledgement is made to the following copyright-holders and publishers:

Collins Publishers, London, for quotations from *Le Milieu Divin* by Teilhard de Chardin (English translation, Fontana Books, 1964).

Penguin Books Ltd, for quotations from Dante, *The Divine Comedy*: *Inferno* translated by Dorothy L. Sayers, 1949; and *Paradiso* translated by Dorothy L. Sayers and Barbara Reynolds, 1962.

SCM Press Ltd, for quotations from D. E. Jenkins, *The Glory of Man*, 1967.

Contents

page

POSTSCRIPT

INTRODUCTION

CHAPTER 1

The scientific and theological enterprises

I. ATTITUDES AND PRESUPPOSITIONS

This essay is written with the intention, and under the constraint, of maintaining consistently two principal attitudes. The first takes seriously the knowledge of the structure and development of the world and of man which the perspective of modern science affords. Although our present knowledge must represent only a fragment of the understanding yet to be acquired, certain broad features have been established sufficiently securely to justify this talking of 'the perspective of modern science'. The human sciences, other than medicine, and the social sciences are still only relatively recent in their growth and will almost certainly radically change our outlook on ourselves. Part I of this essay is confined to the perspective of the physical and biological sciences, not only because of the author's limitations, which are real enough, but also because it seems that a generally agreed body of knowledge in the social sciences (with perhaps the exception of economics) is only just beginning to emerge. There is much to re-think in Christian theology in the light of a science confined to the physical and biological worlds and the present essay attempts to contribute to this limited objective with the hope that others will eventually concern themselves with the impact of the social sciences. This process of taking seriously the perspective and content of modern science so as to build it into the fabric of theological thought has scarcely begun, no doubt because most theologians have little scientific training and vice versa. The need for this dialogue is perennial and is as urgent as ever, judging by the number of sermons, for example, on the nature of man which ignore the biological perspective.

The other main intent of this essay is also to take seriously the theological enterprise. The collapse of the medieval theological citadel during the last 300 years and its recent

3

undermining from within has tended to hide a soundness in its foundations which is greater than is usually conceded by those whose education has lacked any disciplined inquiry into the intellectual development of Christianity. Those who have undergone the process of higher education in Great Britain seem to be entirely unaware of the rigorous and careful thinking and investigation to which Christian origins and theological conceptions have been and are being subjected, so that the 'new theology' with its apparent emphasis on intellectual honesty and a thoroughgoing scepticism is thought to be a new departure and is attended to on this account. The 'new theology' and the 'new reformation', which some would see come from it, originate in the concern to show the relevance of the Gospel to the life of modern industrial man and to make explicit the deep involvement of God in man's secular life. These are proper concerns but in this recovery of relevance it has, I think, been too readily overlooked that men may be failing to respond to the Gospel not simply because it appears irrelevant but because it appears untrue. Much of the 'new theology' is anti-theological in the sense that it eschews affirmations and propositions about the realities of nature, man and God, as seen in the light of Christ and of the experience of the people of Israel, and prefers to see the relevance of the Gospel in existential terms. For example, the seventh thesis of a compilation of '95 Theses for the New Reformation'[1] affirms that 'Theology is part of man's search for God. God is beyond the limits of human reason, so when theology claims to present the truth it is making gods of men.' What has never been made clear by the exponents of the new theology of the new reformation is how God can be known to be present and experienced in any particular situation in life, whether personal, family, industrial, or national, unless the experiencing individual has already some concept and inkling of him to whose voice he is attending within that particular situation. If nothing can ever be said about God, it is not surprising if men experience nothing of him in life. In other words, the sharp cutting edge of man's desire and willingness to live the Christian life in a complete secular mode and context is blunted if he remains unaware of the intellectual content of men's reflection upon God, which I take to be the essence of

---

[1] *New Christian*, 19 Oct. 1967, No. 54, p. 12.

theology. I do not think that the whole of Christian theology has to be dismantled before the new synthesis required by modern man can be effected. I can only hope to urge my scientific and other contemporaries to look, perhaps for the first time, at the intellectual foundations and development of Christianity. I do not pretend they will be satisfied with all they see. Indeed, I am sure that the edifice of Christian theology needs extensive reconstruction and extension by acquiring new symbols, new interpretative principles, new imaginative analogies and connections between its own and other modes of thought. These are indeed precisely the needs of any lively and vigorous human inquiry, such as that of natural science, which is not respected the less for being in part rigorous and established and in part tentative and speculative.

In both the scientific and theological enterprises the primary question must be 'Why?'; in both, the grounds and evidence for hypotheses and beliefs summarized in apparently propositional terms must be sought, with the realization that different types of evidence are relevant to particular types of question. This questioning approach, this asking 'Why?', will mean that we adopt a sceptical attitude to authority, whether that of the Bible, the Church, or of those speaking in the name of science ('the Bible says', 'the Church says', 'Science says'). This does not mean that all authority must be repudiated: only that authority must be authenticated to be heeded. The approach intended may tentatively be described as experimental (in the sense discussed in 3 (c) below) in the theological as well as in the scientific context. A sense of adventure and a zest in inquiry is, or should be, as much a part of the Christian and theological enterprise as it is of the scientific; for Christian theology affirms that God as creative Word was and is expressed in the stuff of the world, both in its whole ongoing process and in a particular human being. On these Christian assumptions, there is to be found in the world that which makes search worth while by means of both the scientific and theological enterprises, the courses of which should therefore also be expected ultimately to converge.

In Part I of this essay the perspective of the world which is provided by the various sciences is sketched, and in Part II an attempt is made to re-consider some of the major themes and

features of Christian thinking set in this perspective. Only in the
process of setting the two expositions alongside each other as
fairly and impartially as possible within the compass of a short
essay, can any complementarity be detected and the tentative
emergence of any new synthesis be discerned. We shall be concerned with such questions as 'What is the significance of matter
and of the created world?'; 'What is the Christian doctrine of
creation?'; 'What is the relation of the traditional doctrine of
the triune nature of the Godhead to our understanding of God's
creative activity?'; 'What is the relation of the idea of the immanence of God to the scientific account of cosmic evolution?';
'How is human personality to be understood in the light of both
evolution and of the Christian affirmation that God became a
man in history?' Such an inquiry may often lead to a 'reverent
agnosticism' concerning particular events such as the Virgin
Birth or a particular miracle. For the evidence may be inconclusive, even when the *a priori* possibility of such an event occurring has not been ruled out in advance of the examination of
the evidence. This reverent agnosticism may well prove to be
a permissible, even permanent, attitude towards some events
but not necessarily towards all. For in their character certain
of the Christian understandings, especially those about the person of Christ, are so all-pervasive in their consequences that
living demands a commitment from us one way or the other.
Our inquiries can only provide pointers to or a basis for such
an existential commitment, and cannot be coercive. At this
point intellectual discourse must make way for that word which
demands challenge and response—a different exercise.

Setting the scientific and theological endeavours alongside
each other seems also to me to be worth while because they both
concern human experiences and, for some of us, different experiences of the same individual. The 'I' who notes an observation
in the laboratory and who tries to link this observation with
others and so to create a satisfying model or 'explanation' of it,
is the same 'I' who reflects on his own destiny and on the meaning and purpose, if any, of the cosmos, and who has intimations
of that Other, that ground of Being, whose presence echoes
through the literature and prayers of the centuries. The contrast
between these two experiences became very apparent to me one
summer when working in a multi-million-pound laboratory

while my lodgings were in a cathedral close justly famed for its quiet beauty. There could have been no greater contrast between the world of science and that of the Christian faith: the one apparently confident, forward-looking, efficient, intellectual, alert and completely secular; the other, apparently traditional, somnolent, conservative, evocative—and claiming to testify to a world other than that which meets the senses. Yet it was twentieth-century men who were involved in the central activities of both. Man is indeed the greatest of his own problems to himself. 'Homo sum; humani nil a me alienum puto'—'I am a man and reckon nothing human alien to me'—and this alone would justify the exercise of comparing the experience of scientist and Christian thinker.

2. THE VISION OF UNITY

Men seek an integrated understanding of nature, of themselves and of their place in nature. Yet this urge which drives forward the sciences, by its very success and the increase of knowledge which it engenders, seems to render even more unattainable the aim for which the whole enterprise was first undertaken. Many have even given up any hope of a unified view of the inorganic and organic worlds, of the life of man and of human societies. When they catch a glimpse of a great synthesis, at once poetic and true to the science of its day, such as Dante unfolds in *The Divine Comedy*, they can only, it seems, wistfully regret that such integration is no longer possible. It is as though man has, by his intellectual, technological and creative efforts planted many seeds which have burgeoned into the 'dark wood' out of which Dante[1] had to be led so painfully, first by Virgil, the image of human wisdom, and then by Beatrice, the bearer and transmitter of experience of the divine. The famous opening of the *Inferno*, and so of the whole work, is peculiarly descriptive of the state of many minds today:

> Nel mezzo del cammin di nostra vita
> mi ritrovai per una selva oscura,
> chè la diritta via era smarrita.

---

[1] Dante the man, Dante-in-the-poem, and Dante as representative of all men. Here and elsewhere Dante quotations are from the translations of Dorothy Sayers and Barbara Reynolds (London, 1949, 1955, 1962).

Midway this way of life we're bound upon,
I woke to find myself in a dark wood,
Where the right road was wholly lost and gone.

Even for Dante, who lived in a world rendered simpler by its ignorance of complexities of which we are only too well aware, the journey from the 'dark wood' to the final vision of unity was long and arduous and frightful, in the full sense of the word. Yet the instinct that in some sense the world, all life, and ourselves are one, are part of some great unity, still haunts us and provides the intellectual passion behind our scientific endeavours when ambition and self-interest are pared away. Men will not be satisfied with a perspective of the world which indefinitely fragments their experience; they need a framework which will enable them to weld their individual and corporate lives and thought into an integrated whole. This essay has been written from the conviction that not only is this quest worthwhile, but that at the present it is far from being hopeless; that there are pointers to a new synthesis of the disparate enterprises of science and theology which might surprise our immediate predecessors, though perhaps not Dante. Such a vision of a new unity in diversity must never become a straitjacket and will always have a provisional character. Even the medieval synthesis of Dante was not a resting-point, for the Love he glimpses at the close of the *Paradiso* is a 'love that moves the sun and the other stars': and he describes his state as one in which 'all speech is vanquished and must lag behind' (Canto xxxiii, l. 56), as though he is still following, however falteringly.

This is a lofty aim and many have abandoned it as hopeless during the last few decades as the growth of knowledge has overwhelmed us. However, our very awareness of the fragmentation of knowledge has heightened our desire and need to seek a new unity. The breakdown of our intellectual life into two cultures, in the terminology of C. P. Snow, has been much discussed. Two has always seemed to be a gross underestimate:[1] the physicist is divided from the physiologist and the psychologist from both as much as all three are divided from the man of letters, and all four from the theologian. The division involves not only a lack of knowledge of the content of each others'

---

[1] As, to be fair, it also seemed to Snow himself.

activities, which could scarcely be culpable in view of our finite time and capacities, but also, and more importantly, frequently an incomprehension of the nature of the others' inquiry and even scepticism as to its value. This situation has been much commented upon, and was focused in Sir Walter Moberly's *Crisis in the Universities* (1949). It is becoming increasingly difficult in intellectual and academic circles to enter into effective discourse with one's colleagues about the actual content of one's intellectual work, and conversation is inevitably confined to the banalities of academic politics, or worse.

This fragmentation of our intellectual life is, however, not only experienced socially, with perturbing effects on academic and intellectual life, but extends to the individual himself. The scientist or technologist, as such, is from his outward aspect confident, optimistic and always driving forward in his enterprises. He apparently never questions the right of science to continue its researches or of technology to reap its fruits, however bitter they ultimately prove. He appears to conform to the professed aims of a scientific and technological society to reshape the world to man's convenience. Yet, concurrently with this outward optimism, the literature of existentialism shows men of sensitivity reacting with nausea when confronted with the Absurd, or urging courage before despair. The extremes of these two approaches are rarely completely represented in one individual, but something of each colours the mood of most modern men at one time or another. As a recent Bampton lecturer has put it:

When operating on the scientific and material side he [modern man] is optimistic and purposeful. When reflecting on the human and spiritual side he is pessimistic and hopeless, so much so that he is prepared in one way or another to write off the achievements of his scientific side and his own personalness with them.[1]

Perhaps this ambivalence in modern man, and in the modern scientist in particular, is the root of that other curious anomaly whereby the scientist is assigned the role of oracle, clairvoyant and seer by society as a whole, yet scientists themselves on the whole avoid involvement in political and social activity, even when it concerns the application of their scientific knowledge.

[1] David E. Jenkins, *The Glory of Man* (London, 1967), p. 74.

This division of man from man through the fragmentation of knowledge, and this division within man through lack of a unified vision of the world may be a natural result of the economy of time and effort which stems from specialization. But the cost is now becoming crippling to man's inner and outer life and the dangers more apparent. For in addition to the widely recognized danger to man of a science increasingly divorced from human values, there is a much less recognized danger to science itself. For the very possibility of the human enterprise which we now call science is based, as Polanyi[1] urged, on the existence of a society which makes certain common value judgements. Even the actual development of scientific knowledge itself requires scientists to be able to bridge the chasms which have been dividing the different sciences from each other (as witness the varied backgrounds of 'molecular biologists'), for nature is still one, even if the sciences are many. So, even for the sake of science itself, we are required to seek a wider perspective, as well as for man and for the quality of life which is available to him in a world increasingly dominated by science and its progeny, technology.

I suspect that at the present time the situation is peculiarly fluid and men of very different intellectual disciplines are willing to ask the wider questions to which theology has sought to provide an answer based on religious experience. Physical and biological scientists are less arrogantly confident than in the past that their disciplines can provide the cure of men's ills and are more willing to recognize the human dimension in existence, and the mystery of human personality. Recently in Western Europe and America a smaller proportion of university entrants than before has preferred science to the humanities. This tendency disturbs those who try to plan economies, but very few scientists have had the confidence to affirm that these young people are actually mistaken in their choice, for they themselves are not entirely sure where science is leading.

Although for two or three generations the case for secular humanism[2] has been strongly urged as the only doctrine compatible with the sciences, there has in fact been a notable lack

---

[1] M. Polanyi, *Science, Faith and Society* (London, 1946).

[2] As distinct from Christian humanism, which has other and, I would say, deeper roots (see Chapter 6 (3) (c)).

of general response among scientists to these counsels. Indeed, it is likely that the proportion of practising, convinced Christians among scientists is no less, and, to my observation, possibly larger, than in the population as a whole. Although most scientists are vaguely agnostic and uncommitted to any position, they have not notably embraced the secular humanist view either. It is impossible, without further investigation, to say why this is so; perhaps it is because, as one senior scientist put it to me, secular humanism 'lacks the resonance' which is possessed by the Christian faith, with its centuries of associated music, art, literature and architecture and its ability to evoke the sense of the numinous. Be this as it may, it is clear that scientists, *qua* scientists, have not as a whole opted strongly or uniformly for any one particular world-view,[1] and the present situation seems to me to be more open in this respect than for some time past.

The preceding apologia is not meant to conceal the difficulties in the way of any attempt at synthesis, however provisional, even if, as I intend, the attempt which follows is confined to seeking and describing the method by which unity and integration are to be sought rather than that unity itself. The difficulties of any author who makes such an attempt are his own very partial and limited knowledge, with the attendant dangers of appearing half-baked to the expert, unconvincing to the novice, and satisfying to none. The task is a many-sided and formidable one and should be the work of a generation. This attempt, because of the author's interests, as well as his limited competence, is concerned with only one of the supposed tears in the robe of knowledge and experience—that between the activities of scientific and theological inquiry, between experience of the natural world and experience of God.

To whom should such a work be addressed? Until recent years with new developments in educational methods, especially in the arts, the education of scientists and technologists, and of many others, has been peculiarly lacking in its ability to evoke imagination which is the basis of any sensitive awareness of the full dimensions of human existence. On the other hand, those whose education has been dominated by the humanities have

---

[1] Perhaps we should qualify this by adding 'in Britain', for here the relation between Christian thinkers and scientists has developed quite differently, and more amicably, than in the rest of Europe.

understood and caught so little of the spirit of scientific inquiry that they have never acquired even that sense of wonder at the world which the perspectives of modern science can evoke. New developments in educational methods in science may eventually rectify this but these have appeared noticeably later than in the teaching of the arts—and this tardiness may, indeed, have been partly responsible for the 'swing from science'. The consequence of this double impoverishment in contemporary education is that few aspire to the ancient ideal, of both Greek and Christian humanism, that of the whole man to whom all human knowledge and activity is significant and who, while recognizing his limitations, desires to integrate his intellectual, moral, aesthetic, personal and religious experiences. I can only hope that this essay, in attempting to set alongside each other the nature and content of the particular human experiences which constitute science and theological inquiry, may help to refurbish and resuscitate this ideal.

3. THE SCIENTIFIC AND THEOLOGICAL ENTERPRISES COMPARED

Before going any further with this examination of the results which have accrued from the two activities of science and theology, it is worth comparing their character as experienced by those involved in them. Certain similarities and differences appear to the participants, and the balance and emphasis is not always quite the same as in the logical analyses made, quite properly, by philosophers of both science and religion. They are worth examining because it is usually the character of these experiences, with their complex interplay of intellect and emotion, which determines attitudes to the affirmations of a more general and propositional kind made by scientists and theologians in their respective intellectual systems. Hence, in the following sections, it is the experienced characters of the two activities which are compared. No attempt is made at that more rational and logical analysis of the principles and possibility of knowledge of the universe and of God which philosophers must continue to pursue.

A difficulty in terminology is encountered at the outset. The word 'science' denotes a fairly well-defined activity, both practical and intellectual, aimed at understanding the physical and biological world or, as is often said, 'discovering' its nature and structure. There are, of course, complex and difficult questions about the status of the hypotheses, laws, models and structures of the scientist and their relation to what he observes in the world. Nevertheless, the word 'science' stands for a recognizable and, on the whole, respectable activity. However, this is not the case with the word 'religion', which denotes a whole complex of human phenomena operating at various personal and social levels and at various levels of emotion, will and intellect. According to one's prejudices and preferences, the word 'religion' can evoke in the first instance, a picture of the horrors of the Inquisition, the fervour surrounding the visit of a Pope to the shrine of Fatima, the narrowness of Protestant social taboos, the quiet sanctity of a saint, Billy Graham campaigns, or the ordered dignity of an English cathedral evensong. It rarely suggests an activity directed at understanding. Indeed, there seems to be no generally accepted word for the activity itself in which man attempts to understand his personal and social experiences and destiny in relation to the nature and destiny of the cosmos and to its ground of Being, to God. The word 'theology' unfortunately suggests a purely academic, scholarly, not to say bookish, occupation little related to life and experience. But at least it has the virtue of suggesting an inquiring, searching activity, even if its field of operation, its laboratory as it were, is as wide as life itself. For this reason, in spite of its limitations, and its cold and distant aspect to the average Christian, I have preferred to use the word 'theology' or the term 'theological enterprise' to describe that reflective and rational analysis of man's religious experiences which I wish to relate to man's scientific activity.

(a) *Abstraction and personal involvement*

The beginner in learning science and the non-scientist who can only examine science from the outside by noting the tone and content of scientific papers and books might well be forgiven for thinking that science is an entirely impersonal activity. For scientific thinking is apparently highly abstract: for its particular purpose, it seems to be precluded from considering any common phenomenon in its wholeness. The beauty of a sunset and the graceful lines of a taree, as appreciated by an observer, the poet, or even 'l'homme moyen sensuel', are personal reactions which are excluded from the purview of science so that the elements which are observed and noted are only those capable of quantitative formulation, and which can be generalized for comparison and correlation with the same features of other parallel phenomena (sunsets, trees, etc.).

This process of abstraction from the experience which constitutes any commonly observed phenomenon also extends to the more formalized phenomena of laboratory experiments. Only certain features are recorded and noted, many variables are not recorded at all and much of the judgement which a scientist acquires by training and research experience is concerned with discerning which observations are relevant to a particular problem. How far this process of abstraction distorts, or even replaces, the picture of the world which science constructs has been much discussed. A. N. Whitehead[1] described this process of abstraction, as represented in Locke's distinction between primary and secondary qualities, in a famous passage:

The primary qualities are the essential qualities of substances whose spatio-temporal relationships constitute nature. The orderliness of these relationships constitutes the order of nature. . . . But the mind in apprehending also experiences sensations which, properly speaking, are qualities of the mind alone. These sensations are projected by the mind so as to clothe appropriate bodies in external nature. . . . Thus nature gets credit which should in truth be reserved for ourselves; the rose for its scent; the nightingale for his song; and the sun for his radiance. The poets are entirely mistaken. They should address their lyrics to themselves, and should turn them into odes of self-congratulation on the excellency of the human mind. Nature is a dull affair, soundless, scentless, colourless; merely the hurrying of material, endlessly, meaninglessly.

He goes on to discuss how this practical outcome of the characteristic scientific philosophy of the close of the seventeenth century has dominated even the organization of our academic studies. He continues:

No alternative system of organising the pursuit of scientific truth has been suggested. It is not only reigning, but it is without a rival.

[1] A. N. Whitehead, *Science and the Modern World* (Mentor Books ed., New York, 1949), pp. 55–6.

And yet—it is quite unbelievable. This conception of the universe is surely framed in terms of high abstractions, and the paradox only arises because we have mistaken our abstraction for concrete realities.

I am not concerned now to follow further the discussion and counter-argument which this judgement has engendered, important as it is for arriving at an understanding of the relation between the world and scientific laws and models. My present concern is to stress that scientific experiment and observation involve a process of abstraction from man's experience—a process necessary for the construction of scientific concepts, models and hypotheses, but a process of abstraction nevertheless. Awareness by acquaintance cannot be fully subsumed into knowledge by description; or, to use Polanyi's terms, 'tacit' knowing is a *Gestalt* phenomenon with its own valid form of awareness and is distinct from explicit knowledge of particulars. The content of public, scientific knowledge is, once ascertained, of the descriptive, explicit kind and cannot, in principle, afford a comprehensive account of the fullness of our experience of the world, which is 'by acquaintance' and 'tacit'—and, least of all, of our experience of each other. The scientific method provides an analysis of the content of human experience which is partial and abstractive (in Whitehead's sense) and complementary, but not alternative, to that afforded by the humanities, including theology.

The preceding section has referred to the non-personal, explicit character of scientific knowledge once it is obtained. However, the process by which statements gain general and approved currency in the scientific community, and the way in which the individual makes his discoveries are both intimately related to the scientific enterprise as an activity of persons. The co-operative character of its inquiries and the role of the free community of scientists in transmitting new paradigms, concepts, models and hypotheses, and in formulating criteria of judgement, are absolutely essential to science. This is part of the experience of every practising scientist. Scientific work would be impossible but for the existence of this community characterized by value judgements, even if these are implicitly assumed rather than explicitly enforced.

The role of the community in the theological enterprise is

perhaps more obvious, though frequently misunderstood. The community in this context appears to have as its chief function the formulation of its teaching and the regulation of corporate worship. However, these are only the external and legalistic aspects of a process of description and transmission of a common experience which has both a past and present reference. The Christian community looks back to those events in history from which it stems, the life and resurrection of Christ; and also communicates and invites to a contemporary common experience through the general interchange of ideas and through common worship. The community of Judaism similarly has its historical reference point in the Exodus and Covenant at Sinai and its contemporary ongoing life which looks to, but is not limited by, that past experience. Both the scientific and theological enterprises would be impossible except as the activity of a community of persons.

The individual, personal element in theological activity perhaps needs no stressing; indeed it is too often regarded, in the Protestant world at least, as entirely individual, personal and subjective with little inter-personal reference. However, the involvement of the individual in scientific discovery is often overlooked, apparent though it is to working scientists, most of whom have their occasional moments of personal insight. The role of personal imagination and intuition in the development of concepts, models and hypotheses from other sources has been emphasized, by a number of authors.[1] Although the hypothetico-deductive view of the scientific method, combined with Popper's emphasis[2] on the role of falsification in rejecting unsuitable hypotheses, is in many ways an adequate description of the explicit conscious processes of science, it gives little account of how concepts, models and hypotheses actually arise and are selected from the multitude of possibilities or, if falsified, are replaced or modified. Extension, analogies and previously

---

[1] P. B. Medawar, 'Hypothesis and imagination', in *The Art of the Soluble* (London, 1967), p. 131; W. I. B. Beveridge, *The Art of Scientific Investigation* (London, 1950), Chaps. v and vi; I. G. Barbour, *Issues in Science and Religion* (London, 1966), pp. 142–4; M. Polanyi, op. cit., and *The Study of Man* (London, 1959); J. Bronowski, *Science and Human Values* (New York, 1956); A. Koestler, *The Act of Creation* (New York, 1964); B. Ghiselin, ed., *The Creative Process* (Berkeley, 1952); R. Harré, *Theories and Things* (London and New York, 1961), Sect. 2, and *The Principles of Scientfiic Thinking* (London, 1970).

[2] K. R. Popper, *The Logic of Scientific Discovery* (London, 1959).

unthought-of juxtapositions of observations and ideas[1] all seem to play their part but the total act is itself elusive and wholly personal—there appear, indeed, to be no defined procedures, no clear-cut recipes, no readily ascertainable personal qualities that will ensure success.[2] There are, of course, in the history of science many striking recorded instances of the role of the imagination in making a new creative synthesis of former ideas or sometimes an entirely new leap: as, for example, Kekulé's half-dreaming of the ring form of benzene, Darwin's reading of Malthus and joining this with the idea of *natural* selection to provide the key to understanding evolution, and Watson and Crick's realization that DNA[3] is a double helix. Everyday science proceeds less dramatically and is conducted by very widely different kinds of persons, but the creation of new concepts, models, hypotheses and techniques[4] still involves some kind of individual, personal, imaginative act.

The process of testing these products of the creative scientific imagination is one in which deductive, verifying and falsifying activities, both theoretical and experimental, of the originator and of others are all necessary: at this level the model, hypothesis, etc., becomes open to public discourse and test and becomes a candidate for acceptance as part of the explicit knowledge of the scientific community.

In summary, it may be said that both the scientific and theological enterprises are personal activities in the context of a community and that this personal dimension is a necessary element in the attainment of their ends. The terminology of the statements which constitute the resulting scientific knowledge have an abstracted and de-personalized character[5] which is less marked in theological statements, which retain even in their most credal forms analogical and symbolic terms with personal overtones.

---

[1] Koestler, op. cit., Ghiselin, op. cit.

[2] C. W. Taylor and F. Barron, eds., *Scientific Creativity; Its Recognition and Development* (New York, 1963); W. Platt and R. A. Baker, *J. Chem. Educ.*, 1931, **8**, p. 1969.

[3] DNA = deoxyribonucleic acid—the carrier of genetic information in the cell nucleus.

[4] Often forgotten, but vital to the development of experimental science.

[5] Cf. P. B. Medawar, 'Is the Scientific Paper a Fraud?', *Listener*, 12 Sept. 1963.

(b) *The new and the traditional*

The idea of discovery and research dominates science and is, indeed, its very life. Publicity given to reports of scientific discoveries tends to build up the impression that only the new is true in science and that the old is continually being cast away. Such an impression inevitably clashes with the public image of the Christian faith, which appears traditional, antiquarian even, clinging to creeds and dogmas apparently based on the assumption that only the old and tried is true. Both impressions are superficial and do justice neither to the scientific nor to the theological enterprises. For scientific discovery is rarely simply a replacement of the old by the new—the popular view is a perversion of the facts. There are, it is true, occasional and outstanding displacements in what the scientific community accepts for its conceptual and instrumental framework of 'paradigms', as Kuhn[1] calls them—the 'standard examples' of past scientific work which guide teaching and research at any particular time. Kuhn has argued that the establishment of new paradigms requires the overthrow of the old, but has probably overstated his case (especially when applied to chemistry and biochemistry) in so far as those involved in undergoing such a transition see the way the new theories and paradigms have built on the foundations of the old, which are frequently still retained as limiting forms of the new. For example, for slowly moving objects Einstein's equations of relativity reduce to Newton's laws, and at high enough temperatures quantum statistics reduce to classical accounts of gas behaviour. So, although science is not strictly cumulative, as Kuhn argues, yet even in the most radical revolutions of its paradigms much is retained and the results of old well-founded experiments are still brought into a coherent scheme with new observations. This is reflected in the structure of the teaching of science which is so cumulative and sequential in its development that it is vulnerable to the criticism of being stultifying to creativity and of minimizing the role of reflection and imagination. That science can be so codified and taught is, at least, testimony to the confidence scientists have at any given time in their models and intellectual formulations and in the repeatability of the observations on which they are based. There

---

[1] T. S. Kuhn, *The Structure of Scientific Revolutions* (Chicago and London, 1962).

is in practice a kind of constant dialogue between the old and established, on the one hand, and the new and tentative on the other. Science widens the scope of its concepts, models and hypotheses and revises them by a process in which new observations are explained in terms of the previously known, and in which new hypotheses are often imaginative transformations of earlier ones. A scientist may well be described in the same terms as the scribe who was 'like a householder who can produce from his store both the new and the old'.[1]

This remark was, of course, applied in this report of the words of Jesus, not to our modern scientist but to that 'teacher of the law', who had become a 'learner in the kingdom of Heaven'. The law was to Jesus's contemporaries the total intellectual, legal, moral and ritualistic structure which shaped the whole life of the people of Israel. Yet, Jesus is saying that even a teacher in this field must bring out of his store things 'new and old' if he is to participate in that 'kingdom of Heaven' which, as we see elsewhere in the Gospels, is the new adventure which Jesus's own coming among the people of Israel was initiating. This aspect of the theological enterprise has been muted and dulled by the antiquarian traditional trappings which surround the Christian life and religion, but it is the authentic note of the 'New' Testament.

When anyone is united to Christ, there is a new world; the old order has gone, and a new order has already begun.[2]

Put on the new nature of God's creating.[3]

Then he who sat on the throne said, 'Behold! I am making all things new!'[4]

The only thing that counts is new creation.[5]

It stretches back to Abraham himself, the founder of the community of the people of God into which Christ was born. He 'obeyed the call to go out to a land destined for himself and his heirs, and left home without knowing where he was to go'.[6] This eleventh chapter of the Epistle to the Hebrews recalls other men of faith too and describes them all as 'having confessed that

---

[1] Matt. 13:52.   [2] 2 Cor. 5:17.   [3] Eph. 4:24.
[4] Rev. 21:5.   [5] Gal. 6:16.   [6] Heb. 11:9.
(All these six quotations from N.E.B.)

they were strangers and pilgrims on earth'.[1] This sense of the adventure of faith has often been lost in times when Christianity was conventional and respectable, but today we are fortunately more aware of it, even if sometimes a little bewildered by the 'new' theologies and 'new' moralities which claim our attention as the authentic expressions of Christian faith and practice in the mid-twentieth century. Certainly, the Christian faith, to this scientist at least, could never have become acceptable in any form unless it had been open-ended in the sense that it affords a glimpse of a vision of God, men, and nature which is continually being made more comprehensive and meaningful as it is brought into relation with wider spheres of experience. Indeed, this aspect of the Christian affirmation is simply the doctrine of God as Holy Spirit who is leading the followers of Christ into that greater truth and 'greater works'[2] which stems from Christ's presence amongst men. The giver of such a life of openness to greater vision is none other than God the Holy Spirit himself, according to Christian teaching, who operates in the community which he creates. Here is where real discovery lies, here is the research for which a man should give his all—the pearl of great price, the treasure hidden in the field. Entry into the life of faith is not, as is frequently thought, a hedging around of intellectual endeavour by a series of barriers which confine the free play of the mind, but an initiation into a more comprehensive liberty in which all life is interpreted in terms of the purpose which called it into existence. Thus at the level of actual experience the role of the old and that of the new in both the scientific and theological enterprises are more akin than the external, social forms of the two activities would suggest—and also in their conservatism and caution, for scientists exhibit both features when faced with radically new ideas, for example, in the early opposition amongst scientists to Darwin and Wallace, to the ionic theory and to the theory of relativity.

(c) *The role of experiment*

Modern science is based on the devising and application of the experimental method. Even the relevance of that most logical of human constructs, mathematics, to the interpretation

---

[1] Heb. 11:13.
[2] John 14:12 (R.V.).

of the external world has to be subjected to the test of its coherence with observations. It has been well said that the discovery of this method and its first thorough application in the seventeenth century constitute one of those great displacements in human culture which has transformed the way man regards the world and himself. Butterfield[1] has expressed this as follows:

[the scientific culture] outshines everything since the rise of Christianity and reduces the Renaissance and Reformation to the rank of mere episodes, mere internal displacements, within the system of mediaeval Christendom. Since it changed the character of men's habitual mental operations even in the conduct of the non-material sciences, while transforming the whole diagram of the physical universe and the very texture of human life itself, it looms so large as the real origin both of the modern world and of the modern mentality that our customary periodisation of European history has become an anachronism and an encumbrance.

The authenticity and reliability of the experimental method as a means of apprehending the external world has, by virtue of its successes, gained an overwhelming reputation, so that few activities of the human mind have not had to bear comparison with it, including theology. This comparison is usually, at first sight, unfavourable to theology. Thus science points to repeatable, observable experiments, under controlled conditions, which are publicly verifiable by any scientist, in principle at least. The 'observations' in science have a public, interpersonal reference which inspires confidence in the concepts, hypotheses and models derived from them, or, rather, used to 'explain' them. Theology, however, can only point, for the 'observations' on which it founds its intellectual structure, to the experiences and reflections on these experiences of many, very human, Christians. The credal statements of theology can, however, be regarded as bearing the same relation to the common experiences[2] of Christians as does a scientific 'law' or 'model' to

[1] H. Butterfield, *The Origins of Modern Science* (London, 1949), Preface.

[2] The word 'experience' refers here not to ecstatic, mystical experiences of the numinous—though it does not exclude them—but rather to the reflective interplay which occurs between the Christian's understanding of what he believes to be the historical revelation of God in Jesus Christ and the rich diversity of his encounter with the world and with his fellow men. Of course, amongst these experiences those of the primary witnesses of the historical Jesus and of the community he engendered are of key significance in determining the explicit, credal formulations of Christian belief, as discussed in the following paragraphs and in later chapters.

the observations of which it is the generalization or representation (recognizing that these ways of speaking of the principles of scientific thinking need much further elaboration and qualification). Theology attempts to register correspondences between the experiences of men of the ways of God with them and to form these into a coherent framework by elaborating suitable concepts or models, as a basis for future action and experiences.

In one respect, Christian theology also has a public reference, 'external' to all Christians in the role it assigns to the 'things concerning Jesus'—the teaching, birth, life, death and resurrection of Jesus of Nazareth. The extent and importance of such an historical reference is especially strong in Christianity and its intensity comparable only with that of the faith of the people of Israel themselves. Christianity claims an historical origin which is subject to historical tests. In this it is both like and unlike science. It is like in so far as it claims that the events to which it points actually happened. The historical evidence for the character of Jesus and of his impact on his contemporaries may be weighed and sifted, by the proper criteria of historical and literary criticism of the Gospel narratives. It is unlike the 'public' observations of the experimental sciences in that these critical events, being historical, are unrepeatable.

Even so, the accessibility of the historical grounds of Christianity to the inquirer is often overlooked and the subjective character of Christian 'evidence' frequently over-stressed. The Christian theologian points to the 'things concerning Jesus' as his primary data requiring analysis and explanation, and the development of Christian theology has, and seeks, no other reference. It is because these events have such immense and profound implications which need to be thought through again in every generation that Christian theology is a continuing enterprise.[1]

The formulation of reliable concepts, hypotheses and models concerning man in his relation to God involves a constant dialectical and rhythmical interplay between, on the one hand,

---

[1] For a recent exposition showing how the 'things concerning Jesus' lead both to a view of human 'personalness' otherwise not perceived and to the need for the Chalcedonian Definition of the 'two natures in one person' of Christ, see the Bampton Lectures of D. E. Jenkins, *The Glory of Man* (London, 1967).

such theological concepts, hypotheses and models (as expressed in creeds and other traditional phrases) and, on the other hand, both the historical 'things concerning Jesus' and the experiences of Christians in life. This constant interaction of both the contemporary individual and the past historical experience with more public formulations is at least analogous to the corresponding exchange between experiment and theory in science. I do not claim that the nature of the relation is exactly the same in the two enterprises, but I do assert that the reference to 'experiment' cannot be uniquely ascribed to science and denied to theology. For the Christian experience is a kind of empirical testing of the worthwhileness in life of the public formulations which summarize past Christian experience and events.

(d) *The dynamic and the static*

One of the commonest images in the biological and physical sciences in that of process. Ideas of patterns, structures and organisms in the physical and biological worlds which undergo modification in time, and the mechanisms which account for these modifications, are characteristic of much scientific description and 'explanation'. Geology is concerned with the transformation of the materials in the earth's crust; chemistry with the reassortment of atoms and groups into different molecular patterns and chemical kinetics with the rate with which these changes occur; biochemistry with the rate and mode of utilization of food and energy by cells and higher organisms; and biology with (*inter alia*) the nature and rate of genetic changes and transformations of living species in evolution.

The scientist has, ever since the Greeks, adjusted himself to examining a world in flux. He has learned not to seek for eternal and static verities standing behind nature and, as it were, veiled in events, but has learned by experience that the unravelling of the processes and mechanisms by which these changes occur is a satisfying enough aim in itself. The description and analysis of processes set against a time scale have become inherent in the scientific view of the world. This way of looking at the world, has, like so much else, spread far beyond the confines of the scientific community so that the static images of previous times can be admired but no longer embraced. Hence the work of scientific, theological, and poetic synthesis of a Dante has to begin all over again. Modern man no longer thinks, can no longer think, in static terms; his images are dynamic and developmental and tend to be constructed from entities that move and participate in a process in time. He is nearer than he might think to the world of Moses, of the Hebrew prophets, and of Jesus and those who wrote about him. To all these God was the 'living God', active in the processes of nature and in history. What God is in himself only the Son might know (cf. the Fourth Gospel), but he *could* be seen in what he had done in Israel's history, and supremely in what he was doing in the life, death, resurrection and ascension of Christ—a process continued in the life of the Church.

For many centuries, the Christian faith has been presented in terms of static images, of events which happened once and for all and which, if apprehended by faith, could alter the relationship of a believer to God. However, an expression of the Christian faith in dynamic terms has always been possible and is in fact closer to the Biblical attitude just described—if we may dare to use one adjective to summarize a whole development and culture. For example, the creative and redemptive acts of God in Christ which the Christian affirms may legitimately be regarded as a process as well as a great dramatic once-for-all resolution of the tension between God's perfect being and man's imperfection and sin. This is a process in which God in Christ actively re-creates and redeems men here and now in the dynamic action of his Holy Spirit, continuing to make effective that which God did for man in Christ. The Christian faith refers to past events not because of the final accomplishment therein achieved but because there and then processes were initiated which can now lead to a fulfilment of man's destiny with God. Such a re-presentation of the Christian faith in dynamic terms would require theological elaboration and justification, biblically based though it is. I do suggest that it is only with some such dynamic terminology and imagery that the Christian faith is likely to engage the attention and imagination of men accustomed by science to moving and not static images. The construction of such a way of thinking of the Christian affirmations is vital to the creation of a unified vision and I hope that later sections of this essay will be able to contribute to this task.

(e) *Authority and intellectual integrity*

The communal context of both the scientific and theological enterprises has already been briefly discussed. One way in which the community exercises its influence on the individual belonging to it is in terms of its authority. By 'authority', I refer not to the power and control which one group of people may exercise over the actions of others under the aegis of some set of laws, but the recognition which may be freely accorded to an individual, or a group of individuals, concerning the validity of their ideas and/or the trustworthiness of their account of their own experiments or experiences. It is not generally realized how much the scientist relies on the authority of his teachers and of his predecessors for his concepts and modes of experimentation. No one individual can ever repeat all the possible experiments and carry through all the theoretical arguments which he has to accept as the basis of his own research and teaching. He relies on the authority of his teachers and predecessors for the reliability of these experiments and theories. This is indeed a publicly assessable reliability, but even subsequent tests of the reproducibility of an experiment or the confirmation of the arguments underlying a theory have frequently been undertaken by only a few investigators, and the majority of scientists rely on these latter. This is inevitable and makes intellectual integrity in the individual a prerequisite of scientific activity. An individual's authority in any area of science can only be founded on his intellectual integrity which, if once found wanting, immediately undermines his standing, often permanently. The mechanisms whereby the contemporary scientific community exercises authority over the individual scientist in his work involves the whole process of publication of research papers and the procedures according to which other scientists check the papers before publication: and yet others can repeat the experiments and re-argue the theories in their own subsequent publications. This authority of the scientific community over the individual scientist has been well described by Polanyi.[1] There is constant interplay between the individual scientific research worker and his contemporary community and between the individual

---

[1] M. Polanyi, *Science, Faith and Society* (London, 1946).

scientific teacher and both past and present scientific communities. The element of authority is present in both dialogues.

To tolerant and democratic people the authority of the
Church over individual Christians has often appeared, and has
too often been in fact, simply a case of coercion by a powerful
oligarchy, armed with presumed truths and the power of the
political structure, over the minds of a weaker majority. Hence
the word 'dogma'—which originally meant 'that which has
seemed good' and so (in its Christian usage) that teaching which
has been agreed (e.g., 'resolved' by a Council, etc.)—has acquired its well-known pejorative sense. However, there is a way
in which the individual Christian can recognize an authority in
his thinking, which involves no social or political coercion and
which is very similar to that prevailing in the scientific community. It had for centuries been impossible to be aware of this
proper, right, and not humanly degrading type of authority in
thought because of the political ascendancy of the Christian
Church in many parts of the world, and the temptation, to
which it too often succumbed, to exercise an improper pressure
on men's minds. How the idea of tolerance followed and was
interwoven with the Renaissance and Reformation is a complex
story but at least it can be fairly asserted that the belief in the
individual's direct access to God without resorting to the hierarchical Church was a theological element in the development
of this idea, along with other complex factors, some economic
and some simply anti-clerical. The modification of the concept
of authority in the Church has therefore not surprisingly reached
its fullest development in the less hierarchical churches, but has
now also begun to develop strongly in the Roman Catholic
Church. I have called it a modification rather than the demise
of the concept of authority in the Church because reference to
authority[1] is as essential to the theological enterprise as to the
scientific, and for two major reasons. Firstly, the individual
Christian cannot himself have been present at the events in
history on which his beliefs concerning man and God are based.
He has to rely, in so far as he has a right to do so at all, on the

---

[1] Let me make it clear that I consider the type of authority which prevails in
the scientific community, and which I have attempted to outline, to be entirely
right and proper, to be the only sort of authority which ought to prevail in the
Church—and to be increasingly doing so.

original witnesses of these events, whose trustworthiness he has to assess; their experience has been transmitted in the early writings of the Church and in those features of its structure which persist in time, in the form of ministries and liturgies. As we have argued elsewhere, the witnesses of the 'things concerning Jesus' will have an authority which is paramount. Secondly, a proper understanding of his own limitations and inadequacies impels the Christian to realize, with humility, that his awareness of the God made known to him in Christ through the action of the Holy Spirit is defective in both intellectual content and in obedience. So any Christian who is genuinely seeking God will listen attentively to what men of God have to say. What they have to say can never be conclusive for any individual, but one would be simply foolish to ignore the accumulated wisdom of many men who have sought to follow the same road. In this sense a consensus has built up and creeds can best be regarded as an expression and summary of this consensus of experience, formulated at particular times in the history of the Christian Church, rather than simply a set of propositions of a purely metaphysical kind. The general trend of this consensus, along with the forms, both credal and liturgical, in which it has been expressed, has an authority which, like that in the scientific community, is never unquestionable and never coercive but always has a justifiable *a priori* claim on the individual. The validity of the claim of any such authority (or authorities) in the Church always, in the end, has to be assessed by each individual; but, as in science, because the individual's experience, time, and capacity are limited, he can sometimes only assume elements in his faith simply on the ground of the integrity and trustworthiness of those who had the original experiences or insights. The parallel between the individual scientist and the Christian in their respective communities is not entirely exact, because the mode in which an experience or insight is assessed or re-invoked by another person is not the same in the scientific and theological enterprises. However, enough of a parallel has been shown to exist to discredit the supposed contrast between a free and open science, devoid of any authority, and a Christian Church entirely hidebound by it.

Both enterprises depend ultimately on the personal integrity of those engaged in them. The ideal of a scientist willing to

follow the argument and evidence wherever it leads is still im-
pelling and widely acclaimed, and is one of the great moral
contributions of science to civilization—even though, in practice, the scientist in his work is often a captive of his own ideas,
methods, prejudices and personal ambition. It is, of course, the
ideal of all sound scholarship in all fields of study, with the same
defects in practice as occur in science. It is not generally realized
that it is also the *sine qua non* of theological scholarship, which
is more open-ended and more rigorous in its methods and techniques than most scientists realize. Unfortunately, the intellectual integrity and honesty which characterizes theological study,
if it is to be pursued at all, does not always extend to more
popular presentations of the Christian religion in pulpit and
pamphlet, where the critical inquiries, especially of the last hundred years into, for example, the literary and historical origins
of the Christian faith, seems frepuently to be ignored. The
Christian faith, in so far as it claims to possess any truth, has
nothing to fear from frankness and honesty about the nature
and results of these inquiries. Indeed it stands to gain more
than it will lose, judging by the response to Bishop Robinson's
Honest to God which, whatever its merits or demerits, at least
adopted a stance which encouraged a critical reappraisal. The
answers may not have been adequate, but at least the attitude
underlying this book was the only one likely to convince a
generation accustomed to admire intellectual honesty and integrity in science. The public teaching of the Church will stand
or fall by its ability to satisfy the same exacting criteria as any
other human enterprise claiming to pursue and to arrive at
truth in a particular area. For the contemporary reputation of
science and its obvious success put intellectual integrity and
honesty at a premium in any presentation of theology to the
modern world—and whenever a sermon is preached, or a hymn
sung, or a prayer is said in public, theology is inevitably
propounded.

PART 1

THE SCIENTIFIC PERSPECTIVE

CHAPTER 2

From matter to man

In the previous chapter the scientific and theological enterprises were compared; and I tried to indicate how the experienced characters of these two activities were perhaps less far apart and antipathetic than is usually assumed. The success of the scientific method in achieving public, verifiable, applicable knowledge has also had profound repercussions on the methodologies of the humanities, usually in the direction of discrediting earlier criteria and standards at the expense of newer, more supposedly 'scientific', ones. This displacement is far from complete, or generally agreed, or, indeed necessarily justified for the studies in question. Nevertheless this has been the tendency.

In the case of theology, a further kind of interaction with science has to be recognized, which is usually the one which engages popular discussion in the press. This is the impact of scientific views of various aspects of the world on the actual, or presumed, content of Christian belief. Many authors have given accounts of these famous battles fought out over fields with whose names we are all too familiar: the Copernican revolution in astronomy; Galileo; the Oxford encounter of 1860 when the St. George of free scientific inquiry, in the person of T. H. Huxley, slew the dragon of bigotry, dogma, and prejudice in the person of the then Bishop of Oxford, who had been unwise enough to act as the spokesman of those, and they included scientists, who opposed Darwin's ideas on the origin of species and of man in particular; Freud and the nature of moral responsibility; Freud and God as Father-figure; the impossibility of parthenogenesis, i.e. of a Virgin Birth; the scale of the universe and the 'location' of heaven and hell; the uniqueness, or otherwise, of man as the only intelligent self-conscious organism; alleged miracles and the 'laws' of nature; the scientific and Biblical accounts of the age of the earth and of the universe; the determination of all organisms, including man, by heredity and environment; and so on.

In the compass of the present essay, there is no opportunity for examining these controversies in any detail, although many of them continue in a variety of forms and are worth re-examination. Rather, I propose to outline the panorama of the world which is laid out before the eyes of modern man by the sciences. For the perspective which is now afforded by the whole inter-connecting nexus of the sciences gives a framework for our thinking which is radically different from many in the past. It is now only, as the 'new' theologians are wont to emphasize, that heaven and hell can no longer be respectively 'up' and 'down', but that we see the world fitting together and being inter-connected in new ways. Many of the ideas had, in principle, been mooted in the last century in learned books and meetings but they had not made any general impact; now that they are beginning to be scientific dogma to the popular mind, science itself has already qualified and modified its whole scheme of things. So it is still necessary to set down in as plain and unvarnished a tale as possible the perspective afforded by the sciences on how the variety of objects, events and phenomena we see around us are related and how they came to be as they are now. For a sense of time, of history, has been an increasingly dominant feature of the outlook of the past hundred years and we are not satisfied with an account of 'how things are' unless we also know how they became as they now appear.

Perhaps I can put this point a little more personally. When I began thinking about the contents of this part of the essay, I was fortunate enough to be sitting in a room from which the view could be regarded as a microcosm of the world we know: distant mountains just visible through the mist; sunshine in the middle distance lighting up snow, water, earth, grass, cattle and birds—all other than man; then, in the foreground, man himself and his products, a road, a car, a house, signs, a church. Anachronisms apart, man a few hundred years ago would have seen the non-human features of this scene simply as a backcloth, and a stage, for the human activities of the foreground. But we can no longer see it thus, even if it is often our first uninhibited reaction. For a little reflection on this scene in the light of information and inferences from the sciences soon leads to an awareness of the connections that we human beings have with those other forms of existence we can see. For we know that there was a time when only mountains, earth and water and the like were present and that the animals and we ourselves have been shaped out of the same material as that which constituted the inorganic world. We are, as it were, like adopted children suddenly aware, after years of ignorance, of who their parents really are. Our progenitors are to be found among the structures of the inorganic and biological worlds, which are the direct predecessors of that which we observe as so unlike and other than ourselves.

It seems to be that this provides a new framework for our thinking, not least for that of the theological enterprise. The world is immensely varied and rich in content, often bafflingly so:

this astonishing cataract of bears, babies and bananas, this immoderate deluge of atoms, orchids, oranges, cancers, canaries, fleas, gases, tornadoes and floods,

as C. S. Lewis once described it.[1] I would not wish to detract at all from this kaleidoscope of experience which is there for us all to see through these more poetic spectacles, to perpetrate the 'fallacy of misplaced concreteness' as Whitehead called it, and so to reduce the world to that 'dull affair' which a Lockean science must contrive. Nevertheless it is the power of science, and its *forte*, to see the common basis, connections, and origins of the world which we survey and this pellucid vision must be incorporated into any integrated view of man and the world. Because of our contemporary sense of time and of history, to which I have just referred, there is a special cogency in demonstrating these connections through what is known of the development in time of the cosmos as we know it. Heeding the warnings of Toulmin,[2] I do not wish to construct any great principle of Cosmic Evolution as the foundation stone of some subsequent metaphysical superstructure; but nor do I wish to ignore what scientists can reasonably discover about the development of the

[1] C. S. Lewis, *Miracles* (London, 1947), p. 81.
[2] S. E. Toulmin, 'Contemporary Scientific Mythology' in *Metaphysical Beliefs* by S. E. Toulmin, R. W. Hepburn and A. MacIntyre (London, 1957); see below, Chap. 3 (1).

cosmos we know and to examine the character of the evolutionary process so discerned. The 'plain, unvarnished tale' at which
I aim is impressive enough without introducing any mythological
overtones. So I will now attempt briefly, and inadequately,
to summarize how science sees the development of the cosmos.

One general point needs to be made about the basis of any
account of the development of the cosmos. It is simply that,
being a form of history, many of the events to which it refers
are no longer available to observation and therefore unrepeatable in their uniqueness. However, no inference concerning the
past can be justified unless it is in accord with some law, principle, or model found to work in relation to present-day observations.[1] Sometimes the ideas expressed have evoked new experiments, for example, to test the behaviour of matter at very high
temperatures and pressures, in order to make these extrapolations more reliable; or to look for the formation of amino-acids
and purines and pyrimidines, the building blocks of macromolecules essential to life, by passing an electric discharge
through a mixture of gases of the same composition as is inferred
to be that of the earth's atmosphere at its pre-biotic stage.

A variety of theoretical and experimental techniques contribute to the story. These include: astronomical observations
of other planets and galaxies at a different stage of development
from the Earth; chemical and biochemical observations on processes likely to have occurred during this development; and
present-day observations of the Earth's geology. At every point,
those who have tried to fill out this picture have grounded it
on the scientific account of the world we know. So it is a
genuinely scientific perspective that is generated, albeit in parts
only reasonable guesswork or at times scientific speculation. But
even when it is the last in its most perilous form, it is distinct
from the cosmogonical myths proper, such as the Babylonian,
Greek and Icelandic,[2] which explained why the universe came
to be as it is in terms of a story. We abstain from asking why

---

[1] The process by which science achieves this is the subject matter of much
contemporary discussion in the philosophy of science. It is enough for the present
discussion that such models (or theories or laws) are made and 'work'.

[2] The account in Genesis, chapter 1, probably written in the Babylonian
captivity of the Jews, is deliberately excluded, for, as C. F. von Weizsäcker (*The
Relevance of Science*, London, 1964) has shown, this is strictly an anti-mythical
account.

the universe is as it is, so that we can really discover without prejudice the way it came to be thus. Only when we know that can we move, if ever, to the larger questions, and then only if any features of the discovered process of development justify such a move.

To understand how the world came to be as it is, it is necessary to believe *that* the world is, and then to examine it more closely to discover of what it consists and how the constituent elements interlock and interact with each other to form the world we observe. Scientists act as if they believe there is a world with an existence independent of themselves, so implicitly negating Idealism in its more solipsist forms. Their rationale for this negation is often no better than that of Dr. Johnson's kicking of the stone. Most scientists would believe that a realistic view of the world, the assumption that there is a world to be known by the human subject which is other than the subject, however much the conceptual framework necessary for this operation is a product of human imagination, is continuously validated by the scientist's repeated ability to do meaningful experiments on both the laboratory and technological scales. In this respect, as in several others, science is nothing but 'glorified common sense'. It may be philosophically naïve, but the empirical, pragmatic test tends to override all doubts.

The examination of what the world is like, what forms and organization of forms it contains, has revealed a whole hierarchy of structures of which the more complex are organized assemblies of simpler ones. It is common to speak of the more complex levels as 'higher' but in doing so in the present context, I want to imply nothing more than this greater degree of complexity, as such. In many instances, though far from all, science has been able to discern the temporal processes in which simpler, lower forms are incorporated into the higher and more complex ones, and sometimes the reverse process of degradation. Such observations have proved particularly valuable in the attempt to extrapolate back in time in order to understand how the world we see has developed to the stage we now observe.

I. THE INORGANIC WORLD AND ITS DEVELOPMENT

It would be impertinent to attempt in a few paragraphs to summarize the scope and content of the perspective of the

inorganic world afforded by the physical sciences. These sciences
—which include astronomy, physics, chemistry, geology and the
other earth sciences and the logical structure of mathematics
which supports most of them—have reached too sophisticated
a level to allow the neat generalizations and simplifications
which, for example, a four-element view of the physical world
once allowed. However, in order to provide an indication of the
character of the perspective on the world now provided by the
sciences, I must at least attempt to summarize broadly the principal levels of organization of matter in terms of which the
physical scientist orders his thinking and observations. Then we
can refer to what is known about the transformations between
these entities and so arrive at the least misleading way of describing the development of the inorganic world, in which I include
not only our immediate non-biological environment, but the
wider planetary and galactic systems in which we are placed.

Hydrogen appears to be 'the basic material out of which the
universe is built'.[1] At temperatures in the range of that of the
earth's surface the smallest unit of gaseous hydrogen possessing
its chemical properties is the molecule (H_2) of hydrogen, each
consisting of two atoms, but it is in the form of atoms (H) that
hydrogen occurs throughout most of the universe and these
therefore constitute a convenient point from which to consider
the different levels of organization of matter.[2]

The atom of hydrogen consists of two particles, a heavy one
of positive electrical charge called a proton, whose radius is
effectively smaller by a factor[3] of 10^{-5} than that of the atom as
a whole (this is the ratio of about 100 yards to the radius of the
earth). Not surprisingly nuclear distances are measured in small
numbers (*ca.* 1–10) of 'fermi' units (fe), where 1 fe $= 10^{-13}$ cm,
whereas atomic distances are usually expressed in small numbers of 'Ångstrom' units (Å), where $1 \text{Å} = 10^{-8}$ cm, and the
typical nuclear radius is about 10^{-12} cm, that is, 10,000 times
smaller than the typical atomic radius. Almost all the mass of
the hydrogen atom is intensely concentrated in this nuclear

[1] F. Hoyle, *The Nature of the Universe* (Oxford, 1960).

[2] A molecule is the smallest component unit into which an element or compound
may be subdivided and which still retains the chemical properties that it possesses
in the bulk form, i.e., which retains its powers of combination and reaction with
other substances.

[3] See Appendix A for a representation of this and other powers of ten.

proton, for the only other particle which is present in it is an electron which has a charge equal in magnitude but opposite in sign to that of the proton, and a mass of only about 1/1850 of that of the whole hydrogen atom. This negatively charged electron moves around the central positive nucleus and both together constitute the hydrogen atom, of net zero charge. We have called these constituent units of the atom 'particles' for in many respects they have, like the atom itself, particulate properties: mass, velocity, momentum, kinetic energy. But this is not the whole story for, as the developments in physics over the last fifty years have shown (notably the uncertainty principle of Heisenberg), the smaller the particle the harder it is to describe its behaviour in such terms alone. For one thing, the precise determination and assignment of each of certain pairs of normal,[1] dynamical properties of particles prove to be mutually exclusive, e.g., the uncertainty in the position of a particle is inversely proportional to the uncertainty in its momentum. There is a similar relation between its energy and the time for which a system exists with that energy. However, the proportionality constant in this relation is extremely small (of the order of 10^{-27} erg-secs) so that these mutually exclusive uncertainties (or errors) in these quantities only become of any importance relative to the actual momenta and position coordinates for particles of the order and size of an electron and, in most situations, are not important for whole atoms—and only just so for hydrogen, the smallest.[2] Thus the earlier statements about the electron moving as a particle around the nucleus (the proton) of the hydrogen atom need to be modified in the light

[1] That is, based on macroscopic observations.

[2] The Heisenberg uncertainty principle or principle of indeterminancy (1926) may be written as $\Delta p \cdot \Delta x \geq h/4\pi$ or, more approximately, $\Delta p \cdot \Delta x \sim h$, where h = Planck's constant, 6×10^{-27} erg-sec; Δx = the uncertainty in the position (in cm from a defined origin) of a particle; and Δp = the uncertainty in its momentum (c.g.s. units) = $m \cdot \Delta v$, where m is the mass (in g) and Δv is the uncertainty in its velocity (in cm/sec). That is, $\Delta v \cdot \Delta x \sim \dfrac{6 \times 10^{-27}}{m}$ cm^2 sec^{-1}. For particles of the order of 10^{-3} g (1 mg), these uncertainties are of negligible significance, for their product ($\Delta v \cdot \Delta x$) is only $6 \cdot 5 \times 10^{-27}/10^{-3} = 6 \cdot 5 \times 10^{-24}$ cm^2 sec^{-1}. But for particles of the mass of an electron ($ca.$ 10^{-27} g), this product becomes $6 \cdot 5 \times 10^{-27}/10^{-27}$, i.e., $6 \cdot 5$ cm^2 sec^{-1}. So that if Δx is of the order of the size of an atom (1Å = 10^{-8} cm), the uncertainty (Δv) in the velocity becomes $6 \cdot 5/10^{-8} = 6 \cdot 5 \times 10^8$ cm/sec, which is about equal to its velocity, and so there is a 100 per cent uncertainty in the actual value of its velocity.

38   THE SCIENTIFIC PERSPECTIVE

of this development, and not those which picture atoms themselves as particles. This modification takes several forms, one of which can be expressed by saying that the position of the electron in moving around the proton is determined by an equation (that of Schrödinger) which has the form of that for a stationary wave (cf. the motion of a violin string) and in which the square (roughly speaking) of a quantity called the 'wave function' (ψ) corresponds to what in classical physics would be an amplitude. The value of this amplitude (ψ^2) at any point in space is, analogously with other forms of classical (e.g., sound) waves, proportional to an energy intensity (energy/unit volume) which, for this wave-like equation representing particles, has the significance of the probability of finding the particle at that point in space. Thus solutions of such wave-like equations for, say, an electron moving around the positively charged protonic nucleus of hydrogen, show how the value of ψ (and so of ψ^2) depends on spatial co-ordinates and so gives, as it were, a map of what the probability is of finding the particle (in this case, an electron) at various points in space relative to the origin of the co-ordinate systems (in this case, the proton at the centre of the hydrogen atom). This idea replaces an earlier one of distinct and precise orbits in which electrons and atoms were supposed to move around the nucleus as if in a kind of planetary system. The introduction of the model of a wave to give an account of the position in space of what was initially conceived of as a particle, a move which becomes absolutely essential when dealing with particles as small as the electron, is sometimes referred to as the complementary (or dual) 'nature' of electrons, and the like, as waves and particles. This paradox and its significance for understanding what constitute scientific experiments and the epistemology of science cannot be developed here. It is, of course, closely related to the emergence of the realization that energy cannot be acquired by the units of matter in infinitely subdivisible amounts but only in finite small amounts ('quanta') so that only certain definite energies ('energy levels') can be acquired by all forms of matter. The gaps between these allowed levels are comparable with the energies for systems at the sub-atomic and atomic levels and the quantum theory (and the wave-like equations) replaces, for such systems, the classical Newtonian laws of energy interchange, towards which they increasingly converge as the mass of the systems under consideration increases.

It has been necessary to refer to the complementary wave and particle-like nature of electrons, to emphasize that what we mean by a 'particle' becomes less and less like the macroscopic billiard-ball picture the smaller the entity under consideration. For this, and other reasons, it is easier to visualize the hierarchy of inorganic structures by starting with the hydrogen atom and proceeding to the larger atoms, then molecules and so on, than it is to penetrate into the nature of nuclear particles and forces. (Nevertheless we shall have to look at this inner world of the nucleus if only to obtain some glimpse of the boundaries to our understanding of the mystery of the 'nature' of matter). The hydrogen atom, as well as being the commonest in the universe, is also the simplest. More complex atoms contain a massive, positively-charged nucleus consisting not only of protons but also of 'neutrons', which have almost exactly the same mass as protons but no net electrical charge (see Fig. 1). The total positive charge of the nucleus is called the 'atomic number' (Z). A neutron may be regarded as a combination of a proton with an electron; or both protons and neutrons may be regarded as alternative forms of the same entity, a 'nucleon'.[1] All these particles, just referred to, are still firmly within the compass of the nucleus and are to be distinguished from those particles, the extra-nuclear electrons, which move over the wide space, relative to the scale of the nucleus, of the atom as a whole and whose number (Z) is equal to that of the positive charges (i.e., protons) in the nucleus itself. Atomic nuclei can exist containing up to a total of about 250 nucleons (i.e., protons plus neutrons) in the conditions which pertain when a supernova erupts, but this appears to be the limit of stability and the heavier ones even in this range are characterized by the instability we call radioactivity. On earth the heaviest naturally occurring atom is that of the radioactive element uranium which contains 238 nucleons (92 protons and 146 neutrons). Atoms with nuclei of the same net positive charge, and so with the same number (the atomic number, Z) of nuclear protons and of extra-nuclear electrons,

---

[1] In that case, a 'nucleon' when combined with a 'positron' (a positively charged particle of mass equal to that of the electron) is a proton and when not so combined is a neutron.

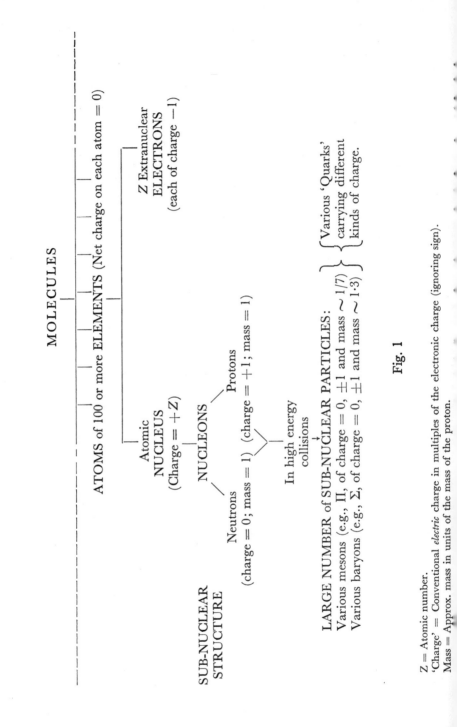

Fig. 1

Z = Atomic number.
'Charge' = Conventional *electric* charge in multiples of the electronic charge (ignoring sign).
Mass = Approx. mass in units of the mass of the proton.

but with different numbers of neutrons and so of different total mass, are called 'isotopes'.

The foregoing description of nuclear and atomic structure has been couched in classical terms, with a few 'particles' specified primarily by their mass and also by their electrostatic charge. However, the unique forces which hold the nucleons together in the nucleus are the strongest existing in the universe, being of the order of 10^{37} to 10^{39} times stronger than those of gravitation and about 100 times stronger than 'electrostatic' or 'electromagnetic' forces (which in the nucleus would in any case be repulsive between the like positive charges). The description of the nucleus as in some way composed of particles of different mass implies the validity of an analytical procedure based on the idea that a system is best understood by reducing it to its component parts and that it is in fact so reducible. This method, P. T. Matthews asserts, 'has been amazingly successful in classical physics',[1] but he continues:

... the Einstein relation, $E = mc^2$, which allows kinetic[2] energy [E] to be converted into rest energy [mc^2]—or mass—makes nonsense of the classical assumption that a whole may be regarded as a sum of its parts,[3] and forces us at least to question our usual interpretation of the analytic approach.

For in recent years physicists have been able to study collisions in which the kinetic energies involved are many times greater than the rest energies of the colliding particles and this has led to a different conception of the relation between and nature of the entities which constitute the nuclei of atoms. At very low energies a proton appears as a structureless point, approximating to our everyday notion of a 'particle',[4] but as the energy increases one can detect the production of mesons, the lightest[5] of which has a mass equal to $\frac{1}{7}$ of that of a nucleon; under these circumstances it appears that the proton is more appropriately conceived of as possessing a core around which a 'meson' is in orbit. However, this meson is only the lightest of

[1] P. T. Matthews, *Endeavour*, 1967, **26**, p. 63.
[2] More strictly, E = total energy. Here m = rest mass; c = velocity of light.
[3] We shall later also have cause for suspecting the applicability of this notion to the relation of biological organisms to their constituent parts.
[4] Although its possession of 'spin' and a magnetic moment, at non-relativistic energies, is evidence of structure.
[5] The Π-meson, or pion.

a whole series of sub-nuclear particles for, as the energy of collision increases, more and more such particles are produced and over 100 are now thought to exist.[1] Each is characterized by a different combination of mass, electric charge, and of two other kinds of 'charge'. These 100 or more subnuclear particles themselves appear to be constituted, in appropriate combinations and according to certain symmetry rules, of at least three kinds of still more 'fundamental' entities called 'quarks' which carry the different kinds of 'charges'. Matthews concludes that:

If a simple description of sub-nuclear matter is possible, it cannot be in the old classical terms of a few particles specified primarily by their mass. The real search now is not for new particles, but for new concepts which will provide the simple basis for a dynamical understanding of the sub-nuclear world.[2]

This brief look at sub-nuclear matter serves at least to remind us of the conceptual barriers to the human understanding of matter and should impede any easy dogmatism concerning our knowledge of what matter is 'in itself' or, rather, of what kind of statements could purport to inform us of the nature of matter.

Fortunately, this mystery of the relationship between experimental observations concerning sub-nuclear matter and the entities which must be conceived to organize these observations in a coherent manner does not impair our understanding of the principal features of atomic structure, the arrangement of the extra-nuclear electrons around the nucleus. For the forces which operate between the various 'particles' within the nucleus, although they are the strongest that exist, are only of very short range and do not reach out beyond the confines of the nucleus and so do not affect at all the extra-nuclear electrons. Hence the number, arrangements in space and energy levels of these outer electrons depend, in the first instance, directly on the value of the positive charge of the nucleus, that is, its atomic number, Z. For, as in hydrogen, more complex atoms are held together by the electrostatic attractive forces (the gravitational ones are here negligible) between this dense, small positively-charged nucleus and the negative extra-nuclear electrons. The

---

[1] These include, besides the two kinds of nucleon (neutron, proton), the lighter mesons and the heavier 'baryons' (Fig. 1).

[2] P. T. Matthews, op. cit., p. 67.

behaviour (including the distribution in space) of these electrons is determined by the atomic number and by the energy levels available to them. These levels are those characteristic of the solutions of the appropriate wave-equation[1] for electrons in this situation under the further constraint of a separate limiting principle, that of Pauli, which excludes many of the possibilities. The arrangement of energy levels and the number of electrons which can be accommodated in the various categories and sub-categories give rise to the characteristic rhythms and repeats in chemical and physical properties which can be discerned when the elements are set out in the Periodic Table, an array which emerges when the elements are placed in order of increasing atomic number. The chemical properties of the 100 or so naturally-occurring elements are classifiable in this Periodic Table, based on atomic number and groupings (by 'quantum numbers') of electrons, because the reactivity of an atom, which is studied by the chemist, is determined by the interactions between its extra-nuclear electrons and those of other atoms, both like and unlike. This chemical reactivity, or ability to combine with other atoms, is ultimately based on the net result of all the various attractions and repulsions which occur when one atom, with its positive nucleus and negative electrons, comes close to another atom also with its positive and negative charges. If the electrons from both atoms can so move round both nuclei jointly that there is a minimum in the energy of the two atoms at a certain close proximity and that this minimum is less than that of the separated atoms then a chemical bond is said to be formed. The theoretical treatment of this problem depends again on solving the appropriate wave equations for the distribution and energy of the electrons in such a situation, and on taking account of an apparent self-motion of electrons called their 'spin'. These studies constitute much of theoretical quantum chemistry and even when the results of such calculations are not entirely predictive, they nevertheless give an illuminating account of the nature of the chemical bond and of the structures and electron distribution in the molecules which result from the formation of bonds between both like and unlike atoms. At this point, one is firmly on the territory of chemistry, which describes and analyses quantitively the possibilities,

[1] See p. 38.

energies and consequent properties of the extraordinary number of atomic combinations into molecules which are possible among the commonest 100 or so elements. Molecules can contain anything from two to millions of atoms, the largest numbers occurring in structures containing a repeating unit linked together by chemical bonds into long chains. These are then called 'macromolecules'. The element carbon has a particular propensity to form such chains both with itself and in conjunction with oxygen, nitrogen and phosphorus atoms.

The energies of building of atoms into molecules, it is worth remembering, are about 10 to 100 times smaller than the energies by which electrons are held by the nuclei in atoms, which in turn are 100,000 to a million times smaller than the energies of binding of the 'particles' in the nucleus. Even the weakest of these binding forces, the net electrostatic attractions which hold the atoms together in a molecule, are still of the order of 10^{35} to 10^{39} times greater than their mutual gravitational attractive forces. In the above both of the terms, 'energy' and 'force', which scientists use to discuss stabilities and tendencies have been used. Force is a convenient description because of its similarity to potential muscular sensations and strictly it can be expressed as the rate of change of an energy with respect to a space co-ordinate. When particles tend to enter some new configuration of lower energy they are said to exert an attractive force; usually it is the total energies before and after entering such configurations which it is the aim of the experimentalist to determine and of the theoretician to calculate.

If atoms and molecules lose or gain a few electrons, the entities as a whole then have a net charge and are known as 'ions'. The configuration of any assembly of atoms and molecules which have become ions is then dominated by the electrostatic forces which these charges engender and this profoundly affects the properties of solids and of solutions containing them. However, even when possessed of no net charge, molecules, and non-combining atoms, can still exert weak attractive forces on each other over distances of up to 5 to 10 times those prevailing between bonded atoms (which are in the range 1 to 3Å). These weak forces, named after van der Waals, are also basically electrostatic or, more strictly, dipolar in origin, and have an energy of the order of $\frac{1}{10}$ of those which hold atoms together in molecules but act over larger distances. Solids in which only these van der Waals forces are present have different properties from the ionic solids and there are other forms in which both forces contribute to the net stability and configuration. In solids and other forms of condensed phase, such as liquids, these ionic and van der Waals forces tend to produce configurations in which the potential energy is minimal but this is not the only consideration. For all molecules (and atoms) undergo various kinds of motions and the possibilities of motion available to them are not the same for different configurations. There is an associated tendency, often running in the opposite direction to that of the tendency to reach a minimum in the potential energy, for systems to remain in that configuration in which the arrangement of molecules in possible energy states can be achieved in the maximum possible number of ways (in the direction of what is called an increase in 'entropy').[1] It is the balance[2] between these two tendencies which determines the actual state of equilibrium of any system, the state which persists in time without further macroscopic observable change.

These principles serve, when properly developed, to account for the varied properties of solids, liquids and gases, the equilibria between them, equilibria in chemical reactions, and for

[1] Entropy is one of those thermodynamic 'properties of the state of a system', which are dependent only on the state of the system and not on how it arrives at that state. Broadly, entropy can be taken to represent the degree of disorder in the system or (which comes to the same thing) the number of alternative ways in which a given state might in principle be attained by a random disposition of its component units. The change in entropy, in a process, in which a system passes from one state to another, is a measure of the change in these quantities (disorder, etc.) and also represents the degree of irreversibility of the process in question. In classical thermodynamics changes in entropy can be brought about by systems undergoing irreversible processes and by absorbing heat. In all real, natural processes taken as a whole (i.e., noting everything that changes including the environment of the system) there is an increase in entropy, and so roughly speaking, in disorder and randomness.

[2] This balance between thermal energy (H) and entropy (S) is represented in thermodynamics by their opposing contributions at constant pressure to a quantity called 'free energy' (G), which is defined as $G = H - TS$, where T is the absolute temperature. Decreases in free energy, also a property of the initial and final states of the system, represent the maximum amount of external work which a system can do reversibly in any given change of state. At equilibrium the free energy is at a minimum with respect to any changes in the parameters defining the system (temperature, pressure, composition, etc.).

the less familiar properties of liquid crystals, rubber-like solids, solutions (including those of macromolecules) of one condensed phase in another, and also of the dispersed phases such as foams, gels, emulsions and colloids.[1]

This level of the organization of matter now verges on the scale of physical phenomena that human beings experience, on the 'immoderate deluge' of C. S. Lewis,[2] or rather on the non-living items in his list. The configuration and varied forms of matter in bulk subjected to forces on a terrestrial scale are the concern of the earth sciences, including geology, geophysics and meteorology, and the properties of matter already described serve to explain these phenomena, except that the time and distance scales are often so much greater that new phenomena frequently appear because complete equilibrium is impossible of achievement and all states are transient, or 'in dynamic equilibrium', like the vortices of a whirlpool or the currents at the edge of a fast-running stream. Moreover, the energies involved in, for example, a natural phenomenon such as a thunderstorm, and the extremity of the conditions (e.g., pressure, electrical charge) are often so great that new manifestations of the behaviour of matter appear in this scale of phenomena. However, the temperature range in which solids and liquids can exist is relatively narrow and low so that the, to us, familiar phenomena of the Earth's surface are relatively rare, cosmologically speaking. Two forces, in particular, take on a new significance with matter in aggregates of the size of the planets and other astronomical bodies. These are the force of gravity and the magnetic fields engendered by the matter in the core of certain planets and in rotating masses of gases in nebulae; such magnetic fields are, in physical theory, another aspect of what up to now we have called electrostatic forces—a more inclusive term which denotes both forms is 'electromagnetic'. On this scale of aggregation, many of the relevant scientific observations are extra-terrestrial, apart from those essential observations of gravita-

---

[1] For a masterly and penetrating survey of the whole hierarchy of atomic and molecular forms of matter and of the principles governing the configurations in which they appear, the reader could not do better than to study *The Structure of Physical Chemistry* by (the late) C. N. Hinshelwood (Oxford, 1951), especially the preface and synopses on pages 1, 111, 162, 227, 280 and 351, to which, and to whom, this author is greatly indebted.

[2] Cf. p. 33.

tional and magnetic effects of the Earth itself, which led to the discovery of such forces. At this point we enter the world of the new cosmology where theoretical calculations have to be made on matter conceived as being under the most extreme conditions of temperature, pressure and density.

It is worth, at this point, reminding ourselves briefly of how our planet, the Earth, appears to the geologist, astronomer and cosmologist.[1] The Earth itself has a core of molten iron and a crust of siliceous rocks[2] and contains all the elements whose nuclei are stable over long enough periods to be observed. It moves round and receives its energy from the Sun; this energy is produced by a reaction in which four hydrogen nuclei give a helium[3] nucleus with the release of the energy equivalent[4] of the mass disappearing in the process. The Sun is indeed composed mostly of hydrogen atoms, with about $\frac{1}{10}$ of this amount of helium and only traces of some other elements on the Earth. It has existed for about 5,000 million years and its hydrogen is likely to last for another 10,000 million years, but not for ever. The Earth, along with the other planets in the 'solar system' moves round its star, the Sun, and this system is itself part of a single galaxy containing 10^{11} stars. The galaxy has the shape of a thin disc and it takes light 60,000 years to travel across it. We look along the thickest part of the disc when we look at the Milky Way. The solar system is near to the edge at a distance of 20–25,000 light years,[5] that is about $\frac{2}{3}$ of its radius, from the centre of the galaxy, about which it rotates once in every 200 million years. The extent of interstellar space relative to the planets is enormous, as strikingly depicted by Hoyle:[6] if the scale is reduced by a factor[7] of 10^{10}, the Sun becomes a ball 6 inches in diameter, Mercury is then 7 yards away, the Earth 18 yards away and the size of a speck of dust, Pluto 710 yards away, and the next nearest stars 2,000 miles. This immensity of

---

[1] An excellent succint account for the general reader is to be found in F. Hoyle, *The Nature of the Universe* (Oxford, 1960).

[2] Minerals containing silicon-oxygen bonds.

[3] Helium has an atomic number of 2 and its nucleus contains 2 protons and 2 neutrons.

[4] According to the Einstein equation, p. 41.

[5] One light year is the distance light can travel in a year, at a speed of 300,000 km/sec (186,000 miles/sec). This distance is $9 \cdot 4 \times 10^{12}$ km, or $5 \cdot 9 \times 10^{12}$ miles.

[6] Hoyle, op. cit., p. 15.

[7] See Appendix A.

interstellar space is not strictly empty but contains mainly hydrogen atoms (*ca.* 90 per cent) in an extremely rarefied form as well as mineral 'dust'. But the cosmologist soon exhausts our available supply of superlatives,[1] for our own galaxy is but one among 10^9 galaxies each containing 10^8 to 10^{11} stars, so that there are roughly 10^{17} to 10^{20} stars in the universe (where our Sun qualifies as a 'star', but the planets do not).

The displacement towards the red end of the spectrum of light from the galaxies has shown that they are all moving apart at a rate which increases with their distance from us. The situation is the three dimensional analogue of an irregular pattern of spots on a sheet of rubber which is being stretched in its two possible directions so that all points on it move apart from each other. This has the important corollary that an observer anywhere else, in another galaxy, would get the same general picture of the universe as we do and that we could learn no more in principle about its large-scale behaviour by being elsewhere. Another curious feature of our observations of these worlds upon worlds becomes important at this point—it is that the further away the galaxy from which we receive a light signal, the longer ago is the time when it was as we see it. If the universe has an origin at a point in time this would constitute a limit to our spatial observations. But this occurs anyway because if a galaxy recedes from us at the speed of light, as it can do if sufficiently far away, because of the relation between distance and speed of recession, then we can no longer receive a signal from it, whether as visible light or as a radio wave to which our modern radio-telescopes are sensitive. So whether or not the universe itself is bounded, our knowledge of it is. Calculation shows that the limit of observation of the universe is at a distance of about 10,000 million light years away, according to Hoyle,[2] and radio telescopes have penetrated as far as about 5,000 million light years.

By examining the spectral lines and their intensities in the light coming from the stars, nebulae, 'white dwarfs', 'red giants', planets and so on, a great body of knowledge has been gained about matter in masses of a scale, and under conditions, which are never attainable in our laboratories. Transformations

---

[1] However, see Appendix A.   [2] Op. cit., p. 85.

are observed there which could only be surmised previously; for example, and most importantly, the transformation of helium to carbon, nitrogen, oxygen and then to heavier elements of iron, silicon and phosphorus which occurs when a star has exhausted its hydrogen. This can be followed by a contraction and the explosion called a supernova, in which the heavy elements are ejected as clouds and can themselves condense. Not surprisingly, young stars are found to contain proportionately much more of the heavy elements than old ones which have undergone supernovae explosions. An important point to be noted is that when we observe the stages leading to supernovae we are seeing the formation of the elements from helium which originated from hydrogen. Once there exist condensed bodies that are the result of supernovae explosions and that contain many elements, there also arises the possibility of the formation of chemical compounds, under the influence of ultra-violet light and electric discharges, as soon as the temperature is low enough for them to exist. It is possible for the geochemist to envisage ways in which the commoner compounds, water, siliceous rocks, metallic ores, etc., could have appeared in a planet such as the Earth. The details need not concern us at this point, but it is worth stressing that ideas on how the physical character of the Earth came to be what we now see are continuously being refined and enlarged by astronomical observations and theoretical calculations on the nuclear processes still occurring in other parts of the universe.

This very rough sketch of the way things are in the physical universe has inevitably involved references to the transformation of one type of configuration of matter into others. This is inevitable because our knowledge of the configuration of matter often only arises in examining the processes of transformation themselves. Thus our knowledge of molecules and of their atomic constitution arose in the context of observing the chemical reactions of substances with each other to produce new compounds. The study of the way in which a pure compound can appear as a solid, liquid or gas has always involved an examination of the conditions of equilibrium between these phases and of the effects of, for example, temperature and pressure on the equilibrium. Similarly, descriptions of the structure of solutions, colloids, liquid crystals and other forms of molecular organization are based on observation of how these states of matter can arise from others. Hence a description of the configurations of matter can be regarded as essentially a shorthand for a vast number of investigations of their mutual interchange and transformations. The actual sequence of events leading from one level to another, on for example the surface of the Earth, is a matter for more detailed inquiry, but there can be little doubt *that* such sequences must in fact have occurred in ways consonant with our understanding of the physical world as it is now.

Proposals concerning the sequence of events leading to the formation of galaxies, stars and planets, and in particular our star and planet (the Sun and Earth) are closely related to our understanding of the varieties of conglomerations of matter in the universe and of the balance of nuclear, electromagnetic and gravitational forces which hold them together. As regards the past history of the assembly of galaxies there are broadly two main theories. The *evolutionary theory* extrapolates back from the speed at which galaxies are moving apart to a point in our present time scale which is 20,000 million years ago and when all the galaxies and intergalactic matter, that is all the matter and energy of the universe, were concentrated in a 'super-nucleus' or 'primeval atom' of almost unimaginable density and temperature, when most of the heavy nuclei would form. The present observed expansion is regarded as the result of a primordial explosion. The *steady state theory* says that the universe has always been in much the same state, in the sense that, as the galaxies move apart, new hydrogen atoms, and so galaxies, appear at a steady rate to replace them, so that the galactic density of the universe remains constant. The rate at which hydrogen atoms would have to appear is extremely slow, about 1 atom every 15 years in a space the size of an average laboratory, and this would be undetectable in terrestial experiments. This second theory has the virtue of making predictions which can be and are being tested, e.g., that the density of the galaxies most distant in time as well as space should be the same as the density of those nearer to us. Radio-astronomical observations are, it seems, beginning to cast doubt on this supposed equality and so on the steady state theory, at least in the form originally proposed, but this does not thereby provide support for the evolutionary theory. For this 'big bang' theory, as it is sometimes called, leaves open the question of the state of the universe before the supernucleus existed. By using the word 'before' in the previous sentence I have presumed that our present time scale could go back beyond the supernucleus, the 'big bang'. Whether this is or is not so cannot be affirmed on this theory and indeed a cyclical process can equally well be envisaged in which the universe, or at least parts of it, oscillate between phases of expansion and contraction. An infinite time scale would then be as much required by the evolutionary theory as by the steady state theory. It is worth remarking, even at this point, that the acceptance or rejection or either theory has no bearing one way or the other on whether the universe is, in the theological sense, 'created' (see Chapter 5).

How one formulates the problem of the formation of galaxies depends on the view taken of the universe, whether evolutionary or steady state. For the latter theory at once poses the problem of the perpetuation of the existing population density of galaxies; whereas the former is bound to raise the question of how galaxies originated. But the steady state theory still requires a primordial galaxy to initiate the processes of steady accretion of new matter and of loss of galaxies from the cluster of galaxies which accumulated upon that first one. It seems that galaxies could form from a whirling disc of gas (hydrogen mainly) through the successive stages of irregularities and eddies, clouds, condensations—possibly on solid hydrogen coating interstellar dust consisting of graphite—and finally stars. The process of coagulation into smaller volumes within each successively con- densed cloud would go on indefinitely with contraction as the mass radiates from its surface, did not the internal temperature rise on contraction and so start the process of nuclear trans- mutation ($4H \rightarrow He$) already mentioned. When the mass of the central core falls below a certain limit there can be a balance between the energy gain and loss and a star is then formed.

Our galaxy appeared 15,000 million years ago, judging from the age of its oldest stars, and the Sun appeared as such a star in this galaxy about 5,000 million years ago. It is thought that, as it contracted, it transferred angular momentum to a disc of gas near its equator and, in order to conserve its momentum,

momentum was transferred to the disc of gas which thereby flowed outwards to the greater radial distances where it now appears in its subsequently condensed forms as the great planets Jupiter, Saturn, Uranus, Neptune and Pluto. Rare solid and liquid material of heavier nuclei, which arose from explosions before the mass had been reduced to its stable limit and which had already condensed out from the gas, could not take up momentum from the Sun and stayed nearer the Sun as the inner circle of planets, Mercury, Venus, Mars and Earth. The 'age' of the Earth is currently deduced to be about 4,500 million years and the processes by which it arose are sufficiently common to make it likely that there are between 10^8 and 10^{18} planetary systems in which the conditions are present for the formation of a planet like the Earth and so for the appearance of living matter. Certain elements of the first row of the Periodic Table were especially abundant, relative to the situation on other planets and stars: in particular hydrogen and oxygen, in water, were both dominant. These light elements of the first row, especially carbon, possess stable nuclei and electronic structures which are conducive to forming large numbers of compounds.

The Earth, because of its origin as a member of the inner circle of planets, contains all the naturally stable elements that exist in the universe. Its primary atmosphere was, according to the geochemical evidence, not unlike those of Jupiter, Saturn and Uranus now, for it was then a reducing, not oxidizing, mixture of methane, hydrogen, ammonia, hydrogen cyanide and hydrogen sulphide as well as water. The earth's crust contained water, iron and aluminium silicates, and nearer the interior, metal carbides. Experiments during the last decade[1] or so have shown how irradiation, heat (volcanic activity), radioactivity, pressure waves (from meteors) and the passage of electric discharges through appropriate mixtures of the gases just listed can, after reaction with water, cause the formation of small quantities of all the amino acids;[2] and, in electric discharges at least, four of the five 'bases' which are present in

---

[1] For a recent account, see *Chemical Evolution* by M. Calvin (Oxford, 1969).

[2] The building blocks of proteins (see later) which contain an amino group —NH_2 and an acidic carboxyl group —CO_2H.

nucleic acids.[1] Polyphosphates,[2] which can phosphorylate at least one of the nucleoside units of nucleic acids (adenosine[3]) can be formed from simple phosphates under some of these conditions, and sugars from formaldehyde.[4] The action of water on carbides[5] can give rise to hydrocarbons[6] and the action of the intense ultraviolet light from the Sun, not then reduced by the upper layers of ozone (O_3) now shielding the earth's surface, could transform these hydrocarbons into a variety of other compounds of carbon containing also hydrogen, oxygen and nitrogen—called generically organic compounds, since the compounds of carbon are so vital to life. Not all of these reactions have necessarily contributed to providing the conditions for life to appear but some of them could well have done so. Solutions in water of this increasing variety of molecules might be concentrated by the influence of the surface absorptive and catalytic activities of silicates (especially as gels) and other minerals, by the chromatographic effects[7] of semi-porous solids, and by evaporation from small pools, and so set the stage for the formation of living matter, to which we must now direct our attention.

---

[1] Deoxyribo- and ribo-nucleic acids, DNA and RNA, the carriers and translators of genetic instructions and information (see below).

[2] Phosphoric acid is
$$HO-\overset{\overset{\displaystyle O}{\|}}{\underset{\underset{\displaystyle OH}{|}}{P}}-OH$$
and a poly-phosphate contains chains of

$$-O-\overset{\overset{\displaystyle O}{\|}}{\underset{\underset{\displaystyle OH}{|}}{P}}-O-\overset{\overset{\displaystyle O}{\|}}{\underset{\underset{\displaystyle OH}{|}}{P}}-O-.$$

[3] Adenosine $= \left\{\begin{matrix}\text{The base}\\\text{adenine}\end{matrix}\right\}-\left\{\begin{matrix}\text{The sugar}\\\text{deoxyribose}\end{matrix}\right\}-\left\{\begin{matrix}\text{Phosphoric}\\\text{acid residue}\end{matrix}\right\}$, where — denotes a chemical bond.

[4] Sugars contain only carbon (C), oxygen (O) and hydrogen (H). Formaldehyde is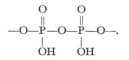

[5] Carbides have the general formula M_xC_y where M = metal, C = carbon and x and y are numbers, but are not always integers.

[6] Hydrocarbons have formulae C_pH_q where p and q are integers.

[7] An effect most familiarly observed when blotting paper separates and ink stain into its component dyes.

2. LIVING MATTER AND ITS ORIGIN

For the first one-and-a-half thousand million years of its existence the Earth must have gradually been accumulating the compounds out of which living matter was to evolve, and in certain localities this must have become concentrated enough to constitute the 'primeval soup', as it is often called in these discussions, in which living matter appeared. One must not think of this appearance as the sudden coagulation of matter to form something like a complete cell as we now know it. For even the simplest of single cells has a complexity at the molecular level which does and will continue to baffle our resources of communication to describe fully, even if we could conceive it in our own minds. What has to be envisaged is that living matter emerged as matter organized in simpler forms of certain of the molecular mechanisms we now know to be essential to life, and that these prototypes became mutually supporting to form a rudimentary organism separated from the surrounding fluid medium by a barrier of some kind. This barrier corresponded to the highly developed membrane of present-day cells and, once formed, enabled it thereafter to lead a separate existence.

No-one, of course, can now observe such crudely organized rudiments of modern complex living matter coming into existence today. Under natural conditions the gases and liquids of the Earth are so teeming with minute living organisms such as bacteriophage, bacteria, bacterial spores, amoeba and so on, that no such potential and rich food material would be left long enough to develop into a multiplying living entity on its own account, but would simply contribute to the life and growth of an already existing organism. But shall we ever be able to achieve this synthesis of life under laboratory conditions when all present forms of life have been excluded from a synthetic mixture corresponding to the primeval soup? The implications of this and the most judicious answer to it can only be formulated after we have examined how matter is organized in living organisms. Although a very large number of key problems remain to be solved, there is no doubt that the most remarkable development in terrestrial science in the last few decades has been the development of modern biochemistry and molecular biology, the second of these two names having arisen to designate the new direction which the study of the molecular organization of living matter has taken during this period. Many historians of science already think these developments parallel the tremendous displacements in thinking about the physical world which the establishment of quantum and relativity theory caused.

When we have summarized briefly the nature of the molecular structures of and dynamic processes in living matter, we can then look again at speculations concerning its origins and the question of the possibility today of 'synthesizing life in the laboratory'. Perhaps the simplest way to begin is first to look at the actual constituents of a typical living cell; whether this be a bacterium, or part of a larger organism, the general picture is broadly as follows. About 70 per cent of the total mass of a living cell is water, which reminds us that living organisms depend completely on the existence of this particular liquid. The remarkable properties of water are often hidden by the contempt bred of familiarity. It is the best solvent known and because of its high dielectric constant and solvating power it dissolves polar (ionic) substances readily but does not entirely exclude non-polar ones; it has a highly ramified structure on account of the unique ability of a hydrogen atom to form an extra, weaker bond to another oxygen atom in addition to the one to which it is covalently linked (i.e., by the usual kind of chemical bond) in the molecule of H_2O; in the solid form as ice, it actually contracts on melting; so that, unlike most other substances, it floats on the water into which it melts; as the temperature rises from the melting-point, its density at first decreases and then passes through a minimum before increasing again; it is a reactive substance frequently involving itself in catalysing chemical reactions, by virtue of both its electronegative oxygen atom and its electropositive hydrogen atom, reactions which would not proceed in any other solvent; and so one could go on. Water is undoubtedly the essential matrix of life and in this matrix the other molecules are embedded. The non-aqueous, dry weight of the cell, which is 30 per cent of the total weight, contains roughly the proportions shown in the following table of different classes of components.

		% of cellular dry weight	Molecular weight*	Nos.† of molecules per cell
Macro-molecules	Proteins	~70	10^4–10^9	~10^6
	Deoxyribonucleic acid (DNA)	5	10^6–10^9	Small number‡
	Ribonucleic acid (RNA)	10	10^4–10^6	~10^4
	Polysaccharides§	~5	10^4–10^6	~10^6
	Lipids	5	} ca. 10^3	~10^7
	Phospholipids	4		~10^7
	Small molecules (metallic ions, vitamins, hormones, co-enzymes metabolites).	~1	ca. 100–400	~10^6 to 10^7

* Weight of each molecule in units of 'daltons'. 1 Dalton = mass of one hydrogen atom.
† Based on weights divided by molecular weights. Only orders of magnitude (within a factor of 10) are given.
‡ One in certain bacteria.
§ Very variable, e.g., plant wall cells contain very large amounts.

Clearly the large molecules, 'macromolecules' as they are called, of individual molecular weights in the range of tens of thousands to a thousand million times that of a hydrogen atom, constitute about 90 per cent of the total dry weight of a living cell. However, a rich variety of small molecules, though contributing little to the mass, are present in very great numbers indeed and are linked together in a complex ramification of interlocking reactions, the unravelling of which constitutes one of the triumphs of modern biochemistry, even before the recent growth of molecular biology.

The different macromolecules play many different roles in the living organism. The lipids and polysaccharides are both important as stores of energy and the latter also have structural and protective roles. Phospholipids have a key role in the structure of membranes; but the two main actors on the stage of life are really the proteins and nucleic acids. The proteins are the most versatile of the two, for some are involved in structural frameworks (e.g., skin, horn); some in doing mechanical work

(e.g., myosin in muscle); some in the transport of small molecules and ions (e.g., haemoglobin carrying oxygen); some in
chemical control of other substances (e.g., insulin on sugar
levels); some in protective systems (e.g., immunoglobulins towards invading antigens); and, most versatile of all, many catalyse specific chemical reactions of the cell (the enzymes). One
class of nucleic acid, DNA, in the nucleus of the cell, where it
is part of the chromosomes, carries in the pattern of its base-
pair sequences the coded 'information', in the communication
engineer's sense, which is the blueprint for that particular organism and is inherited from the cell which preceded it and which,
in a sexually reproducing organism, can eventually be traced
back in a line of cellular forbears to that cell which was the
joint product of a contribution from each parent. The other
type of nucleic acid, RNA, exists in at least three major forms
each of which has a specific role in translating the inherited
genetically controlled message carried in the sequence of base-
pairs in DNA into the 'language' of proteins, i.e., into specific
molecular patterns (amino acid sequences) in proteins, in all
their manifold variety and specificity. How these macromolecules perform these roles has only been discovered and un-
ravelled in the last two decades. I have tried elsewhere[1] to
outline some of the structures and processes involved in this
translation process of DNA-RNA-protein. The details, fascinating as they are, are perhaps less important than the realization
that the special properties of these macromolecules are entirely
due to their special architecture which is, as it were, built up
in a series of levels. DNA is a very long molecule indeed, consisting of two intertwining helical chains linked internally by joining a series of nucleotide units by ordinary chemical bonds.
These double chains are also beginning to be found in a circular
form in which each long chain joins up with its starting-point.
Four types of nucleotide participate, each consisting of one of
four nitrogeneous 'bases' linked to a sugar (deoxyribose) and
a phosphoric acid residue. The four bases (denoted as A, C, T,
G) are arranged in pairs (A–T, G–C) in a variety of sequences
but the common backbone link in the chains is through the

---

[1] In Chapter I of *Biology and Personality*, ed. I. T. Ramsey (Oxford, 1965); and,
with more description of the scientific observations, in *The Molecular Basis of
Heredity*, by R. B. Drysdale and A. R. Peacocke (revised reprint, London, 1967).

regularly repeating sugar-phosphate part of the nucleotide.[1] So DNA is a structure in which along the length of the chain exactly the same bonding unit repeats itself, together with immense variety in the sequence of the pairs of bases. Herein, incidentally, lies the clue to much biological structure—the combination of regularly repeated structures with a high degree of specificity. In DNA the specificity lies in the pairing of bases across and between the polynucleotide chains. The sequence of base-pairs (i.e., the two types A–T and G–C) is entirely specific for each organism and it is this sequence which is inherited from the parent cell or cells and is the blueprint for the organism. This sequence of base-pairs has no meaning except in the context of the organism and although it is indeed a chemical structure it cannot be said to be *chemically* determined for no chemical process would give such a highly *specific* sequence, which it is only possible for the DNA to acquire in the context of the organism. Because of the specificity of pairing (only A with T and only G with C) the sequence of A, T, G, and C[1] along one of the strands determines that along the other and this provides a molecular mechanism for producing 'progeny' DNA molecules of the same base-pair sequence, which is the unique and necessary feature of this macromolecule with its function of hereditary transmission. RNA is only a single polynucleotide chain (it has a different sugar, ribose, and one base different) which is thereby rendered more flexible in the configurations it can assume and this is utilized in the translation mechanism.

Proteins consist of amino acids, of which there are commonly 20, linked together by a common type of bond (the peptide bond)[2]: the variation appears in the side chains of each residue of amino acid so linked. The sequence of these amino acids in a given protein is controlled by the sequence of base pairs in an RNA molecule which copies that in one of the strands of the DNA. The code which links the two is now known: each particular possible triplet of nucleotide bases, with the exception of two, codes for a particular amino acid. The sequence of the

---

[1] A = adenine, C = cytosine, T = thymine, G = guanine.

[2] ---R . C—N . R'---, where R, R' each represent an amino acid residue.
$\qquad$ ‖ |
$\qquad$ O H

building blocks, the amino acids, of the protein chains is called
its primary structure and is highly specific to each protein with
a particular function, for it determines what shape that protein
chain will assume in the three dimensions of space. Such chains
can form regular and irregular bonds within and between
chains which are thereby constrained to take up that particular
convoluted form in space which is necessary to their function—
as has now been verified by the determination of the detailed
structure of the oxygen-carriers myoglobin and haemoglobin,
and also of a number of enzymes (e.g., lysozyme, ribonuclease,
chymotrypsinogen, carbonic anhydrase). These protein chains
so folded can often aggregate specifically with a small number
of other chains to form larger assemblies which may then acquire
special properties by virtue of this new juxtaposition: e.g., the
special oxygen-binding properties of haemoglobin compared
with those of its separated sub-units; the functioning of the
complex of 42 (or possibly 66) protein units of the pyruvate
dehydrogenase enzyme complex. The common principle here,
which is now being worked out in detail in many instances, is
that simple units assembled in a specific array acquire by
virtue of the specificity of that array the ability to perform a
unique function; but that the chemical bonding between these
constitutive units (the amino acids) is the same throughout the
multitude of proteins. This feature of a common bonding together with a high specificity in sequence is similar to that which
we noted also occurred in the genetic transmitter, DNA.

There is one further striking aspect of this fascinating molecular mechanism, which has been implicit in the way I have been
describing it. It is that, as far as a series of wide-ranging investigations can tell, the genetic code (the triplet of bases which
controls the positioning of each amino acid) is universal: that
is, it is common to all forms of life from bacteria and bacteriophage and viruses to plants, animals and man. This is a
striking indication of the common origin of all forms of life from
some common precursor, for this genetic code is only one of
many thousands of possibilities, since there is no particular
chemical basis for any actual triplet (UCA, say) coding for the
one particular amino acid (serine in this case) for which it does
in fact code. It *could* have been some other nucleotide triplet
but once the code was evolved, no variation from it was possible

thereafter. This universality of the code throughout all living organisms on the earth suggests they have originated from one primitive living form.

Viruses have long held a position of some notoriety as occupying the borderland between the clearly non-living and the clearly living. For they are genuinely molecular, being highly ordered complexes of a molecule of RNA, or, less frequently, of DNA, embedded in a jacket consisting of a larger number of small protein molecules, self-assembled in a particular pattern which accommodates the nucleic acid. These entities can be handled in solution like other large macromolecular complexes and have a defined molecular weight, density, velocity in a unit gravitational field, and so on. But injected into the appropriate bacterium, plant or animal they can multiply rapidly, eventually causing the death of the host organism, or at least making it very sickly, if plant or animal. They possess this 'living' property of self-reproduction by taking over, as it were, the protein—and nucleic-acid—synthesizing systems of the host cells. Are they living or non-living? The impossibility of answering this question illustrates well how ideas on the molecular structure of living matter have had to develop.

The DNA which carries the genetic instructions for the organism, whether this consists of only a few cells or millions, resides in the nucleus where it is attached to proteins and most of it is quiescent in so far as it is not producing its specific RNA, and so proteins, most of the time. Indeed, if it did do so there would be no ordered development of the organism with differentiation into the many kinds of cell necessary to different organs (those of bone, nerves, liver, brain, pancreas and so on). For the cells in the various organs still have the same complement of DNA but most of it is somehow 'switched off'. How this mechanism controlling development and differentiation works is scarcely known at all and is likely to prove very complex, for it is a control mechanism which follows a prescribed plan in a time sequence so that, in the developing embryo, for example, particular types of cells with particular functions only appear at a particular stage. Again what little we do know of this mechanism indicates some features common to different organisms. The unity and common basis of the processes at the molecular level in all living organisms has long been recognized in respects other than the genetic processes already outlined. Thus, the carbon compounds in living organisms have been found to exhibit only one set of the two possible (mirror image) arrangements in space of four different groups attached to a given carbon atom. Moreover, there is a striking similarity in a wide range of organisms in the processes used to obtain energy from carbohydrates and fats, both with and without oxygen. This similarity extends to identity of the actual substances intermediate in these cycles and the function of the enzymes catalysing these steps. One fruitful contemporary line of research involves tracing the similarities and differences in their primary structure between proteins in different organisms which perform the same chemical task. This gives a new insight into evolution at the molecular level of these highly specific macromolecules by showing which parts of the primary sequence are essential to its function and which are not, and could lead to better-grounded inferences about the prototype protein which was historically the common precursor of those now having the same function in different organisms.

Another feature of the structure of living organisms at the molecular level which is currently receiving much attention is the nature of membranes. Phospho-lipids and proteins are both implicated and although there is a considerable similarity of membrane structure in a wide variety of cells there is also very often a high degree of specificity in what is or is not allowed to pass. Nerve membranes, for example, are highly selective towards different types of small cations (viz., sodium and potassium ions), otherwise very similar chemically, and it is the movement down the nerve fibre, which is a giant elongated cell, of perturbations in the relative concentrations of these ions which constitute a nerve impulse. At this level, the molecular organization now constitutes the substratum of the larger relationships between different organs of a complex living creature and the chemical substances which flow between them and in and out of the whole creature. This level is that of physiology rather than biochemistry and molecular biology, and there is a gradual transition from the molecular focus of these last-named to the more organismic and holistic approach needed in the study of physiology, behaviour, ecology and the living creature in its wider habitat, at which point the description of molecular processes is only subsidiary to the main story, just as the description of the structure of the atom is subsidiary to the description of the variety of structure and function of protein molecules—subsidiary in that, though essential, it is not alone adequate.

To this general type of relationship between the hierarchy of levels of complexity in the inorganic and biological world we shall have to refer again. For the moment, it may be of interest to summarize the characteristics of living matter in terms which take account of its organization at the molecular level which I have just outlined in the preceding paragraphs. Such attempts have to take into account that matter organized in a form which is living has certain characteristics. These are *inter alia*: ability to self-reproduce the whole inter-ramified structure which constitutes the whole organism; a genetic mutation rate such that self-reproduction is not so absolutely fixed that there is no possibility of further change in that species of organism, but equally is not so rapid that the species never become fully differentiated; ability at the molecular level to replicate particular molecular patterns; ability to maintain highly ordered, improbable structure of low entropy[1] by utilizing the free energy[1] of small and large molecules obtained from both the inorganic and biological environment of the organism; ability to grow and develop in time; and the similarity between the molecular networks of processes and structures in a wide variety of forms of living matter (i.e., different organisms). In the light of these, it may be of interest to quote some attempted descriptions of life by physical scientists aware of the challenge of biology. The first is by J. D. Bernal who has been concerned, as a crystallographer, with the molecular structures in living organisms:

Life is a partial, continuous, progressive, multiform and conditionally inter-active, self-realisation of the potentialities of atomic states.[2]

The terms in this have the following connotations: 'partial' —because only very few of the potentialities of atomic states are realized in terrestrial life; 'continuous'—because each organism proceeds from another; 'progressive'—not in any moral sense,

---

[1] See p. 45, footnotes 1, 2.
[2] J. D. Bernal, *The Origin of Life* (London, 1967), p. 168.

but because new forms are derived from old; 'multiform"—because of the simultaneous existence of a very large range of species; 'conditionally inter-active'—because each organism conditions and is conditioned by the presence of others; 'self-realization'—because of the unique working out by each organism of the interplay of its genetic composition with its environment; 'potentialities of atomic states', together with the initial 'partial'—because all life 'depends' ultimately on the atoms from which its molecules are made.

The second is by C. N. Hinshelwood, who was a physical chemist who applied his understanding of the kinetics of chemical change to explaining the dynamic processes in living organism:

One might in very general terms regard a mass of living matter as a macromolecular, polyfunctional free radical system, of low entropy in virtue of its order, with low activation energy for various reactions in virtue of its centres, and possessing a degree of permanence in virtue of a relatively rigid structure.[1]

The terms used here are taken from the vocabulary of physical chemistry: 'macromolecular'—a macromolecule is a very large molecule composed of many (hundreds or even thousands) of chemically structured units joined by the same kinds of chemical bond; 'polyfunctional, free radical'—refers to the ability of macromolecules to react in a variety of ways at points where there are unsaturated inter-atomic forces; 'low entropy'—in thermodynamics entropy is as we have already mentioned,[2] a measure of the degree of disorder in the system, of the number of ways in which a given state can be attained; 'low activation energy'—the lower this energy barrier is in a chemical reaction the more rapidly it will proceed; 'active centres'—refers to the regions of enzyme molecules catalysing specific chemical reactions.

A third biophysical description of life, by H. C. Longuet-Higgins, stresses the ability of living organisms to transmit instructions to succeeding generations so that their DNA acts as a molecular 'tape' exactly analogous to the programme fed

---

[1] C. N. Hinshelwood, *The Structure of Physical Chemistry* (Oxford, 1951), p. 449.
[2] See p. 45, footnote 1.

to a computer. In the character of a biologist talking to a physicist, he says:

What has been the most important biological discovery of recent years? Surely the discovery that the processes of life are directed by programs, in the most professional sense of that word. In nature, as opposed to computing labs, the really distinctive thing about living processes is that they manifest programmed activity, while non-living processes do not. . . . In nature the controlling programs do not merely determine the way in which an organism reacts to its environment. They also control the actual construction of the organism, and its replication, including the replication of the programs themselves. This is very important, because the small variations which sometimes occur during replication lead to phenotypic variations upon which natural selection can then operate. So life is not merely programmed activity but self-programmed activity.[1]

Of course, none of these definitions is, or would claim to be, exhaustively descriptive of living matter, but they serve to show how life appears to three scientific authors whose philosophical presuppositions are otherwise quite different.

We are now in a position to look, in the light of what is known of the molecular organization of living matter, at the problem of the origin of life[2] during the two thousand million years from the formation of the Earth to the oldest evidence of cellular life (algae in Rhodesian limestone and in Canadian gunflint), the period of about 4,500 to 2,500 million years ago. We have seen how the essential constituent building-blocks (amino acids, bases, sugars) for the macromolecules of life must have been formed into the 'primeval soup' at some point long after the formation of the Earth 4,500 million years ago. We have also seen that the atmosphere then contained no oxygen, so no modern biological mechanisms of energy utilization dependent on this gas can be invoked; for the atmosphere was a reducing mixture of methane, hydrogen, ammonia, hydrogen sulphide, hydrogen cyanide and water vapour. The first protein-like macromolecules may have formed by the joining together of amino acids bound to some suitable solid catalyst or may

[1] H. C. Longuet-Higgins, 'The Seat of the Soul' in *Towards a Theoretical Biology*, Vol. 3, ed. C. H. Waddington (Edinburgh, 1970), pp. 239, 240.
[2] A summary of recent literature, together with a bibliography, is given in Appendix B.

have been formed directly as polypeptides (the general word for chains of linked amino acid residues) by the action of water on the products of a reaction between ammonia (NH_3) and hydrogen cyanide (HCN). These polypeptides might then have become more variegated by interchange of one amino acid residue for another. Simple polynucleotides (the general word for chains of nucleotides) could well have arisen by the joining of the appropriate bases but here the requirement is more stringent. For we know the four bases can be formed in the primitive gas mixture but do not know how they could be linked to a sugar; phosphorylation could have come about through the action on base-sugar units of polyphosphates such as those formed when solutions of simple phosphates are heated. At this point in the attempted reconstruction of the origin of living matter one has the mid-twentieth-century version of the 'Which came first, the chicken or the egg?' poser. In current living organisms, nucleic acids control the formation of proteins but enzyme proteins are essential for catalysing the replication and translation processes of nucleic acids. Each is dependent, though in a different way, on the other and this 'molecular symbiosis' underlies the observed exponential growth rate of living matter, as Hinshelwood and Caldwell showed.[1] This problem has not been solved though informed guesses have been made (see Appendix B).

Two considerations clearly dominate at this point of the argument: firstly, mixtures of both like and unlike macromolecules would tend to aggregate in ordered patterns, as in viruses, the simplest 'living' molecular systems; and, secondly, there would be a competition between different aggregates for the limited supply of essential chemical precursors (amino acids, bases, phosphates, etc.), if primitive self-reproducing aggregates containing proto-proteins and proto-nucleic acids came into existence—so that the aggregate with the most efficient organization would rapidly outgrow and outnumber others; that is, 'natural selection' would occur between even these primitive organelles. The acquisition of a phospho-lipid membrane controlling the ingress and egress of building materials and waste

---

[1] P. C. Caldwell and Sir Cyril Hinshelwood, *J. Chem. Soc.* (1950), p. 3156; Sir Cyril Hinshelwood, Faraday Lecture on 'Autosynthesis', *J. Chem. Soc.* (1953), p. 1947.

products would constitute a real advantage in this competition by maintaining a more steady state within the primitive nucleic-acid-protein aggregate and so a steadier rate of growth. This aggregate would naturally form an incipient colloidal phase, a 'coacervate', in any aqueous medium, whose surface would concentrate such surface-active molecules as phospho-lipids, so one can see how a primitive organism might have developed which we could now justifiably call a cell, since it had a limiting membrane. Any such cells which were able to draw in or synthesize proteins with better catalytic properties in the competition for precursor molecules and for energy suppliers would be at an advantage. At this stage, which Bernal puts at between 4,500 and 3,500 million years ago, all the energy had to be supplied by anaerobic mechanisms for no oxygen was present. At some point about 3,000 million years ago, some cells acquired the ability to synthesize carbohydrates, for energy sources and for structural purposes, by means of the action of sunlight on water and the carbon dioxide which had accumulated in the atmosphere because of its production by the anaerobic mechanisms already mentioned. This process of photosynthesis, which arose in green plants, was only possible through the mediation of a metallo-organic complex called chlorophyll and a number of special enzymes; and, of course, the existence of organisms already possessing a membrane.

It is of great interest therefore that fossil remains of algae have been found in a layer of limestone in Southern Rhodesia which is about 2·5 to 2·7 thousand million years old. The wider importance of this photosynthetic process is that oxygen is produced and from the appearance of green plant-like organisms the proportion of oxygen in the earth's atmosphere steadily rose, taking a sharp turn upwards about 600 million years ago. At this point some organisms developed mechanisms for oxidizing carbohydrates by means of oxygen and so gained an extra supply of energy. For this process suitable proteins, especially the cytochromes, had to be developed. At a later stage, 400 million years ago, when the atmospheric oxygen pressure reached about a tenth of its present value, life could spread to the land as well as in the sea and biological evolution could accelerate. Intense ultraviolet radiation has a destructive effect on protein and macromolecules. However, the increasing concentration of oxygen, by forming in the upper atmosphere a thin layer of ultraviolet-absorbing ozone, itself the product of irradiating oxygen with ultraviolet light, afforded protection for this new life on land, and in the upper levels of the sea.

The above account represents broadly the hypotheses of A. I. Oparin and J. B. S. Haldane; a critical account of the current evidence for this theory, with a valuable attempt to construct the most plausible time scale, has been made recently by J. D. Bernal.[1] Other plausible views of the sequence of events have naturally been advanced, but the main feature of all theories is that by utilizing our present knowledge of chemical reactions and of the molecular organization of life, together with careful chemical analysis and dating of rocks at different stages of the Earth's development, it is possible to make reasonable proposals about the origin of life. In other words, no categories other than those pertinent to molecular systems have had to be employed and life is regarded as a form of matter organized in a certain way which has arisen by the operation of 'laws' or by manifestations of the properties of matter which we now know, and that once it has arisen it has the unique properties outlined in the definitions of life already quoted.

We can now return to the question raised earlier about the possibility of synthesizing 'life' in the laboratory. Since we can see that life evolved by the operation of chemical processes which we can reasonably surmise, there is, in principle, no reason why the complete synthesis might not be achieved in the laboratory of a molecular aggregate which satisfies these criteria of living matter, namely, self-reproducibility, etc. Two naturally occurring proteins, the hormone insulin and the enzyme ribonuclease, have now been synthesized by the methods of organic chemistry by groups of Chinese and American scientists, respectively, starting from purely synthetic materials; and 'synthetic DNA' has been made from entirely synthetic nucleotide precursors, but this, inevitably in the present state of biochemical techniques, involved the use of enzymes themselves isolated from living cells. The intricacy of the chemistry and the number of steps required to synthesize even one protein with enzymatic activity or even a modest length of DNA, is

[1] J. D. Bernal, op. cit., Chapter 7.

daunting. For a typical enzyme protein may contain 200 amino acids joined in a specific sequence and the intact DNA of a bacterial cell contains of the order of a million base-pairs in a sequence specific to the organism from which it has been isolated. Thus a complete synthesis *de novo* presents at the moment immense technical problems. Even if an appropriate potentially auto-synthetic group of macromolecules could be achieved, one still has the baffling problem of arranging them to fit together in space (and time) at the molecular level to express their potentiality. Meanwhile, synthesis of parts of living organisms may be achieved if one is allowed to cheat a little by using some isolated enzymes. At the present stage these technical problems almost amount to expecting a watch to be formed by shaking its component parts together long enough. However, this does not mean that in principle living matter can never be synthesized and that some essential, unknown, metaphysical ingredient beyond our ken and control is needed and lacking.

There is a further corollary to this, which has often been pointed out. There are probably, according to Hoyle,[1] about 10^{11} stars of the same type (slow-spinning 'dwarf') as the Sun in our galaxy alone. So in our galaxy there might be of the order of 10^9 planets whose surface temperature and chemical composition of crust and atmosphere, size and distance from its 'parent' star, and whose chemical development in time, have followed a similar sequence to that on the Earth. Since the chemical elements are the same throughout this observable universe there is no sufficient reason why living matter should not also have developed on some of these planets of the right chemical constitution, of which there may be up to 10^{11} in the whole Universe. The factors conditioning the development of self-producing macromolecules would then apply, with the added variant possibilities that the universal genetic code developed elsewhere would probably not be the same as on the Earth and that, since the evolution of higher organisms is a complex interplay of inherited variations and local climatic conditions, the evolved morphologies of living organisms might be different. But *that* living matter could evolve is highly probable.

[1] F. Hoyle, *The Nature of the Universe* (Oxford, 1960) and *Frontiers of Astronomy* (London, 1955).

3. FROM LIVING MATTER TO MAN

The molecular structures of life and their possible origins in time have been given disproportionate treatment, even in this brief sketch, for much of this could only have been written after the great revolution in biochemical studies of the last two decades. The broad outlines of the great sweep of biological evolution have been a part of general knowledge and education for much longer than this, for this way of looking at the living organisms of the world was clearly delineated by Darwin and Wallace over a hundred years ago. The degree of diversity and complexity of living organisms, of the forms of living matter, are so enormous that the achievements of naturalists and biologists in co-ordinating knowledge of the vast variety of living creatures can only be described as one of the great triumphs of the human mind. One need only point to the existence of over a million extant known species (let alone varieties within them) of living creatures, which constitute only a small fraction of those known to have existed at various times in the past. These facts alone testify to the immeasurable ability of living matter to diversify its forms. Anyone attempting to outline a viewpoint or perspective on the whole scene is at this level faced with an overwhelming intricacy and variety to which the reader's attention is perhaps best drawn by asking him to look at the varieties of living organisms to be seen even in a few square yards of his own garden. Fortunately, many excellent accounts of the process are available.[1]

The main evidence for the general evolution of living organisms comes from the fossil record of the earth's crust (palaeontology), comparative anatomy and embryology, the geographical distribution of animals, and the science of heredity of living organisms (genetics). To these, we can now add the comparative study of the amino-acid sequences of proteins, though such work is only just beginning to be fruitful.

There are good biochemical reasons for believing that the earliest unicellular organisms soon diverged into those that utilized photosynthetic processes (light + carbon dioxide +

---

[1] To mention only a few: G. G. Simpson, *The Meaning of Evolution* (London, 1950); J. Huxley, *Evolution: The Modern Synthesis* (London, 1963); J. Maynard Smith, *The Theory of Evolution* (London, 1966); and the interestingly illustrated *Animal and Plant Diversity*, by N. D. Buffaloe (New Jersey, 1968).

chlorophyll, etc.) to build up their essential carbon compounds, thereby evolving oxygen; and into those that could not. Many of these latter then evolved by acquiring mechanisms enabling them to feed either on the plants or on other cells, thereby taking short-cuts in the biochemical network. There is a 'biochemical logic' underlying this necessity, namely, that in order to build up complex structures it is advantageous to begin with pre-formed chemical units, that is, structures synthesized in other living organisms. To do this, colonies of cells and genuinely multi-cellular organisms (*metazoa*) have certain advantages, especially if different groups of cells in one organism can take over different functions in the complex processes of capturing, breaking up, digesting, and eliminating the waste-products of 'food' in the form of other living organisms.

Pre-Cambrian rocks, dating from over 600 million years ago, contain simple photosynthetic algae much like the present blue-green algae, and imprints of soft-bodied animals, but the first calcareous fossils are found in the rocks called Cambrian, which refers to the long period of life in the seas from 570 to 500 million years ago. By then, fairly advanced representatives of the main phyla of the animal kingdom, except the true vertebrates, had come into existence. Thus crustaceans, molluscs, worms and echinoderms are well represented; such multi-cellular creatures presuppose a long evolution. One major and early branching, which occurred even before the Cambrian phase, was the parting of the photosynthetic from non-photosynthetic cells. The development of living forms subsequently to the Cambrian era, as observed in the records of the rocks, is not one continuous line of development with a few side branches, but is much more analogous to a tree which continuously branches out in such a way that no limb can be said to be the main trunk, or a river[1] spreading out at a delta into multitudinous rivulets of many lengths and widths.

The sequence,[2] as inferred from the geological record, was:

[1] Cf. Sir Alister Hardy, *The Living Stream* (London, 1965), Lecture I.
[2] Succinctly delineated by Sir W. Le Gros Clark, in his Presidential Address to the British Association in 1961 on 'The Humanity of Man', *The Advancement of Science*, 1961, xviii, No. 73; see also Hardy, loc. cit., p. 28 f. and Maynard Smith, loc. cit., ch. 17.

Years ago	*Period*	*Principal new living organisms*
More than 600 million	Pre-Cambrian	Simple photosynthetic algae; soft-bodied animals.
570–500 million	Cambrian	Calcareous fossils: crustaceans, molluscs, worms, echinoderms.
500–430 million	Ordovician	First vertebrates—fishes.
430–395 million	Silurian	First known land plants; air-breathing animals; fishes becoming numerous.
395–345 million	Devonian	Early land plants; amphibians; fishes dominant.
345–280 million	Carboniferous	Reptiles, insects and one type of plant (gymnosperms, such as conifers).
280–225 million	Permian	First modern conifers and land vertebrates.
225–190 million	Triassic	First mammals and dinosaurs.
190–135 million	Jurassic	First flowering plants; primitive birds; flying reptiles; dinosaurs and higher insects numerous.
135–65 million	Cretaceous	More primitive mammals; gymnosperms dominant, giving way to flowering plants.
65–26 million	Early Tertiary (Palaeocene, Eocene and Oligocene)	Modern mammals, including the first anthropoid apes; birds in extensive forests.
26–2 million	Late Tertiary (Miocene and Pliocene)	Man's ancestors, Hominidae; forests less extensive.
2 million to present	Pleistocene and Recent	Great mammals disappear; forbears of modern man (Australopithecus 10^6 to 5×10^5 years B.C.; Pithecanthropus, 500,000 to 200,000 B.C.; Neanderthal man, 60,000(?) to 40,000 B.C.; 'Homo sapiens', ca. 40,000 B.C.

This brief outline merely sketches some of the major new 'shoots' that have appeared at different times on the tree of life and does no justice at all to those forms which have continued through large tracts of geological time spanning many of these periods, or the numerous branches and off-shoots which have come to an end, far more numerous than surviving species.

By giving mere numbers the above outline also does not do justice to the increasing rapidity of the development with time, which might be better plotted on a logarithmic scale, though the reader will no doubt have noticed how this time scale began to contract by factors of 10 as the description of the full development of the 'tree' approached the present. More dramatically, the time scale of the development of the Earth and of life on it may be concentrated as follows into the 48 hours up to a midnight hour representing the present, with each hour standing for a 100 million years.

During the second half of the first 24 'hours' and the following morning and afternoon, primitive living matter evolved chemically, assembling and coagulating; and only at 6.0 p.m. in the evening of this second 'day' do the first fossils appear. From 6.0 to 7.0 p.m. on this second day, the seas fill with shelled creatures, but only at 8.0 p.m. can fishes be recognized. At 9.0 p.m. amphibians appear on land and at 10.30 p.m. the reptiles dominate the earth. By 11.30 p.m., with $23\frac{1}{2}$ hours of our second 'day' of the Earth's development gone, mammals, including the first primates, spread across the globe. At 11.50 p.m. the monkeys and apes among the trees come to the ground. At 11.59 p.m. a primate stands on two legs and in the last 30 seconds of this 'day' we see man appear, but only at the last stroke of the midnight bell can we recognize the earliest tools made by modern man, whom we can at last call *Homo sapiens*.[1]

How did this remarkable, ever-accelerating development occur? The basic outlines of the answer to this question were formulated by Wallace and Darwin in the famous presentation of their papers to the Linnean Society in 1858 and in *The Origin of Species* published by Darwin just over a year later, as the result of twenty years of work. It is based on the perception that it is populations of organisms, not the individual organisms, which evolve and that they do so by 'natural selection' which is perhaps best described in Darwin's own words:[2]

Again, it may be asked, how is it that varieties, which I have called incipient species, become ultimately converted into good and distinct species, which in most cases obviously differ from each other far more than do the varieties of the same species? How do these groups of species, which constitute what are called distinct genera, and which differ from each other more than do the species of the same genus, arise? All these results, . . . follow from the struggle for life. Owing to this struggle, variations, however slight and from whatever

---

[1] I am indebted to my former colleague, Professor D. Nichols, of the University of Exeter, for this striking illustrative reduction of the time scale of evolution.

[2] C. Darwin, *The Origin of Species by means of natural selection*, 6th edit., Chap. iii (Thinkers Library Ed., Watts & Co., London, pp. 46, 97, 98).

cause proceeding, if they be in any degree profitable to the individuals of a species, in their infinitely complex relations to other organic beings and to their physical conditions of life, will tend to the preservation of such individuals, and will generally be inherited by the offspring. The offspring, also, will thus have a better chance of surviving, for, of the many individuals of any species which are periodically born, but a small number can survive. I have called this principle, by which each slight variation, if useful, is preserved, by the term Natural Selection, in order to mark its relation to man's power of selection. But the expression often used by Mr. Herbert Spencer of the Survival of the Fittest is more accurate, and is sometimes equally convenient.

If under changing conditions of life organic beings present individual differences in almost every part of their structure, and this cannot be disputed; if there be, owing to their geometrical rate of increase, a severe struggle for life at some age, season or year, and this certainly cannot be disputed; then, considering the infinite complexity of the relations of all organic beings to each other and to their conditions of life, causing an infinite diversity in structure, constitution, and habits, to be advantageous to them, it would be a most extraordinary fact if no variations had ever occurred useful to each being's own welfare, in the same manner as so many variations have occurred useful to man. But if variations useful to any organic being ever do occur, assuredly individuals thus characterised will have the best chance of being preserved in the struggle for life; and from the strong principle of inheritance, these will tend to produce offspring similarly characterised. This principle of preservation, or the survival of the fittest, I have called Natural Selection. It leads to the improvement of each creature in relation to its organic and inorganic conditions of life; and consequently, in most cases, to what must be regarded as an advance in organisation. Nevertheless, low and simple forms will long endure if well fitted for their simple conditions of life.

This idea, which had also come to Wallace quite independently in 1858, was based on observations of variation in both domesticated creatures (e.g. the varieties of pigeons) and in creatures in the wild (e.g., the various species of finches in the Galapagos islands), on the over-production of offspring by nature, on the apparent competition of all living organisms with each other for limited common food resources and on their predation on each other, and on the inheritance of favourable traits by offspring from their parents (sexual reproduction greatly increasing the combination of variants that are possible).

Throughout the rest of the nineteenth century the discussion of these ideas proceeded without any precise understanding of the principles of inheritance which had been elucidated, unknown to the world, by the Augustinian monk Mendel as early as 1865 but only came to light in 1900. These principles were concerned with the statistical distribution of specific characters among successive generations and led to the postulate of the existence of heredity factors, which determine these characters, which segregate when gametes (the sexual 'half-cells') are formed, and which assort independently. These factors came to be located in the chromosomes of the cell nucleus and eventually in its DNA—which is the story[1] of modern genetics and molecular biology, to which we have referred.

These 'factors' or genes, as we call them, are known to be occasionally subjected to sudden changes, called mutations, whose chemical basis in the DNA structure can often be inferred. These mutations result from the action of radiation (ultraviolet light, γ-rays, cosmic rays), by the action of physical and chemical agents, and from causes not fully known: they are inherited and are random with respect to the biological needs of the organism. Current biological thinking sees the environment acting by natural selection of the type described by Darwin and Wallace, on populations containing occasional individuals which possess a mutated gene(s) affecting their form, functional parts, biochemical and physiological organization or behaviour. Most mutants are not favourable for survival but those that are will quickly spread through the population, so that it is the action of environment on mutations which alters the direction of evolution. From this point of view, natural selection might more properly be called differential reproduction. How quickly this occurs and what the quantitative relationships are at this statistical level have been the subject of study of 'biomathematics' since R. A. Fisher demonstrated how

[1] Outlined in many publications, e.g., the detailed account *The Molecular Biology of the Gene*, by J. D. Watson (New York, 1965); the shorter *Molecular Biology: Genes and the Chemical Control of Cells*, by J. M. Barry (New Jersey, 1964) and the more chemically oriented *The Molecular Basis of Heredity*, by R. B. Drysdale and A. R. Peacocke (revised reprint, London, 1967).

readily and quickly a small advantageous mutant could be established in a population. This combination of ideas is some-times called 'neo-Darwinism', but while most biologists appear to accept this picture, there seems to be an increasing recogni-tion of the complexity of the interaction of the individual, mutated or otherwise, with its environment and the variety of the effects manifested in the population. Thus Huxley[1] can enumerate at least six different types of selection (normalizing, directional, diversifying, balancing, *post hoc* and variability) in addition to the broader categories of survival (phenotypic), reproductive (genotypic) and sexual selection and, he adds, for human beings, social (psychosocial) selection. The subtlety of the interaction is well illustrated by Waddington's[2] demon-stration of what he calls 'genetic assimilation', whereby genes are naturally selected which dispose an organism to become modified in response to a particular environmental change. This might be important when the modifications in question were those of behaviour, in which connection the possibility of 'or-ganic selection' has to be considered. According to this principle of selection, which Sir Alister Hardy[3] has been concerned to re-habilitate (and which he, perhaps more controversially, re-gards as virtually indistinguishable from genetic assimilation), a creature may by changing its behaviour alter its environment and so give structural mutations which adapt it better to this new environment a greater chance of being naturally selected. The mere physical scientist is well advised to handle gently such a complex, interwoven web of cause and effect and not to apply too readily the rough tools of his simplified concepts developed for a less subtle and more readily analysed level of the organiza-tion of matter. We see the world of living organisms as exhibiting a *unity* of structures and forms of molecular organization, a *continuity* with simpler past forms, together with an immense *diversity* arising out of circumstances and restrictions which can only properly be called historical, since they concern the inter-action at a particular time of each particular mutant-containing population of organisms with each particular environment

---

[1] J. S. Huxley, loc. cit., pp. xxi ff.

[2] Described for the general reader in C. H. Waddington, *The Nature of Life* (London, 1963), pp. 88 ff.

[3] Loc. cit., pp. 161 ff., 189 ff.; cf. Huxley, loc. cit., pp. 304 ff, 523 ff.

(including other organisms, as well as the physical environment, in this term). The ability to reproduce, the fact of the death of the individual and the 'biochemical logic' which necessitates that one form of life should utilize some of the molecular structures built up by other forms, are the prerequisites of evolution. But cold logic readily makes way to a sense of wonder at the broad vista of this process, never better expressed than in the words with which Darwin concludes his great work:[1]

It is interesting to contemplate a tangled bank, clothed with many plants of many kinds, with birds singing on the bushes, with various insects flitting about, and with worms crawling through the damp earth, and to reflect that these elaborately constructed forms, so different from each other, and dependent upon each other in so complex a manner, have all been produced by laws acting around us. These laws, taken in the largest sense, being Growth and Reproduction; Inheritance which is almost implied by reproduction; Variability from the indirect and direct action of the conditions of life, and from use and disuse: a Ratio of Increase so high as to lead to a Struggle for Life, and as a consequence to Natural Selection, entailing Divergence of Character and the Extinction of less-improved forms. Thus, from the war of nature, from famine and death, the most exalted object which we are capable of conceiving, namely the production of the higher animals, directly follows. There is grandeur in this view of life, with its several powers, having been originally breathed by the Creator into a few forms or into one; and that, whilst this planet has gone cycling on according to the fixed law of gravity, from so simple a beginning endless forms most beautiful and most wonderful have been, and are being evolved.

[1] C. Darwin, op. cit., 6th ed. (Thinkers Library, Watts, London), p. 408.

CHAPTER 3

Distinctive features of the processes of inorganic and biological evolution

I. 'EVOLUTION—THE COSMIC PROCESS'

Voltaire's shrewd thrust at much of what passed for theology in his day, 'Si Dieu nous a fait à son image, nous le lui avons bien rendu',[1] might well have been directed by him, had he lived now, at many scientists who write on Evolution, with a capital 'E', or the Cosmic Process. Impressed, indeed overawed, by the grandeur and dynamic of the processes that have led from the primeval mass of hydrogen nuclei to *Homo sapiens*, they have understandably allowed a proper sense of wonder to set in motion in their minds inspirations other than the purely scientific: so that, not surprisingly, their ensuing reflections on this impressive development have had incorporated into them their deepest personal aspirations even though they begin by claiming to speak for science as such. The danger is as real as it is understandable. We must accept the strictures and warnings of, for example, Toulmin[2] against the sequence in which a genuine scientific theory, such as that of biological evolution by natural selection, becomes transformed into a metaphysic and sweeps us along with its supposed scientific momentum into positions which have no scientific basis and which are philosophically and theologically indefensible.[3] Thus we have seen interpretations of the 'cosmic process' which are, in turn, ethical but agnostic (J. Huxley), Christian (Teilhard de Chardin) and atheistical and anti-ethical (Nietzsche), according to presuppositions and world-views already adopted for other reasons. Toulmin[4] describes such interpretations in the following terms:

[1] *Le Soltisier*, xxxii: 'If God made us in His image, we have certainly returned the compliment.'

[2] S. Toulmin, 'Contemporary scientific mythology', in *Metaphysical Beliefs* (London, 1957).

[3] See also the similar comments of P. B. Medawar on 'Herbert Spencer and the law of general evolution', in *The Art of the Soluble* (London, 1967).

[4] Toulmin, op. cit., p. 56.

For him [J. Huxley[1]], 'evolution' means more than natural selection. It is a composite notion and a more grandiose one for which the biological term serves only as a starting point. Here is the recipe for producing it. First, select from the countless evolutionary processes that biologists study the particular one which has led up to the appearance of man. . . . Then tack on to the beginning of this historical sequence a series of physico-chemical events leading up to the appearance of the first living creatures, and at the latter end treat the development of civilization and technology as a continuation of the biological trend 'by other means'. . . . Finally, christen your conceptual artefact 'the cosmic process' and present it as a golden thread leading from the remotest past up to the present day and on into the future.

This is undoubtedly a distortion of what Huxley does, but at least it serves to point to the dangers of trying to think on too large a scale. But, *pace* Toulmin, the temporal sequence of: a universe without the Earth; the Earth; life; and then man, are reliable inferences from the available evidence and invite inspection, analysis and interpretation. There are good scientific grounds for postulating the development outlined in the previous chapter and we still need to have some way of referring to it as a whole, if only because each stage has succeeded the other. The word 'evolution' has a genuine general meaning which includes 'appearance (of events, etc.) in due succession' (*O.E.D.*). It was in this sense applied to the biological theory of the origin and development of species and can, it seems to me, properly be applied to the succession of events from matter to man—without any capital 'E' and without any metaphysical or theological overtones. When so applied the appropriate general adjective to be attached to 'evolution' is surely 'cosmic', as pertaining to the universe as an ordered whole, rather than to the Earth alone and as such. Perhaps by introducing any sense of order, by using the word 'cosmic', the metaphysical and theological question appears to have been begged already, but it is intended to refer only to such order as is indicated in the scientific account itself. Thus, 'cosmic evolution' can simply denote, point to, the events outlined in the previous chapter, without any mythological implications. To some, 'development of the cosmos', or 'the cosmic development' may seem more

[1] For example, in his Romanes Lecture, *Evolutionary Ethics* (Oxford, 1943).

satisfactory because more neutral. Less certainly, one might speak of the 'cosmic process' but perhaps this has teleological overtones which might conceal a lurking 'mythology' ready Minerva-like to spring up fully armed later in the argument.

Whichever of these terms are subsequently used in this chapter, my intention is to refer to that sequence of events to which science points, without metaphysical implications. This clarification is necessary as a prelude to the fair discernment of any distinctive features, characteristics, and trends, if any, in the development of the cosmos.

It is the aim of this chapter to make such an examination of both the biological and wider evolutionary development (outlined in chapter 2) so that the perspective on the world, including man, which the scientific enterprise yields may be set alongside the insights resulting from the theological enterprise.

2. CONTINUITY

The continuity of development from one organized form of matter into another is perhaps the most striking feature of the cosmic development. We recall Darwin's[1] reference to the 'few forms or . . . one' into which life was 'originally breathed', and from which all living organisms have evolved. This continuity of material forms is also characteristic of the life of every *individual* organism whose identity and individuality is, at one point in time, entirely contained in a few DNA molecules which are inherited from its parent(s) and from which its whole development then proceeds under the control of the genetic message they carry—in the context, it must be stressed, of the cellular organization in which they are embedded. That the continuity of life has a molecular basis is beginning to become apparent in similarities and differences in the amino-acid sequences of proteins with the same activity but from different species; and in homologies in the case sequences of DNA from different species. Thus it has been reported[2] that 20 per cent of human DNA is identical with the DNA of mammals, 8 per cent with that of birds, 5 per cent with that of fishes and less than 0·01

[1] As quoted on p. 76, end of Chapter 2.
[2] J. De Ley and J. W. Park, *Nature* (London) (1966) **211**, 1002; B. J. McCarthy, E. T. Bolton, *Proc. Nat. Acad. Sci.*, U.S. (1963) **50**, 156; B. H. Hoyer, B. J. McCarthy, and E. T. Bolton, *Science* (1964) **144**, 959.

per cent with that of bacteria; since these sequences carry the genetic blueprint for the organism the evolutionary affinities may well be deduced to correspond, though it has subsequently appeared that this type of homology is difficult to determine and assess.

However, as hinted above, we must be wary of attributing biological properties to any particular type of molecule, even DNA, divorced from the biological milieu (cytoplasm, intracellular fluid, organ, organism) in which it exists *in vivo*. For when DNA is isolated it takes the form of a white fibrous solid which may be stored in a tube in a cold room and dissolved in saline solutions, and can no more be said to be 'alive' than, say, a sample of polystyrene manufactured by the modern plastic industry. The DNA which carries genetic properties does so only in its biological context which gives meaning and opportunity of expression to its particular and unique sequence of base pairs.

So far, it is the material continuity of the biological world which has been stressed. But, as shown in the previous chapter, there are now reasonable grounds for inferring that the whole biological development stemmed from a 'few forms or one' of macromolecular organelles, themselves the resultant of purely chemical processes. This continuity between the biological and inorganic worlds is, of course, not confined to the origins of life but is apparent to the biochemist in the present living world for there he sees carbon dioxide and minerals being imbibed by plants, which are then ingested by animals, so that all living matter is ultimately built up from the inorganic atomic constituents of the physical world.

The stress on this continuity between the living and non-living worlds, with no ancillary evocation of any intruding principle, has been called by some authors[1] a 'materialistic' theory of life and of evolution, and I would not demur at this, but for the implications that have accrued to the word 'materialistic' since the nineteenth century. For there is a hidden implication that we know already what we mean by the word 'matter'; whereas the cosmic evolution which I have outlined can be regarded as revealing, as the aeons unfold, that of which matter is capable when it adopts new forms of organization. Just as we do not know all there is to be known about oxygen and hydrogen

[1] For example, G. G. Simpson, op. cit.

atoms until they combine to form the new entity of a molecule of water with all *its* properties, so we do not know all the properties of oxygen, carbon, nitrogen, hydrogen and phosphorus (or, if one prefers, of sugars, bases and phosphoric acid) until they adopt the form of the DNA molecule in its biological milieu. From this viewpoint, the continuity of the cosmic development serves to reveal the potentialities of the primordial nebular cloud of hydrogen atoms (or its nuclear 'particulate' predecessors, if any). So the description of the cosmic development, including the biological, as 'materialistic' is acceptable if, and only if, we mean by the word 'matter' something very different from the limited billiard-ball concept of a nineteenth-century materialism, based on a mechanistic universe governed by Newtonian mechanics. For, to put it rhetorically, just look at what has become of the 'simple' matter of the nebulae! More explicitly, each level of the development of the cosmos can, it appears, legitimately be regarded as a manifestation of the potentialities of matter which have been implicit in it from the beginning in its simplest forms and have only gradually unfolded.

At the present stage of the discussion, it appears then that there are good scientific grounds for stressing the continuity of the physical with the biological worlds, and so with whatever they are themselves continuous with; and also for provisionally describing the cosmic process as 'materialistic', provided that term is understood in the light of this, However, the qualification just made of 'materialistic' may in the end be so drastic that some other less misleading term becomes necessary. For 'matter' appears to be far more subtle and its potentialities far richer and more diverse than can be inferred from observations made at any one particular level of the development of the cosmos, particularly if that is the simplest and least complex.

3. BY NATURAL LAW

We have already seen that the development of the cosmos proceeds, or can reasonably be argued to have proceeded, by the operation of natural laws we now know: indeed, to say this, is but another way of expressing the continuity of development discussed above. The continuity not only consists in a due succession in time whereby one state of matter is seen to emerge from its predecessor but also consists in the transitions themselves (hydrogen nuclei–heavier atoms–small molecules–macromolecules–aggregates–primitive cells–living organisms, etc.) being also explicable in terms of natural laws. For these laws are, like much of physical chemistry and biochemistry, concerned with the rates and possibility of such changes. The term 'natural laws' in the preceding sentences is not meant to carry any particular implications concerning the epistemology of science, that is, how and what we really know by applying scientific methods. The phrase 'natural law' is intended as a convenient shorthand for the accumulated knowledge afforded by scientific methods of the regular behaviour of organized matter and of the processes it undergoes; and also of the conceptual schemes or models whereby this knowledge is organized into satisfying and coherent patterns. It is not intended to have any implications of the possible existence of a 'Law-giver' nor is the rigid eighteenth-century concept of laws of nature meant to be implied. Perhaps we could put the situation thus. We are affirming that the relationships and metamorphoses between the various forms of matter which happened during the development of the cosmos are understandable instances of, extrapolations from, or inferences from relationships observed to be existing now between these various forms of matter.

Because biological evolution proceeds as the result of mutations occurring in the genetic material and these are random with respect to the biological needs of the organism, it is sometimes urged that *therefore* this biological development is entirely 'by chance' and this is then made the basis of further deductions. But this is to misconceive (i) the role of random processes underlying regular phenomena governed by 'laws'; and (ii) the biological context in which mutations in DNA, etc. occur. These two points need further elaboration. (i) It might equally be argued that because the motion of the individual molecules in a gas is a series of random collisions governed only by statistical probabilities *therefore* the whole assembly of such molecules cannot behave in a regular way according to 'laws' we can determine. However, the science of statistical thermodynamics and mechanics is directed to showing precisely how it is that an *assembly* of such randomly colliding molecules (to take the simplest case) can behave in the regular way described, for example, by the gas laws (whether the simple $PV=RT$ or more elaborate expressions); or how the statistical tendency of a mixture of molecules which can interchange atoms or groups of atoms in a chemical reaction by randomly seeking ways of minimizing their energy and maximizing the number of ways any state can be attained gives rise to a situation which on the macroscopic scale is called by the scientist 'chemical equilibrium'. Thus the randomness of the occurrence of mutations by itself is no sudden abandonment by nature of the regularity of succession, of 'law', which holds at other levels of matter. For —this is the second point—(ii) the mutations which occur in the macromolecule are (a) the result of chemical and physical agents, so in this respect they are no more governed by 'chance' than any other chemical reaction; and (b) the process of biological evolution refers to mutations occurring in DNA in a biological context with particular physical and ecological environments, and the mutual interplay of mutations with environment is governed by that regularity, or 'law', which is called natural selection. For this is the 'law' which describes the common features, regularities and trends in a population of living organisms comprising the joint complex of mutationsplus-environment. Hence to speak of 'chance' as controlling the cosmic development at this crucial biological level is to speak misleadingly.

Perhaps those who have been concerned to stress the role of 'chance' have had in mind the particularity of biological development, which seems, on the face of it, more analogous to the particularity of events in human history than to the generalities of statistical thermodynamics. In human history, broad historical trends and movements are real and apparently impersonal, as Tolstoy continually stresses in *War and Peace*: yet particular, idiosyncratic, highly individual persons act and make decisions in special and unique situations and also genuinely 'make history'. Similarly in the biological development, the physical scientist may find an uncomfortable individuality in the way a particular living creature has evolved in a particular environment—so individualistic that 'chance' is said to dominate. But this is not a legitimate use of the word 'chance', for the emergence of new form in a particular environment is governed by the laws of mutation-plus-environment, that is, of natural selection, and even the particular environment is itself but the product of a sequence of causes and effects both physical and biological, all of which obey natural 'laws'. Moreover, there are trends in evolution, as we shall discuss later, and similar environments in different places can produce similar ranges of organisms of quite different genetic origins and history, as witness the many parallels between the placental mammals and the corresponding marsupials. It would do more justice to this special feature of biological evolution, if it were stressed that as life evolves the operation of natural laws produces organisms (that is forms of living matter) of increasing individuality and particularity. This is why the rich diversity of the biological world is so bafflingly complex to the mind of the physical scientist trained to abstract from the totality of any observed event. The habits of the more mathematically and physically oriented scientist must not here dominate what we mean by the regularities and 'laws' of science, an idea which first emerged in full strength under the influence of Newtonian mechanics. For in the biological world we see matter changing and developing its organization in regular ways, that is according to natural 'laws', but in doing so producing a rich diversity of forms unique to particular environments.

4. EMERGENCE AND CREATIVITY

The account of the cosmic development outlined in the previous chapter is a story of the appearance of new forms of matter at successive times. These new forms exhibit a series of levels of organization, one level (e.g., the living cell) being an organized assembly in space and time of component units (macromolecules and small molecules), which are themselves assemblies of atoms, and so on. Many authors[1] have stressed how each new level of organism is not fully explicable in terms of the level of organization of matter which constitutes it and out of which it has evolved, using the latter word now of non-living as well as of living forms of matter. The word 'emergent' has frequently been used to refer to this feature of the processes of evolutionary

---

[1] For example, S. Alexander, *Space, Time and Deity* (New York, 1920); C. Lloyd Morgan, *Emergent Evolution* (London, 1923); H. Bergson, *Creative Evolution* (London, 1920).

change. The new 'wholes' are not reducible or describable entirely in terms of the former 'parts'. But in what does the difference consist? One type of answer common to authors of otherwise different philosophical and theological positions postulates some extra-physical drive which brings the emergent form into existence, especially when this new form is living—for example, the 'élan vital' of Bergson, the 'entelechy' of Driesch, the 'life force' of Shaw. These views, collectively known as 'vitalism', will be referred to again in the next section. For the moment it is enough to point out that their particular postulates are unnecessary for preserving the idea of emergence; indeed, they are an embarrassment. For there are cogent considerations which help us to find a more precise way of talking about the 'emergence' of one form from another. These have recently been stressed especially by Polanyi who has been uniquely placed to understand the various types of intellectual exploration involved in the various sciences concerned with different levels of organization of matter. His argument is developed fully by him in his major work, *Personal Knowledge*, and in a number of articles,[1] as well as by others.[2] His main point is that in the more complex forms of matter (say, a steam engine) there are boundary conditions which shape initially the configuration (e.g., arrangement, positions and initial velocities of levers, pistons, tube connections, etc.). The principles which determine these boundary conditions and so the configuration of the constituent units are those of mechanical engineering and are not themselves derivable from a knowledge of the properties of these units (the sciences of physics and chemistry which analyse and 'explain' the properties of steel, etc.). The laws of physics and chemistry are not in any way abrogated; but we require further categories of explanation for the machine peculiar to the level of organization of matter to which it belongs. The argument has been worked out with reference to a machine but applies with even greater force and clarity to, say, a living cell, with its complex configuration in space and time, with its flow of constantly changing substances both within and across the cell membrane

[1] M. Polanyi, *Personal Knowledge* (London, 1958); *The Study of Man* (London, 1959); *The Tacit Dimension* (London, 1967), 2nd lecture especially.
[2] W. H. Thorpe, *Science, Man and Morals* (London, 1965), p. 20 ff; M. Grene, *The Knower and the Known* (London, 1966).

and with its possession of an individual 'life-cycle'. The same point may be made about molecular structures with biological specificity and has already been referred[1] to in Chapter 2, when discussing the sequence of base-pairs in DNA. The chemical structure of DNA, the covalent and hydrogen bonds which link them, thereby enabling specific base-pairs (A–T, G–C) to be formed, are describable in terms of the categories of physics and chemistry and are studied on this basis by 'physical biochemists' and 'biophysicists'. However, the particular and unique sequence of base pairs (e.g., $\begin{smallmatrix} A & G & C & A & G & T \\ | & | & | & | & | & | \\ T & C & G & T & C & A \end{smallmatrix}$ .....) that occurs in any DNA molecule present in the nuclei of the cells of a particular organism can never be explained by any purely chemical process. Chemical processes are, indeed, the means whereby bases are incorporated into chains of DNA but the sequence in which the bases are assembled in the DNA is a property of the whole organism. For the DNA can only be so assembled in that organism and have its biochemical function as the genetic 'blue-print' for the production of specific proteins in due order, when it functions in the milieu of the whole organism. No 'laws' or regularities of physics or chemistry describing the nature and stability of the chemical bonds in the DNA can specify the actual *sequence* of base-pairs in any given case, any more than the physics of a piece of steel or of water can describe a steam engine. This treatment of the problem brings out more clearly than any other why one can legitimately speak of the emergence of new forms of organized matter as a feature of the developing cosmos and justifies this usage by clarifying our ways of describing and understanding them.

This view of emergence also has an inverse corollary, namely that there is no basis for inferring from the observed emergence of new features at a 'higher' level of organization of matter that these same features must be present in some rudimentary, primitive or partial manner in the simpler, 'lower' forms. Indeed, there is no meaning which one can attach to the idea, say, of some

---

[1] Also by M. Polanyi, 'Life transcending physics and chemistry', *Chem. & Eng. News*, 1967, **45**, 54; 'Life's irreducible structure', *Science*, 1968, **160**, 1308; chapter 14 in *Knowing and Being* (London, 1969); and, most recently and in the wider context of the whole nature and direction of science, in his Nuffield Lecture to the Royal Society of Medicine (5 Feb. 1970), *Proc. roy. Soc. Med.*, 1970, Vol. **63**.

rudimentary form of wetness, a characteristic of assemblies of water molecules, composed of hydrogen and oxygen atoms, being present in some 'rudimentary form' in hydrogen and oxygen atoms. Yet it is an assertion of just this kind which some authors[1] have been prepared to make about consciousness which, in the present context, is just one of these features emergent in higher levels of the organization of matter. In, rightly, stressing the significance of this emergence of consciousness, they have thought it necessary to propose that there is some rudimentary form of consciousness in unicellular organisms and even in inorganic matter. From the viewpoint outlined above this is simply a mistake and renders less credible their primary emphasis that evolution is *towards* consciousness.

The proposition that in the development of the cosmos new forms are genuinely emergent and are not describable in categories appropriate to the forms of matter from which they originate can now be affirmed without at the same time implying the operation in the cosmic development of any of those obscure entities postulated by some of the earlier proponents of 'emergent evolution' and of 'vitalism'. Nevertheless, the emergent forms do, in fact, culminate in a living organism, man, who thinks self-consciously and explores both the world around him and the path by which he has emerged on the scene. The vitalists were right at least in their concern that this should not be forgotten for it cannot fail to have implications about the character of the cosmic development ((q.v., section 7, below). Furthermore, recognition that our knowledge of the forms of matter has a hierarchical character, which corresponds to the interrelation of these forms themselves, has important implications which may be quite as uncongenial to the opponents of 'vitalism' as are the 'élan vital', and its cognates.

Thus it appears that the laws governing matter in a higher level of organization can never be entirely deduced from the properties of the lower levels, in particular from the properties of the fundamental particles[2] that constitute all material systems—even though each level relies on its constituent units to

---

[1] Teilhard de Chardin, *The Phenomenon of Man* (London, 1959) and in other of his writings; L. C. Birch, *Nature and God* (London, 1965).

[2] Some of which, it must be remembered, can be transformed into electromagnetic energy.

obey the laws appropriate to them. For this reason the cosmic development, especially at its biological level, may be said to be 'creative'. where the word is employed to express the real parallel between what happens in this development and what happens in human creativity, looking at both objectively and not from within. In human creativity out of words, sounds, materials, personal situations, ideas and so on are made unpredictable, previously almost unthinkable, collations, conjunctions and patterns, which could not *in principle* have been predicted before they were so integrated. Afterwards these patterns are perceived and experienced, by those who care to acquire the appropriate sensitivity, as a unique and expressive unity which then, and only then, appears almost inevitable. Similarly in biological evolution, in the course of time the improbable eventually occurs, and new forms emerge. The possibilities open to one level of molecular and macromolecular organization become actualized. Biological evolution by natural selection, like human creativity, also runs the risk of failure, for there is always the possibility of disaster in any molecular patterns. We must not too readily look upon all extinct species simply as discarded experiments *en route* to man, since what 'value' they may have had in themselves and for themselves we cannot know.

The idea of creativity would not usually be regarded as applicable to the processes of nature as we now observe them, since at both the inorganic and biological levels they go on repeating former patterns (disregarding for the moment the property of individuality in the higher organisms). However, when this hierarchy of forms of matter is set out on the time scale of the cosmic development, it appears as a creative process, with its evolution of 'endless forms most beautiful and most wonderful'.[1]

5. MECHANISM AND VITALISM

The view opposed to vitalism is usually called 'mechanism'. It may best be summarized in the words of one of its recent proponents—'The ultimate aim of the modern movement in biology is in fact to explain *all* biology in terms of physics and chemistry',[2] and the same author regards vitalism, which he

---

[1] Darwin, loc. cit. (see above, end of Chapter 2).
[2] F. H. C. Crick, *Of Molecules and Men* (Seattle and London, 1966), p. 10.

rejects, as the view that 'there must be something else in a biological system which cannot be included under the heading of physics and chemistry.'[1] These statements, which, though brief, are fairly indicative of a general position, are attributing to physics-and-chemistry, the sciences of the component units of living organisms, an explanatory power which they logically cannot possess. Such statements are category mistakes which, to put biology on one side, are of the same kind as if we say 'a machine is entirely explained by the laws of physics and chemistry'. As we argued in the previous section, this kind of assertion is not based on an adequate description either of the relation between different levels of organization of matter or of our knowledge of these levels. For it takes no account of the boundary conditions and of the configurations which constitute the higher levels of organization of matter and which cannot, logically cannot, be subsumed under the laws which describe the behaviour of the component units not so organized. Thus the principles of mechanical engineering, let alone biology, cannot be described in terms of 'nothing but' physics and chemistry, for nothing in these sciences describes the configuration of, say, a steam engine. The operation of the engine relies on its parts obeying the laws of these sciences but they do not themselves describe the principles of engines. Were this hierarchy in our levels of explanation to be accepted, the word 'mechanism' could be rehabilitated for application to the biological process. However, if, as Crick says, those who adhere to the mechanistic view of biological organization are thereby expressing the 'nothing-but-physics-and-chemistry' position, then this rehabilitation of the word 'mechanism' is unlikely, at least for the moment, and other terms are needed. In opposing the usual mechanistic view as defined above, I am still asserting the continuity of evolution, its submission to scientific laws without the intervention of any special entity not inherent in matter itself. As new forms of matter, non-living and living, emerge in the universe, new categories of description of their form and properties (their configurations and boundary conditions, to use Polanyi's terms) are necessary and these categories will be other than those of the physics and chemistry appropriate to the subnuclear, atomic and molecular levels. The study of the various

[1] Op. cit., p. 26.

organic wholes which constitute the universe have led men to develop concepts, methods and languages appropriate to the levels of organization they represent and these must not be set aside because of our very real need to understand better the molecular organization of higher organisms. We can agree with A. N. Whitehead that 'Biology is the study of the larger organisms and physics the study of the smaller ones', without accepting all his metaphysics. The view supported here might be called organismic, rather than mechanistic, in the old sense. As Crick suggests, those who adopt this mechanistic position, as he describes it, are consciously rejecting the vitalism of Bergson and others, and perhaps, though less consciously, are also motivated by a desire to leave no loophole for any supernaturalistic interpretation of the universe. There is also a tendency to expand what is meant by physics and chemistry to other levels of organization so that to understand the molecular structure of, say, the chromosome is thought to be explaining the whole genetic process in terms of physics and chemistry, whereas, even in the case of DNA, its specific function *in vivo* is explicable, as we have seen already, only in terms of its incorporation into the whole organism.

Mutatis mutandis, vitalists have been vulnerable to the criticism that they have adopted this position in order to leave open the possibility for supernaturalism. Some Christian apologists have certainly been in the vitalist camp for this reason, thinking that Christians must be vitalists. This was a mistake, even on their own theological grounds, an argument which it is not appropriate to develop in this chapter, where we are trying to confine ourselves to the knowledge of the development of the cosmos which science affords. From this scientific point of view, the continuity of the whole development according to natural laws and regularities which we can observe or infer from observation of the world today seems to me to render all vitalist views superfluous on the grounds of not unnecessarily multiplying hypotheses. This is certainly one of these hypotheses of which we have no need, although its devising was understandable when the alternative was a mechanistic view seeing everywhere 'nothing-but-physics-and-chemistry'. An organismic viewpoint which accepts the outlines of the scientific perspective and does not introduce any vitalistic entities, but nevertheless recognizes the emergent character of the succession of new organisms, avoids the old mechanism-*versus*-vitalism controversy, and can, as it should, set aside any ulterior motives which may have been present in the proponents of both mechanisms and vitalism.

6. DIRECTIONS IN EVOLUTION

Are there any discernible trends in the process of cosmic development unfolded by the sciences? There is a natural predilection, in attempting to answer this question, to see all trends as pointing to man. This is understandable but unscientific and unobjective in any initial approach to the matter. For could we see the world through the eyes of another creature, we might see all evolutionary paths as culminating there—rather like the fish of Rupert Brooke's poem[1] who cries:

> And, sure, the reverent eye must see
> A Purpose in Liquidity.
> We darkly know, by Faith we cry,
> The future is not Wholly Dry.
> . . .
> And there (they trust) there swimmeth one
> Who swam ere rivers were begun,
> Immense, of fishy form and mind,
> Squamous, omnipotent, and kind;
> And under that Almighty Fin,
> The littlest fish may enter in.
> . . .
> And in that Heaven of all their wish,
> There shall be no more land, say fish.

We must begin by examining the development of the cosmos, and in particular, biological evolution, by means of criteria which do not implicitly assume that man is the culmination of it all. For too often in the past, as Simpson caustically remarks,

The extreme view that evolution is basically or over all an orthogenetic[2] process is evidence that some scientists' minds tend to move in straight lines, not that evolution does.[3]

[1] 'Heaven' from *The Collected Poems of Rupert Brooke* (New York, 1915).
[2] 'Orthogenesis' has almost as many meanings as authors, but, broadly, it means evolution in a straight line, in one clear direction, or, at least, evolution which is not completely random. It usually carries an implication of an inherent tendency for evolution to continue in a given direction.
[3] G. G. Simpson, op. cit., p. 14.

This means that the first task is to examine by non-anthropological criteria the process of biological evolution to see if any trends are apparent and to see where man, *Homo sapiens*, stands in relation to these trends. Then, the field of examination must be widened to include the development of the inorganic in the universe and to ask if any of the trends in biological evolution can be seen also in the pre-biotic development.

Up to this point, the whole discussion will have proceeded without any account of what man knows about himself. The omission of such considerations will however have left the whole inquiry unsatisfyingly incomplete. Man and his experience stand within the whole process of cosmic development and, however difficult and unfamiliar the context of such considerations is to scientists, no scientist is being objective if he simply ignores the human experience in attempting to assess the direction of, or at least trends in, the whole cosmic development. This will be the concern of the next section.

Most of the writers on biological evolution referred to earlier, and many others besides, have attempted, following in the footsteps of Darwin's elucidation of the principle of natural selection, to discern trends in biological evolution. For the purpose of this present section, it is best to follow one who repudiates the vitalist position and adopts what he describes as the materialist view of evolution: I refer to the survey of G. G. Simpson in *The Meaning of Evolution*[1] in which he is looking for evidence of 'progress' in evolution. The history of life includes such a diversity of histories of individual species that one can find examples not only of what might be called progress but also of its obverse, degeneration. He claims it is almost impossible to find an acceptable definition of progress which could be applied to all manifestations of life—but this does not mean that progress is absent from evolution. Simpson reviews a number of criteria of progress or of trends in biological evolution, where the word 'trends' is deliberately used in order to impart as few hidden presuppositions as possible. His discussion of the principal criteria is summarized in the following, with the addition of his estimate of man's place in nature with reference to each criterion.

(i) *The tendency for living organisms to expand to fill in all available*

---

[1] Op. cit., Chapters xv, xvii.

spaces in the livable environments. This is true of life as a whole, and not just groups, but it is not invariable with time, for retreat often occurs temporarily. This expansion can be considered in terms of the number of individual organisms, total bulk of living tissue, or gross turnover of substance and energy. According to this criterion, *Homo sapiens* is the most rapidly 'progressing' organism, especially if the plants and domesticated animals grown by him are included, and is now the spearhead of the spread of life all over the Earth, and perhaps beyond in an age of space travel. It is this explosive growth of the 'biosphere'—the layer of life on the Earth—which Teilhard de Chardin emphasized in his most influential work.[1] But this criterion is not very helpful in discerning trends in the whole process. The parallel in the inorganic sphere would be to point to the 'success', under particular conditions, of molecules in filling the Earth, as distinct from atoms. We would then see that this supposed criterion is only another way of describing the fact of evolution. So although it helps to make clearer what we mean by evolution, it does not elucidate much further the character of the evolutionary process itself.

(ii) *The succession of dominant types in biological evolution.* However, at various times a number of groups have been simultaneously dominant (e.g., Arthropoda and some classes of the vertebrates such as Osteichthyes, Aves, and Mammalia) though often in different spheres: thus leading to, e.g., an 'Age of Fishes', followed by an 'Age of Amphibians', etc., up to the 'Age of Man'. Only if one has some other criterion which sets species in order can one then speak of a succession of dominant types as in any sense a trend or as indicating progress—such criteria could be the objective one of relationships of descent or the anthropological one of approximation to men. The former is a different matter from dominance and the latter does not fulfil our initial conditions. There is no single line of dominant types. This having been said, it may be asserted as a matter of observation that *Homo sapiens* has, in fact, been a member of groups which have been successively dominant: medium-sized, self-propelled organisms (vertebrates dominant) and terrestrial forms (mammals dominant). Man is a vertebrate mammal, and in a dominant line within the Mammalia. So this criterion does not make

[1] Teilhard de Chardin, *The Phenomenon of Man* (London, 1955).

man the highest form of life but at least places him among the highest in his own sphere.

(iii) *The successive invasion and development of environmental and adaptive spheres.* The succession is, again, multiple, and reveals no one line of progress for all evolution. The major transition from the sphere of water to that of land did lead to an enormous total expansion of life (criterion (i)), but the lines are multiple. Man's general environment was among the last to be filled and

man's particular adaptive type was the latest to be developed up to now in the history of life, one radically new, never before exemplified, and with extreme potentialities for expansion. In the spreading sequence of adaptive types there is thus a criterion that seems quite definitely to place man at the top, as the highest type of organism in this particular respect.[1]

(iv) *Increasing specialization with its corollary of improvement in efficiency and adaptability.* Increasing specialization sharpens a given adaptation but often narrows its scope, so that although its first effect is to cause an expansion of the form of life which has this adaptation specific to a particular environment, it often leads in the end to its extinction. For specialization may reduce the possibility of further change in any other direction. Two kinds of progress are here under consideration:

there is a progress in adaptability which often tends to conflict with or be restricted by progress in adaptation (specialization), but which only comes into play if, in fact, further adaptation does occur and that adaptability is utilized in a way that can be considered progressive.[2]

Only on the criterion of specialization can *Homo sapiens* be regarded as a low type of animal. For man made his way by a broadening and not a narrowing of the specificity of his adaptation (e.g., by acquiring clothing, tools, houses, means of transport and communication, etc.). In this respect, the development of man is unique in the history of life. This development of adaptability provides an ability to cope with a greater variety of environments and is peculiarly human, so it cannot be taken as a feature of evolution as a whole. But this peculiar success of the human form of life goes further, for man not only protects

---

[1] G. G. Simpson, op. cit., p. 248.   [2] G. G. Simpson, op. cit., p. 251.

himself from his varied environments, like many other creatures, but also controls them.

Man is a new sort of animal that has discovered new possibilities in ways of life—and this is progress whether referred specifically to the human view-point or not.[1]

(v) *Increasing complexity.* Increase in *structural* complexity was clearly important in the earlier stages of biological evolution, for example from protozoa to multi-cellular animals, and increase in complexity was involved in a broad way, in the spread of life to new spheres. This is a simplified picture of biological evolution which has great appeal. But are there any objective criteria of structural complexity which distinguish different multicellular organisms? As Simpson says,[2]

It would be a brave anatomist who would attempt to prove that Recent man is more complicated than a Devonian octracoderm.

Indeed on the purely structural criterion, in many cases evolution has been accompanied by structural simplification. Thus, once multi-cellular organisms have been reached it is exceedingly hard to find an objective method of determining what is meant by an increase in structural complexity. This is a major problem for it is evolution of multi-cellular organisms which dominates the 'biosphere'. The situation is eased somewhat by recognizing that the cases of structural simplification, just referred to, do not represent usually any loss of functions, so that the sought-for criterion may be located in function and in structures as related to function.

This approach has taken on a new character in view of our present understanding of the molecular basis of control of structure and function in living organisms. The knowledge is still only fragmentary but at least it is clear that the sequence of base-pairs in the DNA of the fertilized cell from which an organism stems carries the genetic 'message', although as stressed earlier, the environment must be involved in the reading-out of this message. This has encouraged attempts to apply the ideas of the 'information theory' of the communication engineer

---

[1] Op. cit., p. 252.　　　　[2] Op. cit., p. 253.

to this problem of assessing complexity.[1] This new science was developed strictly for the purpose of assessing and making quantitative the number of messages and the distinct 'information' they could convey over a network of channels of communication. It clearly has relevance to the genetic coding problem but its applicability to the assessment of biological organization (meaning by this structure-and-function) is less certain and has been criticized[2] for ignoring the very real increase in biological organization which occurs in the development of the individual organism, whose 'information content' cannot have changed from that encoded in its chromosomes. The assembly of a pattern is amenable to calculations of the 'information' needed to specify it and on this basis (and on others related to thermodynamics) attempts have been made to calculate the 'information' in a bacterial cell, for example. It is clear that any such calculations are bound to reveal successive increases in information content in the sequence, say, of a small molecule, a molecule of DNA, a bacterium, an amoeba and a mammal. In this sense, there have developed in the universe a series of forms of matter of increasing 'information content', that is, organized forms which require successively increasing amounts of information to specify them. However, it is still an open question whether or not this approach will solve either the problem already mentioned, the need for a quantitative yardstick of complexity; or another one which has been the concern of some authors,[3] namely, whether or not any extra information over and above that encoded in the DNA has to be supplied by some other principle or from some other source (e.g., the environment). It is to be hoped that eventually some quantitative measure of complexity will be forthcoming from information theory or some other course. When it does do so, it will have to incorporate in its measure of complexity not only structure and function but also behaviour, the intricacy and complexity

---

[1] An outline of this approach is given by W. H. Thorpe, in his Fremantle lectures, *Science, Man and Morals* (London, 1965); see also *Information Theory in Biology*, ed. H. Quastler (Illinois, 1953); and *The Physical Foundation of Biology*, by W. M. Elsasser (London, 1958). ('Information' here has a technical meaning which is outlined, e.g., by Thorpe, op. cit., p. 33 f.)

[2] e.g., by P. B. Medawar, *The Art of the Soluble* (London, 1967), p. 57.

[3] e.g. W. M. Elsasser, op. cit., and W. H. Thorpe, op. cit., p. 41.

of which is only now being brought out by the relatively new techniques of ethology (the scientific study of behaviour).

Nevertheless, without any quantitative yardstick there does seem to be a sense in which a dog is more complex than an immobile crustacean and a man more than both, so that the association of an increase of complexity with biological evolution has seemed natural and inevitable to most writers on the subject. The idea has gained widespread currency through the writings of Teilhard de Chardin, where it forms the first part of his 'law of complexity-consciousness'.

If behaviour is included with structure and function among the elements contributing to 'complexity', then man, with his diversity of behaviour, and at different historical periods, must surely qualify as the most complex of all living creatures. But this is only so if his behaviour, which is the outward expression of his consciousness, is to count. Otherwise, he possesses the same degree of complexity as other mammals of comparable size.

We can conclude that biological organisms of increasing degree of complexity have emerged during biological evolution, that this is far from being a single-track process, that the more complex are not necessarily the most successful biologically in their various spheres, and that, especially amongst multi-cellular organisms, relative degrees of complexity are almost impossible to assess, unless behaviour is included, in which case *Homo sapiens* is the most complex of biological species.

(vi) *Increase in the general energy or maintained level of vital processes.*[1] This is a somewhat vague criterion, but not too difficult of application. Thus by this criterion mammals come above reptiles and high among animals in general: man is a typical mammal in this respect. So the criterion is useful for application within any one line of development but not for comparison of different lines.

(vii) *Protected reproduction and care of young.* This reaches a very high level of development among birds, but it is clear that mammals are the most highly developed in this respect, not only on account of the protection and uniformity of internal

---

[1] G. G. Simpson, op. cit., p. 256 f., where he refers to the work of A. N. Sewertzoff, *Morphologische Gesetzmissigkeiten der Evolution* (Fischer, Jena, 1931), as the source of this criterion.

gestation, but through elaborate and controlled post-natal care —and according to this criterion man is decisively the highest amongst mammals, and so amongst all living organisms, since he has the longest and most elaborate post-natal care (to which we can now add education up to the late 'teens or longer). An efficient mode of reproduction in man which allows careful selection of partners and of care of the young has a great influence on the action of natural selection which, as we have seen, may be more accurately regarded as differential reproduction.

(viii) *Change in the direction of increase in the range and variety of adjustments of the organism to its environment.*[1] What is referred to here is not increased control over and independence of but increased awareness[2] of the environment and ability to react accordingly to it. The trend is for organisms appearing later in evolution to be better able to gather more and different kinds of information about their respective environments and to develop apparatus for making appropriate adjustments. This trend depends on the increasing development of organs of sensitivity ranging from a diffuse sensibility to motion, temperature and chemical differentials, etc., in the environment to complex sensory organs and associated nervous and co-ordinating systems, which at its most subtle level involves the development of the mammalian brain. It is these developments which make possible some degree of control over and independence of environment. Huxley[3] regards this feature of evolution which he describes as an 'advance in organization which leaves the door open for further advance' as the most significant of all types of improvement. This criterion is a purely biological one and not man-centred as such but, nevertheless, it indubitably sets man at the highest level of evolutionary progress for, as Simpson says, 'man's associated perceptual, co-ordinating and reacting apparatus is incomparably the best ever evolved'[4]—and to this may be added the social structures and means of communication and

---

[1] C. J. Herrick, *Science*, 1946, **104**, 469, quoted by G. G. Simpson, op. cit. p. 258.

[2] No implication is intended about the extent and nature of consciousness in animals. It is sufficient that sentient creatures act as if they are aware, and their consequent behaviour provides evidence of what in man would be called perception of its features.

[3] Op. cit., p. xxxiii.

[4] Op. cit., p. 260.

of transmitting learning which now characterize human evolution or, rather, history.

(ix) *Individualization.* An increase in adaptability to, and awareness of, and variety of reactions to the environment necessarily means that each individual organism is more independent as a unit and more distinctive and individual in its reactions and interrelationships. Mammals and birds are broadly more individualized in reaction patterns and behaviour than are invertebrates or plants. In man, individualization in evolution reaches an entirely new high level and makes possible the socialization (diversity in co-operation) on which his development has depended.

The above examination of trends in biological evolution has been conducted with only biological considerations in mind. Of biological evolution as a whole, we can say it is not invariably accompanied by progress, according to the biological criteria that have been elaborated above. There have been many directions, each exemplifying different strands of progress; there has been no one single line towards a single perfect form. Even from the point of view of man, it cannot be said that the line of man's ancestry is the central line of evolution as a whole; indeed there is no such central line. Yet all the biological criteria, except (ii), (vi) and possible (iv),[1] place man at a level at which the trends in question reach their maximum expression and culmination, as far as observed evolution goes. In ordinary parlance, it is quite usual to use the word 'higher' of that member of a series in which some characteristic is more developed than in some other member. Thus, all the criteria, except those mentioned above, may be said to show that man is at the highest level of development in biological evolution, and even one of the omitted criteria (iv) testifies to his uniqueness. The other omitted criteria, (ii) and (vi), place man amongst the highest groups of organisms in the relevant respects but not in an outstanding position within these groups. Simpson, whom we have

[1] For (iv), extreme adaptability, is unique in its level of development in men so that it is not quite accurate to call it the culmination of a *general* trend. (v), complexity is taken here to include behaviour.

followed so closely in this argument, concludes his chapter (xv) on these biological criteria thus:

Man is among the highest products of evolution and a balance of them [the criteria] warrants the conclusion that man is, on the whole, but not in every single respect, the pinnacle so far of evolutionary progress.[1]

So although it is clear that man is a member of the kingdom of animals, of the sub-phylum of vertebrates, of the class of mammalia, and of the order of primates, it is, even on biological criteria alone, highly misleading to say he is 'nothing but' an animal vertebrate, mammal, and primate. For such statements are never true, biologically speaking, of any living organism which has been classified, for each has essential attributes of its own. The error is greater when the 'nothing but' label is attached to man, for he is an entirely new kind of animal in the biological world, with characteristics which set him off sharply from any other animal and in the end make an absolute difference in kind and not only in degree. We have already instanced the following criteria according to which man stands at a uniquely high point in evolution: ability to expand over the livable environment, successive invasion and development of environmental and adaptive spheres, complexity—if behaviour is included, reproduction and care of the young, adjustment and sensitivity to environment, individualization ((i), (iii), (v), (vii), (viii), (ix) above). His uniqueness is, however, to be seen especially in his adaptability, individualization, ((iv) and (ix)), intelligence and socialization which jointly are the features, referred to above, which make him different in kind, as well as in degree, from all other living organisms. Was man's arrival probable? There is no answer to such a question but at least we can concur with Simpson that 'Not all the chances favoured his [man's] appearance, none *might* have, but enough did.'[2]

So far in this analysis, that has followed Simpson's so closely, we have exercised a self-denying ordinance not to admit into our assessment of the trends in biological development any man-centred viewpoints. But the pressure of the actual situation cannot much longer allow us to continue under such a restriction. For as Polanyi rightly remarks:

---

[1] Op. cit., p. 262.   [2] Op. cit., p. 292.

It is the height of intellectual perversity to renounce, in the name of scientific objectivity, our position as the highest form of life on earth, and our own advent by a process of evolution as the most important problem of evolution.[1]

To this we must respond in the next section, but before doing so the development of the cosmos as a whole must be considered again to see if any of the criteria of change applicable to biological evolution apply over a wider range.

Most of the criteria just referred to have specific reference to aspects of living organisms and cannot be carried over into any account of the pre-biological development. Nevertheless, the criterion of an increase in complexity appears to be more readily applicable. For each successive development has led to the emergence of a form of matter which is more complex than the units from which it is assembled, whether this be nuclei from protons, neutrons, baryons, etc.; atoms from nuclei and electrons; molecules from atoms; macromolecules from repeating blocks of atom groupings; or, from atoms and molecules, the larger entities of natural phenomena on the Earth's surface, and the larger assemblies which constitute stars, planets, asteroids, supernovae, etc. The forces that lead to this patterned assembly of smaller units have already been discussed. The transitions certainly can all be described as instances of an increase in complexity and thus it appears that there has been a tendency in evolution for matter to assume increasingly complex forms of organization in a hierarchy whereby the more complex are assembled out of the less so. This has been called by Teilhard de Chardin 'the law of complexification'.[2]

The other general trend which we saw in biological evolution which is applicable to the pre-biological development is increasing individualization. All atoms of, say, a given isotope of lead are identical and so are all molecules of water or of the amino-acid serine, and are indistinguishable from each other. But macromolecules made up of different building blocks (proteins of amino acids, nucleic acids of nucleotides) can have a specific and individual sequence of these units. Any two molecules of a particular protein, e.g., haemoglobin, performing the same task in a given organism appear to be identical in amino-acid

[1] M. Polanyi, *The Tacit Dimension* (London, 1967), p. 47.
[2] Op. cit., p. 48.

sequence but small variations may be allowable and certainly occur between the haemoglobin from different sub-groups of the same species and as between species. No two single-celled organisms of the same strain, derived from the same parent cell, are exactly alike in all their molecular particulars and this individualization increases up the evolutionary tree of life. Such individualization is really a function of the increase of complexity, for the number of members in any class of organism is extremely small compared with the number of microscopic configurations which are available to the members of the class on account of their complexity.[1]

7. THE SIGNIFICANCE OF THE PRESENCE OF MAN IN THE UNIVERSE

When we were looking at the succession of forms of matter, at first non-living and then living, which constitutes the evolutionary process, we found that for each particular level, science had developed concepts, methods and forms of language appropriate to that level in the whole hierarchy of forms. Moreover, in examining in what emergence consisted, we found that we had to recognize that the configuration and boundary conditions characteristic of a particular level of organization of matter could not be subsumed or explained in terms of the language and concepts which had been developed for the simpler units of the level 'below', and usually preceding this particular form of matter. Put another way, chemistry is not 'nothing but nuclear physics', nor is physiology 'nothing but chemistry', or ethology 'nothing but physiology' and so on. This is characteristic both of the relation between our knowledge of these levels of the organization of matter and of the actual relation between the levels themselves.[2] Thus to look at a biological organism simply as a complicated piece of physics and chemistry would be to ignore those features of it which are characteristic of it as a total living organism and which could not, in principle, be properties of the individual separate molecules that constitute it. In other words, to close our minds to the emergent properties characteristic of each level of organization of matter when we are considering the evolutionary sequence is inadmissible and renders

---

[1] Cf. W. M. Elsasser, op. cit.
[2] As worked out more fully by Polanyi in *Personal Knowledge*.

us blind to the really significant feature of that particular emergent entity and of the processes giving rise to it.

This preamble is necessary to stress that if we are to interpret the whole cosmic development accurately then we must look at all the facts, however uncongenial to our presuppositions. As the previous section has adumbrated, the outstanding fact of biological evolution is that, along many unknown paths, interspersed with long periods of apparent stagnation, and concomitant with many other lines of development, it has given rise to a unique creature, man, who, by the criteria listed, stands at a high point of evolution. Whether or not one is prepared to affirm, on the basis of man's complexity of life and behaviour and his adaptability, that man stands at the highest point—and the examination made in the previous section strongly indicates this—is less important than the fact that in the life of man new features and properties of matter have emerged when it is organized in the human form. This could be stated epigrammatically by saying that in man evolution has now become history. For, from the strictly biological viewpoint, the unique feature of human society is the ability of man to choose and shape his environment through the knowledge he obtains of it by use of his sense organs, extended by technology, and by use of his reflective organization of these perceptions, which we call knowledge. Moreover, this acquired knowledge now exhibits the 'Lamarckian' property of being inherited, for man's methods of storing and communicating knowledge allow him to transmit his knowledge to his successors, as well as rapidly to his contemporaries. Man is the first animal who, by consciously shaping and choosing his own environment, has stepped outside the process of evolution by natural selection operating on mutations. Huxley[1] calls this form of evolution or selection 'psychosocial': this may be a useful term to point to the very different basis of the processes of change in human society and those in other species, but it could be misleading when the term is used as an adjective preceding 'evolution' or 'selection', for it might then be thought to mean that biological evolution and selection continue in the same way in man. The term 'history' reminds us that men who are conscious of themselves and their purposes now shape the human story and is therefore to be preferred.

[1] *Evolution as a Process* (London, 1954), p. 13.

Whatever terminology we employ, the fact remains that man has emerged from the evolutionary process we have delineated and, as with other emergent forms, displays new characteristics which can only be described by their appropriate languages and concepts and which necessitate modes of inquiry and elaboration peculiar to themselves. We have already seen that some of the features of man can be regarded as special extensions of characteristics to be seen in less-developed forms in other biological organisms. Far more important, because they are uniquely human, are those activities for which man has developed modes of discourse to allow his diverse experiences to be shared. The interrelation of these modes of discourse, the rules by which the 'game' of each language is played, it is the task of philosophy to unravel. My purpose here is simply to emphasize that the fact that we use such a variety of special modes of discourse about man is itself witness to the special character of the human animal who has emerged from the evolutionary process: and that this is as much an observable fact about the development of the cosmos as the need to use, say, the language of chemistry for molecules, of physiology for the interrelation between organs in living organisms, of ethology for animal behaviour, etc. The stuff of which the universe is made has become man who is only describable in terms of the modes of discourse which have developed out of the human experience. This is why earlier I stressed that it was legitimate to describe the whole process of evolution as 'materialistic', if, and only if, one was prepared to recognize that the substantive 'matter', from which the adjective is derived, must refer to an entity which, organized in the way we called human, could exhibit the properties characteristic of that *human* state, as well as of the others which 'materialists' have always recognized. But what is that state? Many words and claims crowd in, waiting to be employed to denote the special features of man: at the danger of appearing to describe the obvious, let me state a few.

Man has the feature of being conscious of his environment. Higher animals probably also have some form of consciousness[1] but at its best it seems to be only a fragmentary and reduced

---

[1] Also will, aesthetic sensitivity and even a kind of moral sense; e.g., see W. H. Thorpe, *Biology and the Nature of Man* (Oxford, 1962) and *Science, Man and Morals* (London, 1965).

version of man's, fascinating as are the attempts to determine its content. But man is also self-conscious, he knows that he knows, he uses the word 'I' of himself in ways which are, in many respects, semantically peculiar. The human mind has an ability to transcend its own environment. One thinks of Hamlet's 'I could be bounded in a nut-shell, and count myself a king of infinite space . . .', or, more soberly, Pascal's 'All bodies, the firmaments, the stars, the earth and its kingdoms, are not equal to the lowest mind; for mind knows all these and itself; and these bodies nothing.' The affirmation of the reality of conscious and self-conscious activities is not dependent on any particular philosophy of the relation of an entity called 'mind' to one called 'body'. All I am concerned with here is that there are human activities and experiences which demand this special language, and that to which these languages refer is uniquely and characteristically human.[1] These include, *inter alia*, the activities referred to when we say men are capable of rational action, of making moral choices, of choosing between beliefs, of forming personal affections; that men are 'persons' in the sense that each is a bearer of rights, is unique and is someone with whom we can imagine ourselves changing places; that men explore their environment and formulate concepts to organize what they find; they are creative and worship and pray; and that they have consciously to come to terms with the anticipation of their own individual death.

All this, according to the evidence we have outlined, is the outcome of the continuous evolution of matter according to natural laws. Of what sort of 'material' is the universe constituted if in the course of time it becomes organized to form the brain of man, the creative thought of a Newton, a Beethoven or a Shakespeare, the person of Buddha or of Jesus of Nazareth? Even when we were thinking about the 'materialist' interpretation of evolution we had cause to wonder what meaning to attach to 'matter'. Now, *a fortiori*, the question presses itself more strongly upon us, especially as the problem turns itself inside out when one realizes the baffling subtleties faced by theoretical physicists in attempting to describe those fundamental

---

[1] The uniqueness of man in his specifically human activities is well expressed by Le Gros Clark in his British Association address, 1961, *The Humanity of Man*, op. cit.

particles, of which the whole universe is but an assembly—an endeavour in which they have to resort to abstract and mathematical forms (wave functions, matrices, etc.) devised by the most sophisticated of human imaginings and ratiocinations.

This question was sharply focused by the announcement[1] in 1968 by Sir Bernard Lovell that the Jodrell Bank radio telescope had been able to pick up a signal which had come from a point 5,000 million light years away. This signal had started on its journey through space 5,000 million years ago, that is before the Earth had come into existence and before man had evolved with the sensory apparatus (including their extension in radio telescopes) and with the intellectual powers which could allow him to know that it had arrived, and had undergone this journey. What is the meaning of, what are the appropriate terms in which to describe, such a universe?

The perspective which science has provided of the inorganic and biological worlds, culminating in man, poses us this question but is not able to answer it within its own terms. For the techniques and languages scientists have fashioned to analyse and make coherent their investigations of the various levels of the organization of matter have not been contrived to answer questions about the scope and direction of the whole process which these investigations unravel. The content of science, its account of the different levels of organization and processes which matter has undergone and is undergoing, pose the questions but, because what is now being looked at is the development as a whole, the present gamut of the sciences cannot, in principle, provide the necessary conceptual and linguistic tools for giving an account of the whole development—cannot 'in principle' by the same argument that was used above when the ability of physics and chemistry to give an account of the cell, of cell biology to give an account of physiology, and so on, were at issue. However, the content of the sciences, the perspective now afforded by them, has served to clarify to what sort of universe any question about its meaning is referring. The scientific perspective serves to show in what direction our statements in answer to these questions are to be referred. It serves as an arrow, pointing the direction of the road ahead without specifying what we shall find along that unexplored way. The

[1] *Guardian*, 24 May 1968.

head of the arrow, if we may continue the metaphor, is the fact of the presence of man in the universe and all that he is and does, so briefly and inadequately hinted at above. The shaft is the evolutionary process which has led to him and the metaphor is meant to suggest that we can only find the direction to which our answers to questions about the meaning of the whole cosmic process should be referred by looking at what his emergence from that process implies about its nature and about the matter, the world-stuff, which is undergoing these successive transformations. For if we are looking for new over-arching concepts to describe the whole cosmic process we have to include man as the most developed product, to our knowledge, of that process. Hence the clue to the significance and meaning of the whole cosmic process is more likely to be found in that in which it has culminated, man, than in any of the previous intermediate levels, fascinating and beautiful though many of them are. What 'value' these other forms have 'in themselves' is a question on which we might be exercised, but we cannot avoid the fact of man in the universe. It is unscientific and unobjective to ignore and renounce the position of man as the product of the evolutionary process, with all that man is and does.[1] Life probably exists on other planets, man's life is both recent and may be brief as the cosmic aeons measure time, but the fact of man has to be incorporated into any view of what the universe is like, what it is for and where it is going. For the greatest mystery in evolution is man himself.

8. CONCLUSION

The new perspective afforded by the sciences has revealed a continuity from atomic nuclei to the mind of man. It is a continuity of development and of emergence of forms of matter, according to regularities and laws of nature, which we now know at least in their broad outlines, up to the threshold of man himself. At this point we meet the discontinuity in our thinking which meets us in our experience, the discontinuity between objects, including other people, and the 'I' who experiences and knows. To be true to the actual situation, we have no other resources to describe the human experience except to employ modes of discourse which men have fashioned and developed to describe

[1] We recall also Polanyi's strong assertion of the matter, p. 101 above.

their experiences—the languages which use 'I', languages of personal relationship, of art, poetry, literature, science, philosophy, religion and theology. In availing ourselves of the experience of the human condition we are not thereby betraying the scientific method in the interest of an unjustifiable mysticism. We are simply doing what science has always done—namely, recognizing that each level within the hierarchy of the organized forms of matter has language and methods of inquiry appropriate to it. It is just that the human being is orders of magnitude more complex and diverse than any other entity which men study, and that in making this study man is then reflecting on himself. There could be nothing more unscientific and unobjective than refusing to look at all the facts because of mechanistic or 'materialist' presuppositions of an old-fashioned kind. I urge that our consideration of the continuity of the whole cosmic process now sharpens to the point where we can no longer avoid the question of the significance of a cosmic process which has culminated in man.

THE THEOLOGICAL ENTERPRISE IN THE PERSPECTIVE OF SCIENCE

CHAPTER 4

Introduction to Part II: the Christian experiment

The broad perspective of the nature and origin of man and of the world he inhabits which mid-twentieth-century science now affords, and which was outlined in Part I, has been discernible in outline to the perspicacious for over a hundred years. However, only in the last twenty years have many of the gaps in our understanding of the development of the cosmos definitely begun to close, for example that dividing the living and non-living. In contrast, the beliefs and practices of Christianity have been developing relatively slowly over 1,900 years as they have adapted themselves to the cultural, intellectual and social framework of many races and nations and to people of varying levels of education, particularly scientific. The energy and intellectual vigour which has enabled Christianity to last so long and spread so far is often under-estimated by a sceptical and, theologically at least, relatively ill-informed generation of Western thinkers. For the existence of a world-wide Christian fellowship is, as William Temple once said, 'the great new fact of our era'.[1] So it is in no spirit of carping criticism that I now stress that, with very few exceptions, Christian thinking has scarcely begun to adapt itself to the conditions of working on its new frontiers— those with the explosively expanding territories of the knowledge of man and the world which the scientific method provides. I am convinced that until the Christian faith has learnt how to explore and penetrate this frontier its ability to extend, or even to hold its own, in its former cultural and social footholds will be vitiated and enfeebled. The proclamation of the Christian church makes a claim on men by virtue of certain realities which it affirms and expresses in its life and worship. This proclamation is now made to men who are increasingly aware of the new

---

[1] F. A. Iremonger, *William Temple* (London, 1948), p. 387; said on his enthronement in Canterbury Cathedral, April 1942.

scientific knowledge of themselves, their origin, and the world they live in: this is real to them when they weigh the evidence, and the Christian proclamation can make no claim on them unless it recognizes this new world which men's minds inhabit. Thus, however much one is conscious of and sensitive to the accumulated insights of Christian thinkers, and however much one recognizes the extent to which their thinking has often been validated in the experience of millions of humble Christians, one cannot avoid the demand now made upon Christians to relate their received insights into the nature and destiny of man and his world to the new scientific knowledge of these matters. Contemporary philosophical inquiries have accustomed us to recognizing the appropriateness of different linguistic usages, or 'languages', to different forms of experience and the organized concepts they engender. However, to assign the scientific and Christian interpretations of man and the world to two different language systems, thereafter not expected to impinge and interact on each other, is as unsatisfactory as the resort of many Christian apologists in the post-Darwinian era who assigned the body of man to science and his 'soul' or 'spirit' to religion. The unity of our experience can never make sense of such dichotomous assignments and the urge, referred to in Chapter I, for a unified view of existence as a basis for the integration for each one of us in his own individual life, continually undermines any barriers erected between our different modes of experience.

So for the sake of the individual and of both the Christian and, as I hope to indicate, the scientific communities it is urgent that attempts be made to set Christian affirmations in their scientific context and to see the new scientific knowledge in a Christian perspective. We can suspect in advance that neither will emerge entirely unscathed from this encounter and both may be rendered more effective in giving man that unified vision without which his life, however materially comfortable, will not be worth while.

A problem arises at the outset in such an attempt. What *is* the Christian faith?—the Gospels, the Nicene creed, confessional declarations, the consensus of Christian thought today (or at some specified point in the past when doctrine is presumed to have been pure and undefiled), the pronouncements of the

Lambeth Conference, of the Pope, or of the World Council of Churches? There is the further problem that Christian thought has an interlocking character which makes it difficult to discuss one doctrine without implicating another; for example, the doctrine of man, without going into the question of God's creative activity and the meaning of the life, death and resurrection of Christ in Christian thinking, and so on to doctrines of redemption, and the rest. It is not possible, within the scope of an essay of this kind, to provide an adequate short summary of the Christian faith. So in the chapters of Part II which follow, those aspects of the Christian faith which seem to me to most need reconsideration in the light of the scientific perspective will alone be referred to and will be discussed as they arise and so, inevitably, out of their natural context in the whole body of Christian ideas and affirmations. At this stage, perhaps it is worth making clear how a modern Christian might arrive at an understanding whose intellectual context is coherent and reasonable and whose experiential implications are both fruitful and self-authenticating.

At some point in his life, sooner or later, an individual begins to ask himself 'Who am I?', 'What am I here for?', 'What is the purpose of (my) life, if any?', 'Is life essentially meaningless and absurd?'. Frequently such questions arise for the individual in a personal context of some *angst* in which the whole, carefully contrived superstructure of his existence has revealed cracks and weaknesses through the light cast on it by some experience of his own (usually of loss) or by a sympathetic entry into that of another, either through his close contact with them or through the media of the arts; or the pointlessness and frenzied waste of much of man's corporate activity has made itself poignantly manifest in some striking way. Whatever the proximate cause, the individual finds himself standing often contrary to all his previous confidence, at the edge of an abyss of despair of himself, of men: nihilism threatens and nausea in face of the Absurd.

Whether the questions are invested with such overtones, or are part of the growing of an adolescent, or are the cool reflections of the study, the further questions 'Why is there anything at all?', 'Why are things the way they are?' begin to have a pressing pertinency, since the world need not have been; it is not self-explanatory, but appears to be derived rather than underived.[1] The questions about the nature and destiny of man in the world he relates to other intuitions of varying strength according to his upbringing and aptitudes, which nevertheless impinge upon his growing consciousness of what have traditionally been called 'values': the experience that there are moral demands upon him; that beauty in nature, words, music, and visual art comes to the individual as something which seizes him from beyond; that the world in which he lives is, amazingly, amenable to the exploration and organizing powers of his mind; and that, for example, the abstract constructions of some mathematical systems are means of ordering observations of the world. All these 'values', especially the last-mentioned for a scientist,[2] appear to make demands on him or to come to him from some inexplicable 'beyond' which is other than himself and yet deeper within his being and consciousness than anything else he knows. As he matures in his relationships to other people, and often to one or two in particular, those relationships too begin to be seen in the same way as expressions of, or originating from, that 'other' in which he moves and has his being and for many indeed are their deepest experience of it. If he has been brought up, as was the writer, in the semi-Christian cultural environment of English education, he begins to be aware that these deepest intimations of his existence are not unique to himself alone but have been the formative insights of many of the greatest and noblest of men. If he has been fortunate enough to be inducted into the literature, art and music of the Christian tradition he then comes to realize that the name for that 'other' which is nearer to him than his own life is 'God', of whom many speak but whom none can describe. Like all those who stumble upon a discovery he is tempted to think prematurely that he *can* describe this other who is the ground of his being and source of all that is. If he is fortunate, his experience or his mentors or his contemporaries lead him to ask and to want to know more.

---

[1] The vulnerability of the classic 'proofs of God's existence' to Kant's well-known criticisms does not, it seems to me, reduce the pertinency and meaningfulness of these questions, which are not answerable entirely by reason alone but only when reason is conjoined with a commitment to values, as indicated below (and as expounded by J. A. Baker, *The Foolishness of God* (London, 1970), Part I).

[2] *Qua* scientist, he may also find that the cosmic process itself evokes a disclosure of God, as discussed in Chapter 5 (4), p. 135.

He is, at this stage, confronted with such an array of would-be claimants in the form of religions of the world that he is bewildered in a 'confusion, worse confounded'. Inquiry can be made over a long period into the central tenets of the major religions but this need not delay a more detailed examination of that Hebraic-Christian tradition which, to Western man at least, is most likely to contain those thought-forms, images and words which will describe this 'other' for him and which he can understand most readily. An openness and willingness to learn from other religions should from this point be a life-long policy, but why should he take notice of any of these claimants? The reason is, I think, exactly the same as that which motivates the apprentice scientist, or indeed any other scholar, who in order to learn must initiate himself into a body of knowledge by accepting the intellectual integrity, and to that extent the authority, of his teachers and predecessors, without thereby precluding his right eventually to revise or overthrow this learning. So the man who is seeking to know who, or what, that Other is of whom he has had the intimations at which I have hinted will, if he is genuine in his desire, be prepared to listen to what men have been able to affirm about this inexpressible reality which has nevertheless to be named.[1]

In the Bible he finds he possesses a library of writers from within this Hebraic-Christian tradition. He has, or should have, in principle, no *a priori* reason for believing or disbelieving what these writers affirm, or say, or how they interpreted what they record. There is no doubt in my mind that these writers must be read like any others, with the necessary proviso that, since most of us do not make it a regular habit to read literature written between 1,800 and 2,800 years ago, we must not expect to be able to understand all the thought-forms of these writers or the setting in life of much of what is written. What is surprising is just how much is intelligible and instructive to mid-twentieth-century man without further elaboration.

He will find in the Old Testament part of this library the literature and chronicles of a Semitic people who early in recorded history experienced, primarily through the charismatic leadership of a number of outstanding individuals, the

---

[1] Cf. the story of Moses and the burning bush, Exodus 3:14.

claims upon them of that Other whom the reader seeks. He speaks to them in many ways but always as their Creator and as a claimant on their wills and their moral and social behaviour: he is one and the moral law within is his law. Within this relatively small people there was always to be found an even smaller remnant of these who, in spite of all temptation or oppression, kept this sense of the 'Holy One of Israel' and whose standards of personal and social behaviour and the purity of whose monotheism sets them apart from their racially closely related neighbours in the Middle Eastern cradle of civilization.

The seeker whom we describe finds he can learn from these people while being conscious of their shortcomings, their frequently crude nationalism, and the primitiveness they shared in many respects with their neighbours. As in the history of art, he may come to recognize that the development of the insights of the 'remnant of Israel' was not so much a continuous upward progress, though that is discernible, as a series of revelatory historical events and of illuminated persons, the memory of which and of whom was carefully passed on in small intimate groups gathered around a centre of worship or in a prophetic school. To both of these we owe the preservation of the writings of the Old Testament. Very much more might be said, but my point is that, were our twentieth-century technical society only unprejudiced enough to see it, there is so much which is unique and of value in the literature and tradition of the people of Israel that it demands inclusion in the education of men of all times and places and comes as water in the desert to those who are really seeking God.

By all outward signs, the history of this people ended in disaster after successive expulsions from their lands and captivity elsewhere, for by the time of Jesus we find them under Rome, a tolerated but subject race, turning to religious legalism away from the challenge of some of their later prophets who called them to make their 'house of prayer' to be 'for all nations', so that they might lead other peoples into the light they had seen. Into this unique cultural milieu, with its knowledge of God, Jesus is born at Bethlehem and lives at Nazareth. Such records as we have, allowing for all their inevitable incompleteness, point to a unique personality attended by unique events and making an impact on the history of mankind unequalled by any other before or since. Yet what is known of his life would not fill a current copy of *The Times*. At this point the seeker, whose journey we are hypothetically tracing, may find himself in a dilemma of most demanding and exacting character. For turn how he may, bring what sources of literary and historical criticism he can to bear upon the four brief narratives concerning this man, allow as he will for distortion and wishful thinking in those who wrote these reports, culled from even earlier oral traditions, he cannot avoid the question this Jesus is reported to have directed to his disciples,[1] 'Who do you say that I am?' His character, the moral purity of his teaching, his deliberate association of himself with the fulfilment of the hopes of the prophetic traditions of Israel, his penetrating insight into men and his intimacy with God, his 'Father', his courage in fulfilling his destiny and the evidence for his resurrection all point to a disclosure of the being of God and of the potentialities of human life about which one has eventually to make up one's mind. For however long this is deferred, once one has really looked at the Jesus of the Gospels and really seen him and the role he is taking and what is regarded as having happened to him, he is an inescapable element, either by adoption or by exclusion, in all one's future thinking about both the claimed reality of God and the nature of man.

If at this point, our seeker responds only to the extent of expressing, like Jesus' first disciples, a simple intention to follow this 'man-for-others', then he is in a position at least to listen to what his other followers have been led to understand about the significance of his teaching, life, death and claimed resurrection. Again, he is not compelled to accept these first followers' understanding of Jesus, but at least being nearer to the Jesus of history

[1] Mark 8:29. The rhetorical tone adopted in this paragraph is not meant to imply any diminution in or disparagement of the intellectual effort that is needed in the 'quest of the historical Jesus'. That this quest is, indeed, not hopeless but can lead to a knowledge of the historical Jesus adequate to allow a considered answer to be made to the posed question has recently been impressively argued by J. A. Baker (in *The Foolishness of God* (London, 1970), of which Part II incidentally provides a succinct working example, for the general reader, of New Testament criticism in action). There is no short cut which the present writer can recommend to enable Jesus's question to be answered *today* which will avoid the necessity for anyone genuinely seeking to answer it by himself looking at the evidence in the New Testament and associated literature with the assistance of all the resources of modern scholarly criticism. The paragraph in the text only indicates a few of the results of such an examination which have been of weight with the writer.

they have a special claim on his attention both on this account and on account of the men they were. So it is that he will turn to examine the New Testament writers and try to understand what their experiences were which made them write in the way they did; then the modern reader can answer the question, 'What must the truth have been and be if that is how it looked to men who thought and wrote like that?'[1] As with the Old Testament, he must not expect to understand the meaning of words and phrases or the setting-in-life of reported incidents and sayings as readily as he can yesterday's newspapers. For these writers are still removed from us by nineteen centuries, and a literalist approach does no credit to our percipience or to the intentions and intelligence of the original writers themselves. The writings he will find himself examining soon transpire to be those of a community whose origins are in the small band of people who collected around Jesus himself. So that now the seeker's inquiry opens out like an estuary into the many channels of development of thought within the Christian church, only very partially summarized in credal affirmations or resolution of Councils, and manifested in worship and in attitudes to existence new to the pagan world into which their faith spread—and thence to us here and now. It is impossible here to begin even to sketch the developments which then occurred, but one thing needs to be said. If Jesus was what he implicitly claimed to be, the fulfilment of Israel's hopes, in whose coming the 'Kingdom of God' had come to men, and was, as his earliest disciples affirmed, in some way the expression in a human person of God, that Other who is the ground of our being, then it is not at all surprising that his followers struggled for centuries, indeed still struggle in every generation, to find the most appropriate and least misleading language in which to describe his person and nature, and the implications of what he did and was, and the process which he initiated within mankind. So in our time and place, it is required of Christians that they look again at this man, for if he has the universal significance the Church claims, he has that significance for the world

---

[1] L. Hodgson, *For Faith and Freedom* (Oxford, 1956), p. x; but we have also to recognize that 'when as far as possible we know what the words meant to them then as far as possible we know what the truth was to them' (J. A. Baker, op. cit., pp. 364–5).

whose development we now see in its scientific perspective. But, equally, those in our day who possess this scientific perspective have still to face the Jesus who claims to be the fulfilment of man's history and the initiator of new possibilities for man if he willingly responds. 'Who do you think that I am?' is still addressed to us.

The foregoing is scarcely even an outline of a possible contemporary Christian apologetic, but I hope it gives at least an indication of how a scientifically-disposed inquirer might begin to follow the Christian trail, and might begin to inquire seriously into Christian affirmations as being attempts to come to terms with both the phenomenon of the man Jesus and with men's deepest intimations. I hope too that I have been able to convey the character of this inquiry as an exploration. Any authority that ultimately attaches to the library of Hebraic-Christian literature, the Bible, and to the body of people who constitute the followers of Jesus, the Christian Church, is only to be attributed to them in so far as their authority authenticates itself to the inquiring mind by virtue of the relevance and content of what they transmit, as in the scientific enterprise, and the extent to which this commitment organizes into a coherent whole our increasingly wide range of experiences. A simple and more traditional way of expressing this, in the Church of England, has been the recognition of a threefold authority for Christian teaching: the Bible, the Church, and sound scholarship, a three-legged stool of which no one leg can stand alone. In this, as in some other matters too, the Church of this country has been fortunate in adopting a wise position which enables men to learn from the past but leaves them free to incorporate into their thinking the new knowledge from other sources, notably in this context, that of science. To this task, following this practice, we must turn.

CHAPTER 5

God and the cosmos

I. CREATION

Christians have affirmed, in concord with Hebraic tradition, that the whole cosmos is other than God, but dependent on him and that, more metaphysically, the cosmos has contingent and derived being whereas only God has necessary and underived being, that is, an existence not dependent on any other entity. The classical expression of this belief is to be found in the phrases of the Nicene Creed which attribute creativity to God: God the Father is believed in as 'Maker of heaven and earth, and of all things visible and invisible'; God the Son as he 'by whom all things were made'; and God the Holy Spirit as 'the Lord, the giver of Life'. Without going into Trinitarian doctrine at this point it is notable that in this Creed one God is said to be creator, but that each 'Person' of the Triune God is also explicitly involved with creation.

In its developed form, the classical Christian doctrine of creation was not an assertion that the world had a beginning at a point in time when God set it all going, but that the cosmos continues to exist at all times by the sustaining creative will of God without which it would simply not be at all. For it has long been realized (e.g., by Augustine and even more explicitly by Aquinas) that time itself is an element in the created cosmos and therefore no 'act of creation' can be located at a point within created time itself. For God is other than the created order and so not in any sense himself 'in time' at all. The magnificent passages in the first chapter of Genesis are properly regarded by modern Christians not as literal records of what happened but, firstly, and traditionally, as 'history' in the sense that this account explains how certain features of human life came about as a result of a once-for-all irreversible event; and secondly, and more recently and less faithfully to the intentions of the Biblical writers, as a way of expressing a present situation, an ever-present truth, by telling a story.

120

As was mentioned earlier, the Genesis story is anti-mythical in the sense that it is in opposition to the myths, for example, of Babylon,[1] which always postulated something other than God (or the gods) out of which he (or they) shaped the world, and also gave accounts of the birth of the gods themselves. In Genesis, and in Christian thinking, the world exists entirely by the *fiat* of God 'And God said, Let there be . . .'. In more propositional and less literary terms Genesis is asserting that nothing comes into being but by the one God. It is in this respect an anti-mythical account and was probably intended to controvert the Babylonian creation myths. Thus in the Biblical teaching about creation the prime emphasis is on the dependence of everything that is for its existence on God's will and, correspondingly, that there was and is nothing whose existence is apart from God. This was later condensed into the assertion that creation was *ex nihilo*, 'out of nothing', which thereby denied pantheism, dualism, Manichaeism and, of course, atheism. This assertion may at first appear to be logically absurd, for only nothing can be made out of nothing, as has frequently been pointed out. But the phrase was intended to emphasize that 'creation' itself is not an act at a point in time but an analogical word representing God's relation to the cosmos now, a relation of absolute dependence of the cosmos on God's will for its very being. MacKinnon[2] quotes William Temple as interpreting this as: God minus the world equals God; whereas the world minus God equals nothing at all. Or we may recall the ascription to God in Revelation: '. . . thou didst create all things; by thy will they were created, and have their being.'[3] That this is broadly the classical Christian doctrine of creation is not as generally realized as it should be, partly no doubt because of a literalist interpretation of the Biblical literature to which popular Christianity readily reverts, and partly, so E. L. Mascall argues,[4] because of the influence of eighteenth-century deism in the thought of our nearer predecessors.

---

[1] *q.v.* C. F. von Weizsäcker, *The Relevance of Science* (London, 1964), chapters 2 and 3.

[2] See the discussion between A. Flew and D. M. MacKinnon in *New Essays in Philosophical Theology* (London, 1955), pp. 172–3.

[3] Rev. 4:11 (N.E.B.).

[4] E. L. Mascall, *Christian Theology and Natural Science* (London, 1956), Chapter 4.

I. T. Ramsey[1] has analysed the logical form of 'creation *ex nihilo*' into the analogical model, 'creation', which is a word used of human beings making paintings, symphonies, etc. out of something or by means of something and is here applied to the creation of all that is in the cosmos; and the qualifier, '*ex nihilo*', which has the function of developing a sense of wonder with the universe as its focus and which, by eliciting an awareness of its logical oddity, shows how the word 'God' is being posited in relation to this situation. Ramsey[2] concludes 'whereas creation *ex nihilo* seems, on the face of it, and from its grammar, to be talking of a great occasion in the past, it is rather making a present claim about God, and its logical grammar must be understood appropriately'. He goes on to suggest that perhaps 'creator *ex nihilo*' might have made the point better but that then its connection with the empirical world around us, 'creation', would be concealed. Or we might express it by saying that God is the logically prior source of the being of the world not temporally prior, since time itself is part of the created cosmos which is other than, but dependent on, God.

Much of the preceding exposition has had currency amongst Christian thinkers certainly for the six centuries since Aquinas and in one form or another ever since the origin of Christianity. What impact does the scientific account of the development of the cosmos have upon this position? Historically, there is no doubt that the initial impact was to reveal the inadequacy of much Christian thinking which interpreted the Genesis narrative literally and which saw creation as a definite event at a point in time.

The story has often been told[3] but, in summary, it may be said that the view that creation occurred only at a particular point in time was usually elaborated to mean also that biological species, including man, were individual and special creations of God at particular times. This doctrine of 'special creation' was eventually seen not to be a necessary interpretation, even a literal one, of the Genesis narrative, which simply states, for example, 'And God said, Let the waters bring forth abundantly the moving creature that hath life, and let fowl fly above the

[1] I. T. Ramsey, *Religious Language* (London, 1957), Chapter II.
[2] Op. cit., p. 75.
[3] e.g., by D. Lack, *Evolutionary Theory and Christian Belief* (London, 1957).

earth . . .' (1:20), and asserts nothing explicitly about the mode of creation, even in the story taken literally. Not for the first, or the last, time knowledge from science served to purify Christian belief of associated and unwarranted assertions which were not central to its teachings and which, indeed, barred the way to wider and more inclusive concepts. The idea of God creating through an evolutionary process in now fully accepted by Christians but its implications have not yet been fully realized and worked out.

For the essentially new element which the scientific perspective inevitably introduces into the idea of creation in the 'classical' form described at the beginning of this section is the realization that the cosmos which is sustained and held in being by God (this sustaining and holding itself constituting 'creation') is a cosmos which has always been in process of producing new emergent forms of matter. It is a world which is still being made and, on the surface of the Earth at least, man has emerged from biological life and his history is still developing. Any static conception of the way in which God sustains and holds the cosmos in being is therefore precluded, for the cosmos is in a dynamic state and in the corner which we, as men, can observe it has evolved conscious and self-conscious minds, who shape their environment and choose between ends.

That the world was in flux and change, with all its corollaries for the destiny of the individual man, has been reflected upon since the ancient Greeks. But that the matter of the world developed in a particular direction to more complex and ultimately thinking forms was not established knowledge.

The people of Israel, and following them, the Christian Church, have always believed in the providential hand of God in human history, with the non-human world being regarded simply as the stage for that drama. Science now sees man as part of 'nature' and both together as subject to continuous development. Any static conception of the relation of God and the world is therefore excluded, for if the emergence of new forms of matter in the world is in some way an activity of God, then it must be regarded as his perennial activity and not something already completed. Clearly, if God is 'outside' time in some sense, that is, if time itself is other than God and part of the created cosmos, there is no more difficulty in regarding God as having a creative relationship with the cosmos at all times than postulating a special creative relation only at some posited 'zero' time. Indeed there is less difficulty, for why should God have a relation to one point in time which is different from his relation to any other point if he himself is not in time at all, that is, if his mode of being is not within the temporal process? There is, of course, a conceptual impasse in trying to understand how God the transcendent, the Other, who comes to men from 'beyond', as we have discussed, and discloses himself to man, can be related to time at all. But this is only to say that we cannot assert who or what God is in himself. We can only speak of him by analogy. Briefly, the scientific perspective of a cosmos in development introduces a dynamic element into our understanding of God's relation to the cosmos which was previously obscured, although never excluded.

2. GOD AS IMMANENT AND AS 'HOLY SPIRIT'

The doctrines of God the Holy Spirit and of the immanence of God have in principle always allowed Christian thought to be open to the aforementioned possibility of seeing God as dynamically active in the cosmic process, but the new scientific perspective now renders it a necessary element in any understanding of the relation of God to the world.

Because the world is dependent on God, he has always been presumed to be able to be present and active everywhere in the world, although other than it. God is said to be 'immanent'; he has the attribute of immanence. Since the cosmos has order and regularity the question arises, is God to be sought in the regularities or in the irregularities, or in both? To this question we must turn in the next section, but before doing so another element in Christian thinking must be considered.

In the experience of the early Christians and of those who followed, it has been found that in one mode of relationship between men and God, God is experienced as the one who takes possession of man's inner being and powers so that God speaks as it were deep within man to the man himself. This aspect of the being of God, God the Holy Spirit, came to be seen as describable only in the personal terms which were also applied to God as transcendent (the Father) and God as Incarnate, 'made flesh', in man (God the Son). God the Holy Spirit was in New Testament times largely seen, such was the impact of their experience, as God working within the baptized Christian and within the whole Christian community to point men to Jesus Christ, and thus as the source of the new life of the Christian whose most characteristic note was love. The Holy Spirit of God and the Spirit of Jesus Christ were at first almost synonymous, but gradually Christians were led to affirm a trinity of modes of being,[1] of 'persons', within the one Godhead, to be the origin and content of their experience of God transcendent, incarnate and as possessor. The working in Christians of God as Holy Spirit later came to be seen as but a more personal manifestation of the ever-working immanent activity of God in the whole created cosmos, and there are indications in the Bible that these ideas had already been linked with the concept of God as creator. Thus in the first few verses of the Bible the Spirit of God is said to brood over the face of the chaotic deep[2] out of which God ordered his cosmos; and the other story (J–E) of creation[3] depicts man as being brought into existence by God breathing 'the breath of life' into the dust of the ground, where 'breath' also means 'spirit'.[4] In much of the Old Testament the 'spirit' (*ruach*) of God refers to an invasion of individuals by the divine energy, which thereby enables men to achieve otherwise impossible feats. But with the Exile and afterwards a more personal connotation was given to the term; on the manward side it came to be associated with the voluntary, conscious and intellectual aspects of man and as the unifying centre of a man's personal being and, as such, potentially capable of a harmonious relationship with God, to whom the word was also then ascribed. God is, one could say, described as Holy Spirit when he is operative in the spirit of man which, it must be stressed, was not in the Hebrew psychosomatic concept of the whole man a 'ghost within the machine' or a separate entity of any kind in itself. Rather, man's 'spirit' is the organ of psychic life, of the vitality of a man, and is open

---

[1] The use of the word 'modes' is not meant to imply that the distinction between God the Father, God the Son, and God the Holy Spirit is only transitory (as in 'modalism'). Rather the three modes are meant here and elsewhere (e.g., pp. 139, 159, 173) to denote God's 'ways of being' the one divine reality.

[2] Gen. 1:2.

[3] Gen. 2:7.

[4] See remarks on *ruach*, p. 150, n. 1.

to the influence and direction-giving power of God as 'Holy Spirit'.

Thus the concept of God the Holy Spirit had biblically this double reference to God as immanent in creation and God as active in the 'spirit' of man, with the stress on the latter. It is therefore highly significant that when the purposes of God are consummated, from the Christian viewpoint, in God expressing himself in a man, it is God the Holy Spirit who is said to 'over-shadow' Mary when she accepts her role as the earthly agent of this act: 'The Holy Spirit will come upon you and the power of the Most High will overshadow you.'[1]

These two streams of thought therefore converge in the one man, Jesus, who is both the consummation of the process of creation, of God's action upon men, and the initiator of that new Christian community which the New Testament saw as the characteristic and special sphere of the Holy Spirit. But even while affirming this, we can see that the Hebrew and Christian thought grounded the possibility of such action of God the Holy Spirit in men in his ever-present activity in creation and in individuals. The coming of Christ is seen as now enabling God the Holy Spirit to have free course in re-creating men and thereby opening up new possibilities to mankind.

Thus we see many ideas converging in the New Testament: of God as immanent in the cosmos in contrast to his transcend-ence over it; of God the Holy Spirit as the mode of God's being operative in creation and in the spirit of man; of God the Holy Spirit as God active in bringing Jesus Christ into the world, giving him his role,[2] of raising him from the dead[3] and re-creating man through conversion, baptism and incorporation into the Christian community (the 'body of Christ'). All these affirma-tions, whose justification would take us too deeply into a critical analysis of the Christ-event, must now be reassessed in the light of the scientific perspective. This perspective cannot directly support or in any sense 'prove' the Christian assertions but it

[1] Luke 1:35 (N.E.B.).

[2] At the baptism of Jesus, the Spirit was said to be seen to descend upon him (Mark 1:10 and parallels) and therefore must be regarded as the inner agent of his call to his mission.

[3] Cf. Rom. 1:3–4. 'On the human level he [Jesus] was born of David's stock, but on the level of the spirit—the Holy Spirit—he was declared Son of God by a mighty act in that he rose from the dead' (N.E.B.).

does provide a securely based framework of knowledge to help us understand more fully the character and meaning of the context in and to which these assertions are relevant. The convergence of ideas just summarized which see God the Holy Spirit as immanent in the cosmos in general, in man in particular, and as consummated in Jesus and in the community expressing his Spirit, is peculiarly consonant with this new scientific perspective. For that perspective is of a cosmos in which creativity is ever-present, in which new forms of matter emerge and in which, with many thrusts in many fruitless directions, nevertheless in the end there emerged man, mind, human society, human values, in brief the 'human spirit'. These two perspectives from, on the one hand, the Hebrew and Christian experience and, on the other, the gamut of the sciences, mutually illuminate each other. Each has its own autonomy and justification but, if both are recognized, a combined insight into the cosmic development is then afforded in which the features elaborated by the sciences are in harmony with the experiences which cluster around particular events in history and which theological language expounds. The theological, Christian interpretation complements and develops the scientific account in the significance it attributes to these events in human history. Moreover the theological perspective, if accepted, gives meaning to the present and a sense of direction for the future to a world still regarded as in process and as the matrix of new emergent forms of human life.

The theological perspective itself is correspondingly re-shaped by this consideration of the scientific account of the cosmic development. For the theological account will now be seen to be most meaningful and to correspond best with the scientific one, when it emphasizes that God is immanent, that his action in the world is continuously creative, and that the coming of Christ and the role of the Church are to be understood in such dynamic terms, rather than in the more classical and static images of earlier theological exposition. We shall have cause to stress this again in connection with the understanding of man provided by the two enterprises. Here we are concerned with the impact of the scientific perspective on our understanding of God's relation to the cosmos. It has become clear that this relation must now be conceived with a new emphasis on God as immanent in the whole cosmic process and of God, as Holy

Spirit, as in some way the directing agency in this process leading up to man and the Christian community. The two perspectives are complementary, for the scientific provides the necessary
grounding in material reality which the theological requires,
and the theological provides the means whereby contemporary
man in his community can consciously participate and find
both personal and corporate meaning in a cosmic process which,
without the Christian perspective, would appear impersonal
and even inimical. For just as the first Christians found
themselves inevitably using language which was an extension
of that applied to persons and so corresponded to the highest
they knew, about that power of God, the Holy Spirit, which
through Jesus possessed them, so this Christian insight claims
that the meaning of the cosmic process revealed by science is
ultimately to be expressed in personal terms in the sense that
the language of human personality is the least misleading for
describing the direction in which the process moves. In such a
complementary outlook informed by both the theological and
the scientific enterprises, the individual human being and his
society might well find a hope which is not misplaced and of
which it has too long been bereft.

3. CONTINUITY, REGULARITY, AND VITALISM

The eighteenth-century deist saw the relation of God to the
cosmos rather as that of an instrument or machine to its maker.
The maker fashions the parts, their interconnection and the
principles by which the instrument, say a watch, will work.
Then having been set going, it is left to work by itself, with the
implication that a perfect watch-maker would so construct it
that any interference subsequently needed would be minimal.
The deist thought he could understand how the whole cosmos
kept going but required God to bring it into existence in the
first place. We have seen that this view of creation is not the
classical Christian view which is not necessarily tied even to
believing that the cosmos had a beginning in time as such. Thus,
the Christian doctrine of creation is neutral as regards the 'big
bang' and the 'continuous creation' theories of the origin of the
universe. For as we have seen, it is really making a different
point, namely that the cosmos depends for its being on the will

of God, and is not giving an account of the historical origin of the universe. Time itself is regarded as part of the created order and the act of creation by God is strictly regarded as not in time at all or, rather, as having the same relation to all points in time. The deist view was developed as a result of the enormous impression which Newton's laws of motion and gravitation had made with their sense of an ordered universe obeying 'laws of nature'.

The position now is that, as discussed in Chapter 3, we can see that the development of the cosmos is continuous and that it proceeds according to regularities and relationships which are examples of or reasonable extrapolations from regularities and relationships we can observe now (we have called these 'laws of nature', for brevity). To this extent at least, and only to this extent, some deist presuppositions continue to be valid. However, what we have learnt in the last hundred years is, as Chapter 2 outlined, that matter obeying these laws has in fact been in continuous development so that new forms of matter have emerged up to man himself. This development is genuinely creative, for the higher levels of complexity manifest principles of organization which could not have been predicted from the laws pertaining to the less organized states of which the more complex are patterned assemblies. In summary, whether the cosmos is considered in the light of the classical, non-deist Christian doctrine of creation or of that of the scientific evidence, 'creation' in both senses is an ever-present reality. There is therefore no justification and no adequate motive for separating the creative aspects of the world at all points in time from its creation, again in both senses, at some definite postulated time in the past. Hence the deist view is no longer needed to solve a problem which has become unreal. However, the contemporary Christian theist in urging the immanent creative activity of God in the cosmos must recognize that it is by the 'laws' and through the regularities of nature that God must be presumed to be working. This recognition is linked with the important understanding that matter is of such a kind, and the 'laws' which it obeys are of such a kind, that creativity, in the sense of the emergence of new forms of matter, is a permanent potentiality whose actualization depends on circumstances. This potentiality is not injected into the cosmos from 'outside'

either by God, or by a Life Force, *élan vital*, or other supernatural agency. If God is in the world-process of matter at all,
he is in it all through, in all its potentialities, whether actualized
or not, and he continues to hold it in being by his will with these
potentialities and not otherwise.

We are beginning to see that to postulate a 'God of the gaps'
who is supposed to intervene to fill, for example, the gap between the living and non-living, or to 'explain' the appearance
of new species by special creation, is not only just a tactical
error on the part of those theists who have seen God in these
supposed discontinuities in the cosmos, but is to mistake entirely
the relation between God and the cosmos. It is as if men could
only conceive of a God who could direct the course of his
machine-like universe by making discrete interventions at
crucial stages. No doubt this view owed its limitations to the
prevailing mechanistic understanding of the cosmos which followed from the impressive scope of the Newtonian scheme. But
since Darwin and all the other developments, the mechanistic
model has had to give way to a more developmental and organismic framework of thought so that the motives for postulating
a 'God-of-the-gaps' view of God's relation to the cosmos should
have faded. It is, as already stated, in any case entirely unsatisfactory theologically and should disappear from Christian discourse. For, with hindsight, it seems almost an impertinence of
men not to allow God to be creative in his own way through
the stuff of the cosmos and its regular mutual interrelationships,
or the 'laws' it obeys, and to assert that he had both brought
matter into existence and had to intervene from time to time
to help it on to the next stage which he, presumably, willed—the
transition from non-living to living, or the special creation of
individual species, notably man himself, or the creation of each
individual human 'soul'. It now seems more consistent to urge
that God has been creating all the time through matter and the
'laws' governing its transformations. We have, as it were, like
the Scribes and Pharisees,[1] been asking for signs whereas the
signs were already present there for us to see, if we only had
the eyes to do so.

Hence Christians should have no interest in finding evidence
for any form of vitalism, as they and their critics have frequently

[1] Matt. 12:38 f.

supposed. To postulate a 'special creation' of species or that God injected 'life' into the universe or that God somehow directly and personally directs the processes of biological evolution by means other than that inherent in the nature of matter and its 'laws' are all errors on *Christian* premises. However, as we have discussed in Chapter 3, the 'mechanist' in contrast to the 'vitalist' can gain no comfort from this repudiation of the older vitalism on both scientific and theological grounds. For Polanyi's analysis even of what we mean by a machine shows the involvement in mechanisms of new principles of ordering matter, of boundary conditions, which could not have been predicted from a knowledge of the laws governing the constituent parts. So 'mechanism' as a view of biological evolution has to reckon with this logical feature of the relation of higher organisms to less complex.

To have reached this position concerning the relation of God and the cosmic process, that God works through order and the 'laws' of nature, does not eliminate the question of how the 'boundary conditions' of Polanyi, the principles of organization of more complex forms of matter, came into existence. Is it enough to assert that the biological efficiency gained by acquiring and participating in these higher levels of organization of matter is enough in itself, by natural selection, to explain their survival and dominance and culmination in man? Or is it necessary to postulate, as Polanyi himself does,[1] for example, the existence of a 'phylogenetic field' that governs the process of evolution and in which the organisms are guided by the potentialities which are open to them, drawn on by an active centre from which such striving is directed? Here 'field' is used by Polanyi as it is in physical science, as a field of force, where the force is the gradient of a potential which in this context is a potentiality waiting to be realized, and the proximity of a possible achievement provides the driving force towards its actualization. In Polanyi's own words:

So far as we know, the tiny fragments of the universe embodied in man are the only centres of thought and responsibility in the visible world. If that be so, the appearance of the human mind has been so far the ultimate stage in the awakening of the world; and all that

[1] M. Polanyi, *Personal Knowledge* (London, 1958), pp. 398–400.

has gone before, the strivings of a myriad centres that have taken the risks of living and believing, seem to have all been pursuing, along rival lines, the aim now achieved by us to this point. They are all akin to us. For all these centres—those which led up to our own existence and the far more numerous others which produced different lines of which many are extinct—may be seen engaged in the same endeavour towards liberation. We may envisage then a cosmic field which called forth all these centres by offering them a short-lived, limited, hazardous opportunity for making some progress of their own towards an unthinkable consummation.[1]

Such a postulate is possible only in the context of a wider philosophical position, such as Polanyi's own, but whether or not we adopt his mode of expression (especially his idea of a 'phylogenetic field') the problem remains of explaining how the cosmic process developed in the direction it did. We recall that the attempt to apply information theory to this problem has so far been inconclusive. We may have to learn much more about the way development is controlled in higher organisms before we can even find the most appropriate language in which to discuss the problem. Nevertheless, the logical character of the problem of the relation of higher to lower organisms remains. It would be over-hasty to link the solution of this problem with the immanent activity of God working through matter and the 'laws' it obeys. At least it seems we have been able to reach a more accurate understanding of God's relation to his cosmos as a result of realizing that this cosmos has a continuous creative development governed by its own inherent laws.

4. ORDER AND MIND—AND A COSMIC DISCLOSURE

The perspective on the cosmos which science provides is so magnificent in its scope and scale that it can easily obscure its two most notable features, which are in fact also its presuppositions. These are, firstly, that the things and events of the cosmos are amenable to that rational ordering of which human minds are capable; and secondly, that the minds which effect this ordering are themselves the product of the cosmic process itself, which is thereby engendering that which reflects upon it. The observation of regularity and the susceptibility of the flux of events in the world to the sifting, rationalizing processes of

[1] Op. cit., p. 405.

science, the ability of the concepts, models and hypotheses fashioned by these intellectual processes not only to rationalize past regularities but also to predict future ones with such a degree of reliability that men everywhere trust their lives to the reliable working of modern technological products, has become such a commonplace that few remark on it. This is a pity. For that the world appears to men's mind as an ordered cosmos susceptible to discovery by the combination of experimental study and rational reflection is one of the most significant discoveries made by man. It is scarcely 300 years old and it has transformed human existence and thinking. It is still the single most striking feature of the cosmos, and it is the most frequently forgotten because so implicit in all of modern science and technology. But if we are to find any principle which orders our experience of this world, does not this imply that it is only to be found in categories and language-usages which are those appertaining to 'mind'? For only mind transcends its objects and we find that human minds are gradually transcending and mastering greater and greater tracts of the physical and biological universe around man. For mind knows the universe, which does not know mind. This sequence of thought has always worked strongly in scientists reflecting on the cosmos; it has not always led them to conventional theism but it has frequently protected them from the grosser forms of materialism. The realization that our minds can find the world intelligible, and the implications this has that an explanation for the world process is to be found in mental rather than purely material categories, has been for many scientists who are theists, including the present writer, an essential turning point in their thinking. Why *should* science work at all? That it does so points strongly to a principle of rationality, to an interpretation of the cosmos in terms of mind as its most significant feature. Any thinking which takes science seriously must, it seems to me, start from this. This principle of rationality has been an implication since the secrets of the cosmos began to yield to the methods of scientific empiricism, but we now realize something more, almost as striking: that these minds which possess the capacity to apprehend the cosmic process themselves emerge from that process itself. As Temple put it, 'That the world should give rise to minds which know the world involves a good deal concerning the nature of the world.'[1] There is clearly a kinship between the mind of man and the cosmos, which is real, and which any account of the cosmos cannot ignore, even if the emergence of mind is entirely explicable in terms of the survival advantage it confers on its possessors. This last suggestion is in fact scarcely adequate to the whole range of human activities—what is the survival value to its author or its observers of a Mozart quintet, a Ming vase, a sonnet of Donne, an understanding of relativity? —and in any case, it does not explain the reality of the kinship between human minds and the cosmic process in and by which they emerge.

Again one cannot avoid the conclusion that any explanation of the whole cosmic process is likely to be best describable in terms of that into which it ultimately develops, namely the human mind and personality, and this is likely to provide the least misleading terminology and language for expressing what it is really about. For, to take a simple analogy, the 'explanation' of a pile of bricks, planks, pipes, window frames, glass and cement bags only transpires when they are assembled to form the house for which they were intended, and such an explanation we regard as completely satisfying in ordinary life. We find ourselves living in an immensely variegated and complicated universe but with the two features which stand out beyond all others: the variety is amenable to the ordering of human minds and human minds have emerged out of its very stuff. Hence it seems reasonable to explain the whole process in terms of mind rather than in terms of the constituent units which mind orders and which give rise to minds at a higher level of complexity. The old theistic 'argument from design', in spite of its evocative power,[2] foundered logically in its inability by itself to show that the concept (of an omnipotent Architect and Designer) generated by reflection on the natural order actually had an object; and it was later vulnerable to the further criticism, based on biology, that what appeared to be the result of design, and so of the intention of a Designer, in the biological world could,

---

[1] W. Temple, *Nature, Man and God* (London, 1934), Lecture V, p. 130. The whole chapter is a superb exposition of the points made so briefly in this section.

[2] Strikingly and sympathetically depicted by Kant, while demolishing its strictly rational basis (*Critique of Pure Reason*, trans. N. Kemp Smith (London, 1933), p. 519.)

in principle at least if not always in detail, be more readily explained in terms of the operation of natural selection, however ingenious the contrivances in question. Now, however, the sciences afford a wider perspective, which we have des-cribed in Part I, of a cosmos developing from insentient baryons, nuclei, electrons up to matter organized as man who thinks, loves, prays, creates and reflects on himself and the processes which brought him forth. Any meaning in this process is likely to be found in its end because only from that viewpoint can the process be seen for what it is. As with other theistic arguments, it is at this stage not absolutely compelling but, in the terms of I. T. Ramsey,[1] it serves rather to evoke a disclosure. Indeed, the whole cosmic development itself may be set out like one of the sequences in Ramsey's expositions[2] of which the last term has the function of evoking a situation to which we respond by commitment and, in its logical oddity, points to the appropriate logical status for the word 'God', thus: baryons, nucleons, atoms, molecules, inorganic matter, nucleo-proteins, living matter, cells, cellular assemblies, fishes, mam-mals, conscious organisms, primates, *Homo sapiens*, Stone-age man, the inventor of fire, the inventor of the wheel, intelligent, self-conscious persons, Archimedes, Galileo, Newton, extremely intelligent self-conscious persons—and so on, and so on, taking many different lines of human excellence until the sequence evokes a disclosure and a commitment, 'the light dawns', 'the ice breaks'. It seems that the whole cosmic development is in itself just such a disclosure sequence as Ramsey has shown characterizes religious language, but now it is a sequence not merely of language but of what has actually happened. So re-garded, the scientific perspective is a most compelling pointer to God, that Beyond which is in our midst, to the understanding of whom the theological enterprise is directed.

5. CREATION A COSTLY PROCESS: STRUCTURAL
   RELATIONS AND PAIN

The cosmic development to which science has opened our eyes is a development in which new forms of matter emerge in

---

[1] In his *Religious Language* (London, 1957).
[2] e.g., op. cit., p. 67: Ferdinand Lopez—hardly good; Long John Silver—fairly good; David—very good; St. Francis—intensely good; God—infinitely good.

the assembly of simpler forms into new patterns and arrangements based on new principles or 'boundary conditions'. This means that the higher, more complex forms could not arise unless the simpler forms had preceded them in the cosmic development; and, moreover, once they have come into existence they continue to survive only because new individual examples of the more complex structures can incorporate units of simpler structures from their environment. These simpler units, out of which any existing more complex entity is assembled, are rarely those which immediately precede the complex form in the evolutionary development. To be more particular, animals feed on vegetables and fruit, and often other smaller and weaker animals, but not necessarily on their near predecessors in evolution, if these still exist around them. This is, in fact, rare since the biological success of a species means that it has won a particular niche in the environment for itself in competition with its nearest relatives: bacteria feed on simple salts, gases, and small organic molecules, whereas their predecessors in evolution were simpler single-celled organisms of some macromolecular aggregate; even molecules, to go outside the biological range, exist in nature by chemical reactions which re-assort atoms between different molecules and which do not necessarily correspond to the original processes which first brought these molecules into existence in the early stages of the Earth's history. There is in all this a kind of structural necessity, whereby more complex structures can only be assembled in large numbers if the energy expenditure is minimized by the utilization of substructures already pre-formed in the environment. This structural necessity is as apparent to the chemist and biochemist as any mathematical identity such as $(3 + 5) = 8$. Similarly, just as we cannot conceive of a God for whom $(3 + 5) \neq 8$, because the proposition is analytic, there is the same kind of difficulty in conceiving of a God for whom complex structures of matter could be assembled otherwise than from less complex units, because this too is a necessity, with its own kind of 'logic'. This usually causes no problems when we think of the inorganic world and would generally be regarded as quite obvious. However, when in the biological world we see all living creatures depending for their life and sustenance on other living creatures, emotional considerations have frequently in the past swamped a more balanced judgement with cries of 'nature, red in tooth and claw'. Even on its own ground, this reaction is misplaced, for the memories and anticipation of living organisms other than man appear to be either fleetingly short or non-existent, so that fear and pain in animals is not the continuous blight it can be to man.[1] The earlier picture of Darwin and T. H. Huxley of the biological world as a 'struggle for existence' has given way to a more precise view of the process of survival rather as an advantage in differential reproduction. As Simpson puts it:[2]

Struggle is sometimes involved, but it usually is not, and when it is, it may even work against rather than toward natural selection. Advantage in differential reproduction is usually a peaceful process in which the concept of struggle is really irrelevant. It more often involves such things as better integration with the ecological situation, maintenance of a balance of nature, more efficient utilisation of available food, better care of the young, etc. . . .

Even so, there is a cost when new forms of life emerge which are then dependent on simpler forms for their continued existence. New life can only emerge if other forms of life are, as it were, incorporated into, or sacrificed on behalf of, the higher forms. The structural necessity of this is almost as cogent as that of arithmetic and creation is only conceivably possible on this basis. Thus, to use more emotive terms creation involves a 'cost', of life offered so that forms of new life might emerge and survive. That this is so, should not have surprised Christians, who, in the light of the life and death of Christ, have come to ascribe to God, so far as human speech can indicate, self-offering 'love' as his most distinctive attribute. They have affirmed that God has to be described as 'love' because, in creation, he deliberately limits himself, by allowing a cosmos to remain in being which is other than himself, which is given its own autonomy and so limits his freedom, and which in man can consciously repudiate his creatorhood; they have affirmed that God was revealed as self-offering love in the self-limitation which was his incarnation in Jesus Christ and in the self-offering of Jesus's human life for men; and that God the Holy Spirit is characterized especially by his communicating to those who follow

[1] See, e.g., C. E. Raven, *Natural Religion and Christian Theology* (Cambridge, 1953), pp. 115–16, Vol. II.
[2] G. G. Simpson, op. cit., p. 222 (see also pp. 268, 298).

Christ the ability to love.[1] Thus Christians have been led to the understanding that—and the personal, apparently anthropomorphic, language is inescapable, we have no other higher terms —the creative process is costly to God, that in the created order God strives to bring into existence new forms of matter and ultimately man, and that the self-emptying[2] of God in the incarnation and the self-offering of Christ in life and ultimately death on a cross, all testify to a creative ground of Being whose name is Love, the 'love that moves the Sun and the other stars'.[3] I am only too well aware that the above only begins to touch upon the problem of evil and suffering in human life, which is on an altogether different scale and at a higher level of intensity than in the animal world. But even this 'problem of pain' has to be viewed in its wider biological context. For pain is a warning device necessary to preserve the individual, and so the species, against many dangers. Moreover, if a creature is to evolve which has sensory organs receptive to sounds, smells, taste, sight and touch (and perhaps other signals such as ultrasound or infrared radiation) it must inevitably have an outer surface which is soft enough to contain the delicate and sensitive organs of detection, which means it is inevitably more vulnerable to physical calamities in its environment and more easily attacked by bacteria, viruses and by better-armed, though less-sensitive, organisms. Thus pain appears to be a necessary concomitant of an increase in sensitivity and awareness, which are the prerequisites of the development of consciousness.

There is a structural necessity, often overlooked by Christian and agnostic alike, in the cessation and offering of life for new life to evolve. This offering science now shows to have occurred in the cosmic development. Uniquely among the great world religions, the Christian understanding of God as self-offering Love reckons with this offering of life through what it has learned from the life and death of Jesus. This theme is developed further in the Christian understanding of the One God as a trinity of 'persons', conceived not so much as centres of

---

[1] Rom. 5:5, 'God's love has flooded our inmost heart through the Holy Spirit he has given us'; Gal. 5:22, 'the harvest of the Spirit is love . . .'; Rom. 15:30, 'the love that the Spirit inspires'.

[2] Phil. 2:6, 7.

[3] Dante, *Paradiso*, Canto 33, l. 145 (trans. D. Sayers).

consciousness but rather as individual modes of being.[1] This doctrine is affirmed because of the Christian experience of God as transcendent, incarnate and immanent, but nevertheless as one Godhead. Some thinkers have gone on to stress that this harmonious unity-in-diversity is the supreme expression of what love really is and that what constitutes love is its creating of a unity between persons without ever abrogating or derogating from the diversity and individuality of those whom it unifies. To many this is a mysterious and incomprehensible doctrine: to others it becomes the keystone of the whole Christian understanding of nature, man and God. Be that as it may, it is mentioned at this point to affirm how fundamental to Christian thinking is the concept that within the very being of God love is operative and that self-offering is in the nature of his being and of the creative activity which expresses that being.[2]

[1] See p. 125, n. 1.
[2] In the language of Christian sacrifice and self-offering, the author of Revelation did not shrink from describing Christ as 'The Lamb that hath been slain *from the foundation of the world*' (Rev. 13:8, A.V.).

CHAPTER 6

Man, evolution, and Christ

Scientific endeavour (Part I) has disclosed a continuous process of development in which new forms of matter have
emerged, by 'natural laws', and culminate in man, who has
now spread into every corner of the Earth's surface and is even
beginning to explore the space around the Earth. Man's presence in the universe has already been discussed (Chapter 3 (7))
from the point of view of interpreting the significance and meaning to be attached to the evolutionary process to which matter
is subject. In the present chapter we will be looking in the other
direction—what can we say about the nature of man in view
of his evolutionary origins? We ask this question modestly,
realizing that, if man's proper study is man, the insights of the
poet, the experience of the judge, the intuitions of the lover, the
reflections of philosophers on human language and perception,
indeed all human experience, bear powerfully upon it. However, the aim of this essay is to examine the interaction of the
knowledge and approach of the sciences with the doctrinal
formulation and content of Christian experience and, at this
particular point, especially the view of man which both afford.
We must ask whether these two views of man now complement
or contradict each other, recognizing that both are themselves
developing. What can the doctrines concerning man, and of the
possibility of God revealing himself as a man, be thought to be
affirming in the light of the scientific perspective of an evolving
cosmos of which man is indubitably an inherent part? What
meaning do or can such Christian affirmations continue to
have? First, some implications of the scientific account itself are
considered. We will then attempt to outline some of the relevant
points in the Christian view of man and its claim that God was
in Christ, and, in the third section of this chapter, these two
approaches will be brought into juxtaposition for mutual illumination and, if need be, correction. Certain ideas on a Christian
humanism and on our understanding of the creativity and being

of God which result from this juxtaposition will then be elaborated.

I. MAN IN THE CONTEXT OF EVOLUTION

(a) *Man as a person, a psychosomatic unity*

The continuity of the processes of inorganic and biological evolution, their subjection to 'natural laws' and their culmination in the emergence of man, reveal man as a part of the material structure of the world. A man may be subdivided into brain, organs, cells, macromolecules, small molecules, atoms and so on, like any other observable structure. Yet in evolution at each new level of organization of matter there emerge new features, properties and activities of the new wholes which did not appear in the constituent parts. This, as we have seen (Chapter 3, especially (4)), does not mean that each emergent whole (e.g., the cell compared with its constituent macromolecules) is any less 'physical' in its basis than its components —but it does stress that each emergent whole will require languages and conceptual frameworks of description which are appropriate to the new level of organization and inapplicable to the parts. The level of organization of matter which we call a man is thus as much and as little describable in terms of the physics and chemistry of his constituent atoms and molecules as any other organism. Moreover, in a man new properties and activities of matter emerge which cannot be subsumed or described in terms of languages and concepts used for the forms which preceded him. So when we view man in his evolutionary context it is necessary to affirm both his physical nature and all that which is specific and unique to him as a man, even if rudimentary forms of, for example, his intelligence are to be discerned in other higher mammals, especially the primates. At the end of Chapter 3, in section (7), we referred to some of the distinctive activities of men and, for brevity, we will include all of these (his intelligence, curiosity, adaptability, creativity, ability to form personal relationships, consciousness and self-consciousness, openness to God (his 'spirit'), ability to transcend in thought his environment and survey it as subject, his use of 'I') in the adjective 'mental'. The adjective is applied to activities with the deliberate intention of avoiding any postulate of a distinct entity called the 'mind' which performs these activities. The mental activities are activities which emerge distinctively and characteristically in matter organized at the level we call man. These mental activities are activities of the one entity which includes the hierarchy of levels of structure of matter which we have referred to above. Thus both the physical and mental activities are activities of the same entity which might properly then be given a special name—'person' seems the most appropriate.

This way of describing man does justice to man's evolutionary origins out of the matter of the world, on which he is still dependent for life; and on the truly emergent mental activities which characterize man specifically. Man has been said to be a psychosomatic unity: perhaps one would rather say he is one person possessing both physical and mental attributes, each explicated by appropriate sets of predicates. This way of putting it avoids the posing of misleading questions such as 'At what point in the evolutionary scale, or in the growth of an embryo, does mind or "soul" enter the biological world?' and 'How can a physical entity possess a non-material "mind"?'. For the activities and attributes described as mental are now regarded as one, albeit the most recent and significant, in a whole series which have emerged at different stages in the cosmic evolution. This emergent quality of mind is less obvious than that of, say, the wetness of water from hydrogen and oxygen, or of the first living cell from its constituent macromolecules, because in this instance, and this one alone, in looking at man we are reflecting on that emergent quality which makes reflection on anything possible at all. Moreover, there is a dichotomy in our experience and in the language we have to employ which is not reduced or removed by anything said so far, as we shall discuss in a moment. However, the mental attributes of man are in fact an emergent in evolution and hence have their basis in man's physical organization. The close relation between mental activities and the physical organization of men's bodies and brains has been supported by every advance in psychology, psychiatry, medicine, biology and physiology: for example, the dependence of personality states on hormone balance, and vice versa; the genetic basis of man's bodies, personalities, mental attributes and of defects in these respects—hence their basis in the structure of the DNA inherited in 23 chromosomes per cell from each of the two parents (all men, like all living organisms, begin life as a few molecules of DNA); the effect of diet on personality; the effects of drugs on mental states and of mental states on drug dependence; personality changes after brain operations or injuries—and so the list could continue. These relationships have been considered in many publications[1] and there is no need to go over the same ground here.

It is worth emphasizing again that to ascribe both physical and mental attributes to a single entity, a person; or to affirm, as I have tended to do with reference to the evolutionary context, that mental activities are properties of matter organized in the way we call human brains in human bodies is not to mean that mental processes are *caused* by purely physical, physiological events and that they are 'nothing-but' such events. The emergent mental attributes are attributes of the new whole (man's-brain-in-man's-body), which requires specific and appropriate concepts and language ('laws' even) to describe the inter-relatedness of its activities. These concepts and languages cannot in principle be broken down into those applicable to the component units of structure and activity, in this case anatomical, physiological and biochemical (cf. the discussion of Polanyi's analysis of the relation of the engineering language appropriate to engines *vis-à-vis* the physics of an engine's component pistons, etc., Chapter 3, (4) and (5)).

This way of talking about man has a significant consequence concerning his possible future evolution. Whatever form such evolution might take it is clear that it must be of such a kind that it transcends, or incorporates into a more comprehensive diversity-in-unity, both the physical and mental activities which constitute man as he has emerged from biological evolution. Any prognostication of what this new humanity might be and

---

[1] Just to mention a few: Rushworth, Whitty, Smythies, Price and Cleobury in *Biology and Personality*, ed. I. T. Ramsey (Oxford, 1965); Sherrington, Adrian, Clark, Brain and Penfield in *The Physical Basis of Mind*, ed. P. Laslett (Oxford, 1957); *The Brain*, ed. D. Paterson (B.B.C. Publns., London, 1969); Lord Adrian, *Factors in Mental Evolution* (Oxford, 1960); J. C. Eccles, *The Neuro-physiological Basis of Mind: The Principles of Neurophysiology* (Oxford, 1953); E. C. Rust, *Science and Faith* (New York, 1967), pp. 207–39; I. G. Barbour, *Issues in Science and Religion* (London, 1966), pp. 347–64; and, of course, the classic *Man on his Nature* (Cambridge, 1951) by C. S. Sherrington.

how it might appear is deferred, since it will depend on an understanding of how evolution in men is thought to be proceeding now.

The introduction of the entity of 'person' as that of which both physical and mental attributes may be predicated is consistent with our individual sense of being one person, but it is not, on this account, meant to deny the very real and familiar dichotomy in our experience. The mental event of willing to raise one's arms seems to occur in a quite different milieu of space and time from the actual movement of muscle and bone then set in train after the ionic pulses have passed through brain and nerves. Although it is still *our* consciousness which undergoes this mental experience and *our* arm which rises, nevertheless the dichotomy remains baffling and part of the data of both science and philosophy. The interrelationship of the two sets of data remains unsolved. Linguistic analysis has clarified our ways of speaking of them and rightly exorcized any ghostly entities in hypothetical machines. Man remains a diversity-in-unity and neither the diversity nor the unity can be properly denied as being characteristics of man, who standing at the summit of the evolutionary process, himself reflects on the ladder by which he has climbed out of insentient matter.

(b) *Man evolving: an unfulfilled paradox*

This dichotomy in the human experience and the resulting tension and sense of incompleteness, tragedy even, to which it gives rise at first appears to be a situation specific to man. The nature of the incompleteness is indeed unique to man but further reflection on the character of the evolutionary process and the conditions of emergence of new forms suggest that each stage of evolution represents not only a new attainment but also a more acute inadequacy of realization of potentialities. We have already seen (Chapter 5 (5)) that there is a kind of structural necessity in the evolutionary process in so far as complex forms of matter first emerge in the cosmos by developing out of simpler forms and depend for their continued existence on incorporating (i.e., feeding on) the structures of other simpler forms. Because of these necessary structural relationships, each level at every temporal stage in evolution expresses a potentiality, until then unrealized, of the preceding forms of organization of matter.

Post hoc, we can see that each level was, at that point, also an inadequate realization of the potentialities of matter, which still had the possibilities of taking on many new forms, and the cosmic development shows that eventually it did so. Thus each stage had a 'value' in so far as it represented a new level of organization of matter and so made new developments possible, but it also represented hitherto undeveloped possibilities whose range had been brought into sharper definition by the fact of that stage having been reached at all. Thus, until the small building-blocks (amino acids and bases) of proteins and nucleic acids had arisen by chemical processes in some hidden pools of the water on the Earth's surface, the possibility of living matter emerging based on macromolecular assemblies of these small molecules was extremely remote. As soon as these macromolecules did form, not only did the probability of the emergence of living matter enormously increase, but the forms it would actually take when it did emerge were thereby limited, and made more precise and specific. This is but one illustration of how each stage represents not only the emergence of a new form but the sharpening, defining and focusing of the future possibilities as yet unrealized.

In man, the stuff of the universe (we still have to call it 'matter') has become conscious and self-conscious, aware of its past evolution and, more to the present point, aware that it has a future. In man the evolutionary process has become aware of itself: but man is an organism who uses his intelligence and his organizing and communicating abilities to shape and choose his own environment which then reacts back on himself and so alters his future possibilities. Natural selection has ceased to be the means whereby man's future is shaped in the way it set the course of all his predecessors. Man's evolution is now dependent on man's action on himself and on his environment and these actions depend on his choices, aims, ethics, inherited culture through education (a 'Lamarckian' influence this), his development of creativity, and so on. Huxley summarizes this by asserting that in man evolution has become 'psychosocial', 'internalized, conscious and self-directing'.[1] Earlier I put this epigrammatically in the statement[2] that in man 'evolution' has become

[1] J. Huxley, *Evolution as a Process* (London, 1954), p. 13.
[2] Chapter 3 (7), p. 103.

'history'. Man is the first organism to be conscious of the possibilities and potentialities which are open to him and aware of
his freedom to choose by altering both himself and his environment. The next stage of evolution from man, unlike the earlier
ones, depends on the freely-willed conscious response of the
latest organism (man) to the challenge of what he might become. For in man the evolutionary process has given rise to a
creature conscious of where he has come from and capable of
seeing where he might go—and capable of accepting or refusing
the challenge. Man is challenged by an immense variety of
calls—to creative activity, to loving actions, to duty, to social
justice; but in all these respects the best and wisest of men
recognize the failure of their societies. Man is the only creature
who, aware of the pinnacle on which he stands, is also tragically aware of the possibility of his not fulfilling his own
potentialities.[1]

This sense of paradox and tragedy in human existence imbues
not only his reflections on the wider destinies of man but also the
individual's own self-consciousness. The dichotomy of experience within the single human person, to which we have already
referred, entails a recognition of the finiteness of the individual
human life, for even though our mental acts seem not to be
located in space and time yet we cannot avoid recognizing the
limitation of our bodies to a finite time; and that our inner
experience is vulnerable to the physical disintegration of our
bodies. The individual's sense of incompleteness and inadequacy
is enhanced by the immense growth in human knowledge as a
whole, for the gap between the scope of this knowledge and the
finitude of the individual's intellectual power becomes increasingly marked. Those men who, viewed from any external viewpoint, would often be regarded as the most creative and fulfilled
persons have usually been the most sensitive to the incompleteness of their achievements, and to the brevity of human life, and
have had that sense of travelling to, but never arriving at, any

[1] Cf. The mood of public discussion surrounding the first landing of a man
on the moon in July 1969, which was greeted both with adulation (e.g., 'The
greatest moment since creation' of President Nixon) and with mounting
cynicism, and despair, at the failure of man to feed the undernourished millions
of his own kind and to prevent men from slaughtering men in Vietnam and
Biafra.

resting-place for human strivings where all is fulfilled.[1] We are all so aware of this tragedy and finiteness of human life at our acutest moments and it has been so much the theme of the foremost artists and thinkers that there is no need to stress it further. In this century, modern means of communication have not only, curiously enough, heightened the sense of isolation of the individual, but have also made us more aware than ever of the failures of man as a social animal. For example, we now see that practically no other species of living creature kills its own kind —indeed they kill almost only when they are hungry (in accord with 'structural necessity', Chapter 5, (5)). Yet man, and most savagely in this century, attacks his own kind, and moreover plunders his natural environment, on a scale impossible to and unequalled in other creatures—and this is the organism with all the creative potentialities which we saw as emerging out of the evolutionary process (Chapter 3, (7)). 'Corruptio optimi pessima.'

We have the paradox of man as the pinnacle of the cosmic development so far, for his mental activities transcend it all, yet at the same time tragically aware of his personal and social shortcomings and subject to the tension between the awareness of the finitude of his individual life and the infinity of his longings. He is aware both of that from which he has evolved and also of his tendency always to fall short of the full realization of his own individual and corporate potentialities. Thus the non-realization of the potentialities inherent in the universe has in man become the responsibility of that creature himself. This non-realization when it comes in man does so as a result of his own lack of response to the creative nisus[2] which appears to exist in the universe. This is quite different from the situation of unrealized potentiality in the molecule or cell which is eventually realized in, inter alia, living organisms. That the potential of man is not fully realized is now the result of his own choice. This constitutes a break in the evolutionary process which had hitherto depended on the continuous operation of

---

[1] Cf. (as in Chapter 1) the men of faith in Hebrews 11 who 'confessed that they were strangers and pilgrims on the earth' who 'desire a better country', amongst whom was Abraham who 'went out, not knowing whither he went' but 'looked for the city which hath the foundations whose builder and maker is God' (R.V.).

[2] Nisus = effort, endeavour, impulse (Shorter O.E.D.).

natural 'laws'. For man appears to himself[1] to have a free will allowing him to make choices, and is free to fail to respond to the challenge presented to him. The Genesis story which depicts evil as entering the universe with man when he acquires the 'knowledge of good and evil' is a shrewder diagnosis of the human condition than is usually allowed.

Man's dilemma is real, for how is he to know which way to go, to which challenge he should respond, what his real potentialities might be? What does it involve to be a man, to be fully a person? What should constitute personalness in its richest manifestation? What should a man—what should men—strive to become? Moreover, given that he knew the answers to these questions, how is a man—how are men—going to be able to overcome their inherent limitations and deficiencies freely to will to move in the sought-after direction? For any such change of direction cannot be imposed, if it is to be effective in his 'inner', mental life. The evolutionary sequence clearly shows that the answers to these questions are vital for man and his future but at the same time provides nothing from within the process itself which will tell us what men ought to become, how they should achieve their ends in a way which recognizes their personalness, that psychosomatic unity which differentiates them from the rest of the cosmos.

2. THE CHRISTIAN VIEW OF MAN AND OF HIS FULFILMENT IN CHRIST, AS GOD INCARNATE

It is appropriate at this point to attempt to summarize the Christian account of man, or rather, some important features in this account which have significance in the light of the scientific perspective.

(a) *Man, his sin and 'Fall'*

The early Christian, and especially the New Testament, understanding of man is rooted in its Hebraic background,

[1] The question of the extent to which man is truly free continues to divide philosophers. The present writer accepts that the range of action over which there is genuine freedom for the individual is always more restricted than he thinks. Nevertheless, the mature man's acceptance of responsibility for his actions is a significant indication that there is a range of possibilities within which he is free to choose and, as our conscious lives are dominated by this sense, I have found the use of the phrase 'free will' unavoidable in this context.

though this was sometimes overlaid by later Hellenistic influences. For the Hellenistic distinctions between flesh and spirit, between body and soul, and indeed those between form and matter and between the one and the many, were never made by the Israelites.[1] In particular, the concept of an immaterial entity, the soul, imprisoned in a material frame, the body, is entirely contrary to their whole way of thinking. 'The Hebrew idea of personality is an animated body, and not an incarnated soul' affirmed H. Wheeler Robinson over forty years ago[2] in a famous epigram, and subsequent intensive analysis and philological studies have not substantially altered this assessment of this underlying common theme in the Old Testament view of man. Thus, more recently Eichrodt[3] described this view in the following terms:

Man does not *have* a body and a soul, he *is* both of them at once.

Of the greatest consequence, however, is the realism in biblical psychology, which brings the body into organic connection with the psychic life. Here we have an affirmation of human existence in the body, with all that follows from this. For the body is not an object which we possess, but which stands outside our real being; it is not simply the natural basis and instrument to which we are assigned, but which does not belong to our essential self. It is the living form of that self, the necessary expression of our individual existence, in which the meaning of our life must find its realization. Hence the body cannot be despised as the prison of the soul, or feared as the enemy of the spirit. On the other hand, it is equally not regarded in a materialistic light as the real man, a being who can find the goal and meaning of his existence in physical events. Instead it is understood as in all its parts the medium of a spiritual and personal life, which stands under divine vocation, and finds its nobility in being God's image.

This is not to say that, within this view of man as a psychosomatic unity, there was no awareness of the distinctive character of the inner life of man as contrasted with the external physical processes. For there is a word for the living body of a

[1] J. A. T. Robinson, *The Body* (London, 1957), p. 11.
[2] H. Wheeler Robinson, *The People and the Book*, ed. A. S. Peake (London, 1925), p. 362.
[3] W. Eichrodt, *Theology of the Old Testament* (trans. J. A. Baker) (London, 1967), Vol. 2, pp. 124, 149. The whole section, pp. 131–50, must be referred to for a balanced account of what is here described so briefly and inadequately.

man, namely, *basar*, the 'flesh', which has a distinct range of usage from, and can occur in a certain opposition to other words, such as *ruach* (='vitality'[1]), *nephesh* (='person' or 'living being'[2]) and *leb* (='heart'[3]), which have a closer connection with man's inner, psychic life. For the principal feature of Hebrew anthropology, being the result of the direct experience of the living encounter between man and man, is to see man primarily as a unity with various differentiating organs and functions in any of which the person in his totality can express himself and be apprehended. Man is a unity and does not subdivide into immortal and mortal parts. Indeed, to the Hebrews, personal individuality was constituted not by the boundary of

[1] *Ruach* (q.v., Eichrodt, op. cit., p. 131 ff.) is best thought of as 'vitality'. Its basic and primitive physical meaning is that of 'air in motion, breath, breeze', and this has a natural connection with its meaning the supernatural force that comes on a man ('the *ruach* of Yahweh') or the natural energy within a man. The last-mentioned idea is closely linked with a later development when it came to denote what might be called the individual 'spirit' of a man, the organ of psychic life seen primarily as an ethical direction of the will, and as such coming directly under the influence of God. When this is the stress, it can be used to denote the spirit of Man in the wider sense, the higher spiritual function characteristic of man as a whole. It is the human *ruach* which is open towards the influence (the *ruach*) of God, but *ruach* is never used to mean a spiritual *alter ego* in man, which as his higher self might possess a more permanent mode of existence, superior to death.

[2] *Nephesh* (q.v. Eichrodt, op. cit., p. 134 ff.; J. A. Baker, op. cit. p. 151, n. 1 below, p. 110, n. 4). The common physical connotation was 'neck' or 'throat' and so, by a natural extension, 'breath' or 'breath of life', and then simply 'life'. In contradistinction to *ruach* in the sense of the life force or vitality present everywhere and existing independently of the individual, *nephesh* denotes the 'individual life bound up with a body' and thence 'the living individual himself' or a 'living being'. In the older English version of the Old Testament *nephesh* is often translated as 'soul', which is highly misleading, and is probably better translated today by 'person' (so Baker, loc. cit.). The individualistic reference comes out sharply when the word is used in place of the personal or reflexive pronoun (e.g., 'Why art thou so heavy, O my soul', Ps. 43, v. 5, Coverdale version) and also when it gives rise to another usage of the word, as an expression for being alive, and thence every type of wish, desire and urge, and feelings and emotion of a spiritual kind. In this development it come very close to one of the meanings of *ruach* (though a distinction remains, q.v. Eichrodt, op. cit., p. 140).

[3] *Leb* (q.v. Eichrodt, op. cit., p. 142 ff.) means basically 'heart', the physical organ, but this is conceived of as the organ of feelings, intellectual activities and of the working of the will—roughly, the organ of thought ('to say in one's *heart*'). The emphasis is on intellectional and volitional processes, especially on the element of responsibility, on the conscious and deliberate spiritual activity of the self-contained human ego, even when *leb* acts as a comprehensive term for the personality as a whole, its inner life and character. The *leb* is the centre of the psychic sphere, is not synonymous with flesh and is particularly God-related (cf. Ps. 73:25, Coverdale version, 'My flesh and my heart faileth; but God is the strength of my *heart*, and my portion for ever').

a man's body but by the indivisible responsibility of each man to God and so by the uniqueness of the divine call to him—and certainly not by his 'flesh' (*basar*) as such. The common themes of the variations executed by the Old Testament writers as they depict man in his various activities and relationships to himself, nature and God have been masterfully surveyed in a recent article by J. A. Baker.[1] He stresses both the 'earthiness' and the personal aspects of the Hebrew view of man in describing it in the following succinct terms:

Man is formed of matter. His every thought, feeling, action, his most transcendental conceptions, have their origin in, and are made possible by, the same basic particles as those from which the whole cosmos is built. It is through the body, therefore, that man has to live. His experiences are always physical experiences, even though they may be evoked by either physical or non-physical occasions— things, places, people, psychic events, mental concepts.
    . . . But the paradox of man's being is that, though he is thus physical through and through, he is also something much more—a non-physical reality, a person. This truth is bound up with his self-awareness, which is of such a kind that he can address himself as 'thou', and speak of his own personhood as if it were another being, someone whom he can judge, exhort, comfort. This personhood is a different kind of fact from the fact of his body; indeed, it is the determinative, classifying fact about him, so that it is only right to speak of even a deceased human being as a 'dead person', and not just as a physical object. Accordingly, to treat a dead man or woman as so much debris is a mark of inhumanity, and to be so treated is a just fate for the worst of mankind.

Thus, although it is not easy to develop any intellectually precise anthropology from the Hebrew literature, in this tradition of over a thousand years, a common theme—that of man as a psychosomatic unity—clearly emerges through all its variations.

This Hebraic background is the key to understanding the New Testament writers, especially St. Paul's use of *sarx* ('flesh'), *sōma* ('body'), *kardia* ('heart'), *nous* ('mind'), *pneuma* ('spirit') and *psyche* ('soul'). The relationships of these terms both to each

---

[1] J. A. Baker, 'Man: his nature, predicament and hope, (1) The Old Testament', in *Man: fallen and free*, ed. E. W. Kemp (London, 1969), chapter 5. I am much indebted to Mr. Baker for illuminating discussions on these questions.

other and to the Hebrew terms is a highly complex web which is not rendered less easy by variations of usage and meaning.[1] The consensus of scholarship indicates a view of man in the New Testament very much like that of the Old with respect to its understanding of man as a psychosomatic unity, a personality whose outward expression is his body and whose centre is in heart, mind and spirit. The contrast in some Pauline passages of *sarx* (flesh) and *pneuma* (spirit) is not, as is commonly believed, that of matter and body, conceived as evil, as against disembodied and eternal soul, conceived as good. For *sarx* possesses psychical characteristics and refers rather to man's total created nature in its weakness, in contrast with and distant from God, and sometimes as it directs itself away from God; whereas *pneuma* is that by virtue of which man is open and sensitive to the life of God. Living *kata sarka* ('after, or according to, the flesh') denotes wrong living not in the sense that matter or the body is in any way evil, but in the sense that it is living for the world and directed away from God, and a distortion of a man's relation to God. For further elaboration of the anthropology of the Biblical writers, the reader is referred to the works cited and their sources, but what clearly emerges is an affinity between the view of man as a psychosomatic unity in the Biblical tradition and that stemming from science, an affinity which has been obscured by the strong influence of some elements in Greek thought on the development of Christian ideas. As a result of these Greek influences, the characteristically Christian view has been thought to be of man as a union of two entities, a mortal body and an eternal soul. The preceding paragraphs indicate, at least, that the situation is not so simple, and that the view of man of the Biblical writers is rather of man as a psychosomatic unity and not as the dichotomy, or trichotomy, which much popular Christianity would lead one to suppose. Consistent with this background was the development of ideas in the Biblical tradition about death and its aftermath. The Hebrews did not, like the Greeks, think of the real core of personality, the soul, as naturally immortal and therefore existing beyond death in

[1] See, for example, J. A. T. Robinson, op. cit., and *A Theological Word Book of the Bible*, ed. A. Richardson (London, 1950) under *inter alia*, 'body', 'flesh', 'mind', 'heart', 'Adam, man' and also the wider survey of J. L. Houlden, 'Man: his nature, predicament and hope, (2) The New Testament', in *Man; fallen and free*, ed. E. W. Kemp (London, 1969), chapter 6.

an even more liberated form. The most they could imagine was a shadowy existence which was but a pale reflection of full life. Gradually, the sense that the timeless character of men's relation with God could not be ruptured by death came to the fore and, given their anthropology, a doctrine began to appear in Judaism of resurrection of the total person, which included some form of body, that is, some form of external expression of man's total personality.

The Biblical views of man, and the Christian teaching which stemmed from them, are thoroughly realistic in their recognition of his paradoxical character. It sees the height of his possibilities and his destiny with their occasional and intermittent realization, conjoined to a degradation and wretchedness which can engender only cynicism and a sense of tragedy: it sees his eternal longings and his individual mortality.[1] Man is, like all other beings, regarded by the Biblical writers as existing by the will of God who sustains the cosmos in being. He is furthermore regarded, especially by the 'Priestly' writer of *Genesis*, as created in the 'image'[2] and 'likeness' of God[2] in the sense that:

[On man] personhood is bestowed as the definitive characteristic of his nature. He has a share in the personhood of God; and as a being capable of self-awareness and self-determination he is open to the divine address and capable of responsible conduct.[3]

He is, however, regarded as responding only incompletely to, indeed rebelling against, the call of God to his high destiny and potentialities in relation to himself and his dominance of the earth. This failure to become what God intends him to be is freely willed by man and is, in essence, the setting by man of himself in the centre of his individual and social life. This constitutes 'sin', the breakdown of relationship between God and men or, rather, the non-attainment of that harmonious relation with God, in which God wishes man freely to participate. Only a self-conscious being could freely thwart the divine purposes. The Biblical stories of the 'Fall' in the early chapters of Genesis depict this perennial situation at a supposed point in time. For

[1] See J. L. Houlden, op. cit.
[2] Genesis 1:26.
[3] Eichrodt, op. cit., vol. 2, p. 126. The passage (pp. 122–30) associated with this quotation provides an illuminating account of the profound insight of the 'Priestly' writer of Genesis into man's relation to God.

as soon as a creature, man, became self-conscious (and there
was a real period of time, however imprecise, during which this
happened) and became able to choose, it then became possible
for actions and events to occur in the universe contrary to God's
creative purposes. For men were then, and have been since,
free to act in a way contrary to what they could discern frag-
mentarily of God's creative purposes for them and could repudiate God as the ground, centre, cause and ultimate goal of their
being. Heightened consciousness with acquisition of freedom of
choice could not but imply the possibility of spurning the best
and choosing the worst. Thus 'sin' and 'evil' became possible
and indeed actual, with man. Within this framework of Biblical
ideas, how were men to know what they should do and become?
Even if they knew, how were they to be enabled freely to choose
to do what God required, to act in accordance with his creative
purposes both for men and for their environment? Men need
to know which direction they should take and how to take it.
The Biblical authors thought they had had over the centuries
sufficient signposts from God himself concerning the direction
their lives should take and, speaking from within and out of this
development, the early Church in its preaching and writings
affirmed that this historical revelation had culminated in a particular person, Jesus of Nazareth. I have already given an indication of why I think the early Church were basically right,
allowing for all the particular myopia of their times. A full argument and apologia for this confidence in their evidence cannot
be developed now and we must pass on to summarizing what
is of ultimate significance in what they, and their successors in
the Christian community, believed had happened in and with
the coming of the man Jesus into history.

(b) *The impact of Jesus the Christ: on the understanding of nature,
     God and man*

    Even by the most humanistic criteria the impact of the thirty
or so years of the life of Jesus on human history, thought and
ideals is so complex and far-reaching that it is less like the
ripples emanating from the proverbial stone falling into a pond
than one of those great deluges which Leonardo da Vinci depicts
in his drawings after which the whole landscape has been unrec-
ognizably altered, never to be the same again. The life of Jesus

was brief and by public reckoning relatively obscure, certainly
in its location with respect to the centres of the contemporary
civilization, but as time has passed this man and this life still
have enormous evocative power over men's ideals and aspirations, however discredited, institutionalized and formalized the
body of his official followers may appear to be. *He* cannot at
least be ignored by anyone who is seeking to find and understand any significance in human life.

The early Christians, utterly monotheistic Jews though they
were, found themselves driven to the conclusion that in Jesus
of Nazareth God had in some sense revealed himself and had
acted in a way which had universal significance for man, a significance which was also a revelation of man in the sense of
revealing the full possibilities of human nature, hitherto unrealized and unattained. This conviction was expressed at first
in a variety of terminology and titles primarily of Hebraic origin
(e.g., Son of Man, Messiah (=Christ[1]), Kingdom of God, Son
of God), to be followed later by terms of a more Hellenistic
origin (e.g. Lord, Word (Logos), second 'Person' of the triune
God). Both of these sets of terms and those in which they express
the relation between Jesus and God and the meaning and
nature of what he did cannot be understood by twentieth-
century man without much exploration of the thought of the
first and immediately succeeding centuries A.D., however
familiar the words may be on account of the semi-Christianized
education to which most of us have been exposed. The quality
of this thinking about Jesus and his significance which, especially during the first four centuries A.D. but also ever since,
has engaged some of the most able and penetrating of human
minds is often underestimated and even ignored by otherwise
well-educated and informed people. I can only refer the reader
to the appropriate literature[2] and apologize for the apparently
dogmatic and partial character of the summary which follows,
as a result of a ludicrously severe process of condensation.

[1] See footnote 2, p. 160.
[2] For example: J. F. Bethune-Baker, *Introduction to the Early History of Christian Doctrine* (London, 1903, 1933); J. N. D. Kelly, *Early Christian Doctrines* (London, 1958); D. M. Baillie, *God was in Christ* (London, 1947); M. Wiles, *The Making of Christian Doctrine* (Cambridge, 1967); M. Wiles, *The Christian Fathers* (Philadelphia & New York, 1966); A. Grillmeier, *Christ in Christian Tradition*, trans. J. S. Bowden (London, 1965).

The Christian understanding of God's relations to the world we have already touched upon in earlier chapters. It must be recalled now to understand the significance attributed to Jesus' coming. Briefly it is that the world is dependent upon God for its existence and continues to exist only because of his continuing to will it so. God is not dependent on the world and is other than it, but creation, which is a continuous action of his will, has for God a significance analogous to the personal fulfilment of a human creator. Although other than the world, and so transcendent, God holds the world in being by his will in a way which is further indicative of the nature of God's being, that is, is indicative of the least imprecise ways of thinking of him. The world is created by God, in the timeless sense of the word 'create' which has been used above; but time is created with the world and in this dimension the world is seen to be in process of development, of evolution, in which new forms of its basic stuff emerge continuously, creatively but according to regularities of relationship which we call the 'laws of nature' of the stuff of the world. Through this knowledge of the world, our understanding of God is extended by attributing immanence in the world to him in the sense that it is held in being by his will and that this sustaining involves a continuous process of change. God in his transcendent aspect limits himself by bringing into existence something other than himself with its own laws of development, and to this extent creation is an act of that love which is a true description of God's being since it represents, by analogy, a centre of personalness which is self-limiting on behalf of another. This 'love that moves the sun and the other stars' eventually brings into existence, into the world he has created, through the matter he had endowed with this potentiality, a creature, man, who partakes sufficiently of God's own personalness that he may be described as the 'image of God'. Yet man emerging from, and as a new pattern within, the stuff of the universe is incomplete and unfulfilled and, although through his emergent personalness he now apprehends something of God's being and is aware both of himself and his environment, he invariably repudiates that co-operation with God wherein his potentialities might be fulfilled, and takes courses of his own devising. In all of these, man puts himself at the centre of his universe: this constitutes his 'sin' in the traditional language. His relationship with God is thereby ruptured or, rather, never becomes what God wills it should be.

The next basic and specifically Christian affirmation is rooted in history. It claims that, in a particular time and place in history, the God who had all along been immanent implicitly in the whole temporal creative process then expressed himself personally in and through a particular man, Jesus of Nazareth, who humanly speaking, was completely open to him. The effort to describe with least inaccuracy the nature of that one person who was, to the men who understood their experiences of him, God-and-man, God-made-man, the divine-Word-made-flesh, constituted in the long run a major transition in the way men thought of nature, God and man.

Men's understanding of nature was in the end transformed because if God had become fully man ('incarnate' is the technical word), then the world of matter organized in the form we call a man must have been of such a kind that God could express himself in it explicitly, as well as implicitly by sustaining that world in being. This constituted a repudiation of all attitudes to the stuff of the world which saw it as evil, alien to its Creator, a prison from which a non-material reason, or 'soul', must seek release. God was to be seen as achieving his ends by involvement with, immanence in, expression through the very stuff of the world and its events in space and time. Moreover, the assertion that Jesus was the ultimate revelation of God's being to men in a mode they could understand and appropriate, amounted, we can now see, to an affirmation that 'nature' in its actuality, materiality and evolution, of which Jesus was indubitably a part, is both potentially at least an expression of God's being and the instrument of his action. Paradoxically, the Christian claim asserts that God fulfils man's personalness, and satisfies his most 'spiritual' aspirations, by entering the temporal process of materiality as a man, made like all men of the component units of the stuff of the world.

Men's understanding of God was transformed because it was seen primarily as love—that is he in whom men live and move and have their being was seen primarily to be involved in the cosmos with the end of achieving man's fulfilment, the realization of his potentialities and the satisfaction of his aspirations, even at the cost of acute self-limitation of his own freedom of action. This was the inference ultimately drawn from Jesus's life, death, and resurrection, from two principal standpoints. Either, as with St. Paul for example, Jesus's life of self-offering, sacrifice and obedience to God and service to man in utterly personal encounter led them to see God acting in him and that this life was, above all, love in action. Or, as with the writer ('St. John') of the Fourth Gospel, Jesus's life, death and resurrection, was a revelation of the eternal communion of Jesus with the transcendent God so that Jesus's earthly life was seen as the uniquely true symbol and expression of God's unchanging nature, which could then only be designated as Love, in view of what had actually constituted that human life. Both of these approaches[1] originate in the experience of Jesus, which is recorded in the New Testament; one approach values that earthly life rather for what it effected as an instrument of God's action, the other for what Jesus is in himself as a symbol of God's unchanging nature and so a revelation of eternal truth. There is no contradiction here for what Jesus did is effective because of what he was and is, and what he was and is can be understood from what he effected. Different aspects of and elements in the primary experience of Jesus led to the one approach or the other. Men's experience that they had in some sense encountered God in Christ and that Christ's actions could be identified with God's action and the power of God which was released in their lives by this conviction, whether or not they were the primary witnesses, inevitably led to a new insight into God's being and a search for suitable terms to express this insight. This search was absolutely conditioned by the unity and oneness of God and an important development occurred in the second and third centuries based on the description of Jesus Christ as the *Logos* of God (Eng. trans.—'Word of God'), a term first applied to him in the prologue to the Fourth Gospel at the turn of the first century. In Greek thought *Logos* stood for reason in both the sense of the human capacity to discern and make order and in the sense of the principle of rationality of the cosmos (which strictly means an *ordered* world).

Man and the universe fitted together because of the *Logos* of the *cosmos*. The universe had an underlying essential and rational unity.

---

[1] We follow here the treatment of O. C. Quick, in his *Doctrines of the Creed* (London, 1938).

Man had an essential affinity with this ordering rationality of the universe by virtue of his reason, which was what distinguished him from every other existing thing.[1]

Jewish thinkers in the century or so before Christ had developed the similar conception of the divine 'Wisdom' which was a personification of the activity of God both in creation and in giving discernment to men to understand that creation.[2] Since *Logos* usually also meant 'word',[3] and in Hebrew thought the 'word of God' was his *fiat* and command, not least in creation, the two ideas fused in the minds of Jews familiar with the Greek idea of the *logos* of the *cosmos*. The experience of Jesus was interpreted in the light of this idea but the experience modified the idea, in an interplay which is reminiscent of that which occurs in the experimental sciences. This *Logos* language expressed the Christian understanding that the coming of Jesus Christ had been definitive for the understanding of the way in which man and the universe fit together and that within the being of God there was present a creativity which was personal, which ordered the universe, which awoke the response in man corresponding to this order, which existed eternally but was manifest in the man Jesus in history. 'The Word (*Logos*)' the prologue to the Fourth Gospel asserts, *per impossibile* 'became flesh (*sarx*)'.[4] It must be stressed that it was the experience of and facts about Jesus which led to this adoption of the *Logos* concept and not the concept which controlled the observation.[5] The primary experience determined the applicability of the terms and not vice versa, and because of this we can affirm that this use of the terms represents a new insight into God's being based on men's experience of Jesus. The insight implies that there is within the Divine life a diversity-in-unity which it is legitimate to denote by terms associated with person or mode of being.[6] Thus God in His mode which became incarnate is described as God the Son, the Second Person of what came to be called the Trinity.

[1] D. E. Jenkins, *The Glory of Man* (London, 1967), p. 39.
[2] Cf. Proverbs 8:22–31; Wisdom, 7:22–7; 9:1, 2.
[3] But not in the sense of 'individual unit of speech'.
[4] John 1:14 (N.E.B.).
[5] Jenkins, op. cit., p. 43 ff.
[6] See p. 125, n. 1.

Finally, man's understanding of himself was transformed by
Jesus. In Jesus, men came to see what all men might become:
the full potentialities of human nature are in their essentials
shown to men in Jesus. The title of 'Son of Man' which Jesus
especially appropriated to himself has both individual and corporate[1] references and may well have a Messianic significance;
but, be this as it may, it certainly has a human reference,
especially if in its most reduced meaning it signifies simply 'man'
or 'this man'. The humanity of Jesus stands out starkly in the
text of the Gospels without any attempt at reduction alongside
those actions, claims, and events which constituted the experience which impelled his monotheistic followers to acknow-
ledge him also as God-in-man. His humanity was seen to represent the ultimate in the fulfilment of human life by virtue of his
utter self-offering love to man and obedience to God which was
vindicated by his resurrection. It was the survival of no ghost,
of no eternal soul released from a corrupt body, that turned
upside down the lives of His disciples, but the transformation
of a complete human personality, which had been self-offered
to the point of a shameful death, into a new mode of existence,
able to express himself externally to the physical senses of his
disciples. The resurrection was not proclaimed as the survival
of man's soul—*that* would have caused no surprise in a Hellen-
ized Palestine—but as a distinctive act of God which had
transformed a whole person in his totality. This act of God was
seen first as an indication of the perfection of Jesus's self-offered
humanity, and also formed the basis of the earliest preaching:
'Jesus is Lord', the victor over all the powers and features of
the world apparently hostile to man. It also then formed the
basis of the Christian hope of the destiny of all men, who are
now enabled to partake and participate in that union with God
with is uniquely that of Jesus (the) Christ.[2] The Ascension, the
last of the definitive appearances of the risen Christ to his
disciples, historically clearly carried with it a sense that the
whole being of Jesus is now at the centre of the life of God

---

[1] As in the *locus classicus* of Dan. 7:13 f., where the figure 'like unto a Son of
man' seems to represent corporate Israel, as God intended that people should be
in the fulfilment of the destiny of man.

[2] 'Christ' is the Greek translation of the Hebrew 'Messiah' and means literally
the 'Anointed One'.

(whatever external manifestations accompanied that event as a matter of history). This life of Jesus, 'ascended' to God, includes his human life and so, especially in the Eastern Church, this ultimate event in the history of Jesus was seen as the sign that the destiny of a transformed humanity is to live within the presence of God. Thus by virtue of what that human life was and what it became, it was clear that a new view of man and of his potentialities was necessitated by the 'things about Jesus', and that the realization of these potentialities had been the purpose, in God's sight, of the Incarnation itself and of the life of the historical Jesus. 'Because of his measureless love', wrote Irenaeus in the second century, 'he became what we are in order to enable us to become what he is.'[1] In some Eastern writers, apparently this emphasis on man being raised to God, being 'deified', is particularly strong, e.g., Clement: 'the Word . . . became man so that you might learn from man how man may become God.'[2] Some Christians would regard the latter as too extreme a statement, apparently destroying the distinction between man and God, the created and the Creator, which persists even when man is perfected. This criticism cannot be directed at St. Paul's development of the parallel between Christ and Adam, whom he apparently, like all his contemporaries, takes as a historical figure with whom all men have a solidarity in their human, fallen, nature. He calls Christ 'the last Adam' and 'the second man'.[3] In this mythology, Adam was the 'first man' destined to become the crown and lord of creation, who repudiated his high calling by disobedience and so never became what God intended him to be. In Jesus Christ, in his perfected human nature, God achieves his purpose and Jesus is the new beginning of a fulfilled humanity which is, or is at least becoming, what God intends—so Jesus is a 'second Adam', a second progenitor of a mankind realizing its potentialities. 'If any man is in Christ, there is a new creation.'[4] 'The defaced image of the Creator is being renewed: the old humanity is being put off and the new humanity is being made, in which the former distinctions of

---

[1] *Adv. Haer.* 5, *praef.*
[2] *Protr.* 1, 8, 4.
[3] 1 Cor. 15:45, 47. N.B. 'Adam' = 'man', in Hebrew.
[4] 2 Cor. 5:17 R.V. margin; or, 'new creature' (R.V.); or, 'there is a new world' (N.E.B.); (*kaine ktisis*, in the Greek).

race, religion, culture and class are being done away.'[1] The love of God, which was expressed in creation and in his incarnation, acts in the individual man to fulfil his human nature if that individual will identify himself with Christ and follow his way of life. Thus 'grace', as this loving action is called, does not destroy but completes human nature.

(c) *Jesus the Christ as 'One Person in two Natures'*

These transformations of the understanding of nature, God and man which reflection on the data of Jesus's life, death, resurrection and ascension engendered were only elucidated along with a long development of thought in the Church which culminated in the Definition of the Council of Chalcedon (A.D. 451). In this development it had become clear that, to do justice to the data about him, Jesus Christ must be regarded as: truly God; completely man; indivisibly One Person; and both God and man, without confusion. Chalcedon concentrated on the relation of the human and divine natures and the centre of unity of Jesus Christ and its conclusions may be curtly summarized as 'One Person in Two Natures'. Expressed so tersely, the words are mere ciphers for many complexes of ideas. Thus, as the valuable recent treatment of D. E. Jenkins puts it:

'Person' stands for 'one existent reality', in fact for the personal and historical individual designated Jesus of Nazareth. 'Nature' stands for all that is required to be truly God and all that is required to be truly a man. Thus the Definition asserts that the proper Christian understanding is that our Lord Jesus Christ who is Jesus of Nazareth is all that is required to be God and all that is required to be a man. It also goes on to state that all that is required to be God does not contradict, diminish or distort all that is required to be man, and all that is required to be man does not conflict or lessen or alter all that is required to be God—and that, further, the co-existence of all that is required to be God and of all that is required to be man does not mean any separation or division. There is and remains one Jesus Christ, perfect in Godhead, perfect in manhood, and perfect in unity.[2]

---

[1] A. Richardson, in *A Theological Word Book of the Bible* (London, 1957), referring to Col. 3:9–11 (. . . 'you have discarded the old nature with its deeds and have put on the new nature, which is being constantly renewed in the image of its Creator and brought to know God', N.E.B.).

[2] D. E. Jenkins, op. cit., p. 49.

This same author, whose treatment brings out strikingly the significance of what Jesus was and did, and is and does, for our whole attitude to nature, man and God, goes on to say,

The Christian discovery on the basis of the givenness of Jesus Christ was that the man and the universe hold together because of the involvement of God to that end. Thus materiality and history provide the stuff for the attainment of ultimate reality and the fulfilment of absolute value. The distinctive Christian understanding of man and the universe is that, to do justice to the realities involved therein, and to be experienced by man in and through his life in the world, it is necessary to hold in distinction, and yet in union, that which is transcendent and wholly other to the universe and that which is immanent and wholly continuous with the universe. . . .

. . . Jesus Christ, because he is a man, is, like every other man, continuous as a physical organism with the whole of the rest of the universe. There is no more of an evolutionary break between the cooling of a spiral nebula and the man Jesus than there is in the case of any one of us. Between the cosmic dust and us there is no discontinuity. So Jesus Christ is all that is involved in being man including the possibility of analytical reduction to whatever are the units of the stuff of the universe.

But the Chalcedonian Definition is a symbol of the discovery and assertion that in the purposes of the transcendent and independent God, and by the power of this God, a union has been achieved between that evolutionary product of cosmic dust which is a human being and that transcendent and wholly other purposeful personalness who is God. Transcendent and independent personalness is at one with derived, dependent and evolved personality whose whole basis can be reduced to that impersonal materiality out of which it has developed and on which it depends. And the result is the personal union of God and man who is himself the person, Jesus Christ. In this there is discovered the personal fulfilment both of God and of man. We have the fulfilment of the personalness of God because God has achieved the expression of his purpose of love.[1]

This understanding of the significance of Jesus Christ which the Christian community arrived at with so much difficulty saw in him the hope of a new transformation of all men. To discuss how this transformation can occur in the individual man would take us deep into a discussion of how the apparently past historical fact of Jesus can be made effective here and now[2] in

[1] Op. cit., from pp. 53–5.
[2] In fact, into a discussion of what are technically known as the doctrines of 'redemption' and 'sanctification'.

drawing man into a new and fuller relationship with his Creator and so to an undreamt-of realization of his human, and so utterly personal, potentialities. 'I have come that men may have life, and may have it in all its fulness.'[1] This claim has the awkward quality of authenticating itself only as the consequence of a prior act of willing commitment in which a man identifies himself with Jesus Christ at least to the extent of attempting to follow his way. Theology and philosophy here merge into religion and existential commitment.

3. CHRIST AND EVOLUTION

The principal features both of the scientific perspective on man in the cosmos and of the Christian understanding of nature, man, and God have now been outlined and we cannot defer any longer bringing them into juxtaposition. That they have been kept too long apart, each in an introspective isolation from the other, is one of the causes of the impoverishment, I believe, of both our scientific-technological world and of the Christian community. Evolution takes on a new meaning and dimension if the 'things concerning Jesus' have the significance Christians claim; and he and the community he engendered have a new relevance for modern man if the scientific story is taken seriously enough to provide a new factual and conceptual framework for viewing man and the cosmos.

(a) *Evolution to man: in the light of Jesus Christ*

We have seen (Chapters 2, 3 and section 1 of this chapter) that the spectrum of the sciences demonstrates that man is clearly continuous with the material universe out of which he has evolved. It is therefore a fact, and a highly significant one, that the matter of the universe has been evolving into persons, a word designating *all* that it means to be a man (in the sense of section 7 of Chapter 3). We have seen, moreover, that future transitions in human life depend on man's choices in a way which never arose with his biological predecessors so that human evolution is now 'psychosocial'. But man is an unfulfilled paradox consequent on his being a person rooted in the materiality of the cosmos and tragically unable, and aware of this inability, to effect in any convincing way any transformation of himself

[1] John 10:10 (N.E.B.).

which would fulfil his potentialities. This desired transition, or 'mutation', is unimaginable on a purely scientific basis yet one has the intuition that it would be recognized at sight for what it was were it to appear.

Now in the light of Jesus Christ and the significance attributed to him on account of the data concerning him, it can be affirmed that the derived and evolved personalness[1] of man was in Jesus Christ united with that transcendent personalness who is the ground of all being and that this union is the consummation of human personality for which man yearns both individually and corporately.[2] It is a consummation in which men are invited to participate by identifying themselves with Jesus the Christ and by committing themselves to that to which *his* life was committed. The scientific enterprise leads one to a perspective of the cosmos in which personalness in man is the summit of the evolutionary processes which the matter of the cosmos has undergone. The 'things concerning Jesus' led their witnesses and successors inexorably to the conclusion that, in that Person, man was transformed so that he was a 'new creation' drawn up into the very life of God himself, the originator and sustainer of the creative processes of the cosmos. The results of the scientific and theological enterprises here complement and mutually fulfil each other so that some hybrid terminology seems called for which has reference to both. Thus one might affirm that in Christ a 'trans-mutation' (rather than the 'mutation' of biology) of human life was effected at a new depth of the personality and that men who participate in, or acquire, this new depth of life in Christ are becoming a new sort of human being (dare we say 'species'?). Such terms, although having the virtue of emphasizing the analogy with the earlier biological transitions, could be misleading if they led one to ignore the special character of the 'trans-mutation' effected in Jesus Christ. For this new realization of human potentialities occurs not in man's DNA but within his total personality. It is a function of the *whole* organism of the person including his self-conscious and mental life. The Christian transformation, once accepted as a reality through

---

[1] Employing the mode of expression of D. E. Jenkins, op. cit.

[2] One cannot help recalling here the individual pilgrimage of St. Augustine, as described in his *Confessions*, epitomized in the prayer to God on its first page 'Thou madest us for thyself, and our heart is restless, until it repose in thee', and his great corporate vision in the *Civitate Dei*.

reflection on the historical evidence, can properly be viewed as a new phase of that cosmic development which is disclosed by science and which had hitherto culminated in man, the unfulfilled person and paradox. The results of the two enterprises do indeed fit together with immense mutual illumination of each.

We had already seen reasons for thinking that since human evolution is now psychosocial, any further development depends completely on human choice of ends and ideals, and increasingly so as man extends his control and knowledge of his environment. Likewise, the Christian transformation has always been regarded as a response of the whole person (including an intellectual assent as well as an act of will) to the 'things about Jesus', that is, as a response by the individual to the call of his Creator to participate in and to forward the cosmic process.

Similarly, just as the 'psychosocial' transformation of man which biology now points to as the only possible one, must inevitably be that of a population of individuals to be effective, so the Christian faith has always viewed the response of the individual man to the divine challenge in Christ as the response of a man-in-relation-to-men. For the fact and form of the challenge are regarded as mediated to the individual by a historical community which was initiated by Jesus Christ and is the primary witness to him. Moreover, the individual when he responds can only make his response effective by participating in that historical community so that the response and new relationship can grow ('in grace') and so that his new mode of life can have an effect in transforming society into a new humanity 'in Christ'. The New Testament employs a number of metaphors to describe what this human community, the Church, might effectively come to be, e.g., the 'Body of Christ', the 'people of God'. No overweening arrogance is implied thereby for, like the individual, the community of Christians has not reached its perfection *in via*, it is not yet the 'Kingdom of God' or the 'new Jerusalem', any more than any individual Christian has attained any perfection that he can be aware of. Yet, and this is the Christian conviction, it is a community moving, like the individual, in the direction God intends and co-operating with his creative purposes. So the response to the challenge which is Jesus Christ only heightens the awareness of the individual, and of the Christian community into which he is incorporated, of his and their lack of fulfilment of God's purpose; and it restores that lost experience of hope, to which I have already referred. For if Jesus Christ has the significance which I have tersely summarized in the preceding section, namely that in him there was a union of the two natures of God and of man in one Person and that he effected a reconciliation between God and man, thereby transforming man, then men may know that the cosmic process has a direction which is concordant with the realization of their own personal and corporate potentialities—and so their own aspirations. The historical fact which is Jesus Christ is, when assessed fully, the ground for hope that the cosmic development has not, after all, come to an impasse in man, the unfulfilled paradox, that it is not after all 'played out'. For if Jesus Christ is both truly God-made-man and the only proper Man then he opens up to men the possibility of a new level of existence, which is both exemplified in him and made available to us through him and his continued action through the community he founded.

This transmutation of the individual and of humanity in Christ is entirely in accord with that psychosomatic unity which we saw so clearly stressed in the scientific study of man's origins. Man's spiritual and mental life is an activity of a whole organism and not of some entity other than his body infused into or attached to him. The Christian understanding of Christ was rooted in that Hebraic tradition which, like the scientific, though on a more direct and experiential basis, also saw man as a psychosomatic unity and could only assert the continuity of a man's relation to God beyond death in terms of a 'resurrection' of the whole personality, including some mode of external expression analogous to the physiological body. So too, the Christian church affirms primarily the historical fact of Jesus's resurrection as an act of God and, for this reason and no other,[1] affirms that all men, in so far as they identify themselves with him, have the assurance that God will act to bring their full person, as he did that of Jesus *qua* man,[2] into his presence beyond space and time.

[1] Cf. St. Paul in 1 Cor. 15, 'If Christ was not raised, your faith has nothing in it' (v. 17, N.E.B.).

[2] Cf. St. Paul again, 'As we have worn the likeness of the man made of dust [i.e., Adam], so we shall wear the likeness of the heavenly man [i.e., Christ]. (1 Cor. 15:49, N.E.B.)

Such language is bound to sound strange if we are not attuned to the use of metaphor and extrapolation which are necessary to speak of what is inevitably unobservable. There is, however, no need for our present purposes to be more definite or to go much beyond the primary apostolic experience of the resurrected Christ. Because of the records and testimony of that experience there is no doubt that the early Church affirmed a resurrection of Jesus which had an inevitably materialistic and Hebraic connotation. How 'matter is organized', to use our usual terms, when in the form of resurrected human persons in the 'presence' of God, we have no means of describing. The whole concept of resurrection, in distinction from that of immortality, includes certain key features: firstly, the resurrected human personality is continuous with the living human personality, including his molecular, material aspect, and is derived out of it without loss of individuality; secondly, this transition is effected by a pure act of God which (thirdly) is dependent on the individual's beginning to participate in that new feature of the cosmic process which is the life of men obeying God's will and thereby participating in that new mode of existence which was initiated by Jesus the Christ.

There is a further apparent coherence between the character of the evolutionary process and that of the historical Jesus Christ. The evolutionary process has already been seen to be, in a sense, costly (Chapter 5 (5)), in that newer and more complex forms of matter only emerge by imbibing less complex forms, which, if closely related to the new emergent, may even be superseded. There is at least a parallel in the significance attached to Jesus's suffering and death which are regarded, in the Christian faith, as the explicit manifestation, *qua* man, of Jesus's self-offering and obedience to the Divine will (not to mention the courage and strength of purpose this entailed), and also *qua* God-made-man, of the true character of God as self-offering love. Thus the significance attached to Christ here parallels a principal feature of the creative processes in the cosmos since the Christian believes that this self-offering act on the part of Jesus the Christ was representative and indicative of the true character of his incarnation, and so of God himself, and was also the historical act *par excellence* which shows how men may be 'made whole', that is enables them to become fully what

God intended them to be. So again if we regard this Christian 'trans-mutation' as at least consonant with and culminating the series of biological mutations, the same feature of costly offering appears—though in the case of Jesus it was consciously willed.

(b) *Man, Christ and God: in the light of evolution*

We have already seen (Chapter 5) that the evolutionary and continuous character of the cosmic processes of evolution emphasizes the immanence of God in the sense that God holds in being by his will the whole world of space and time, with matter and energy. The matter, etc., so held in being by God, has such properties and potentialities that it has, in the course of time, led to the emergence of more complex atomic, molecular, macromolecular and biological forms, up to man. God's immanence is expressed in the nature of matter, etc., as it in fact is or might become and not by any special 'spiritual' influence guiding or infusing the processes of evolution, at particular critical points. The creativity of God finds its expression in and through the matter itself—not as some separate entity infusing matter. There is no room for any *deus ex machina* or 'God of the gaps'. Yet the stuff of the world is of such a kind that in man persons emerge out of materiality. The connection between the personal (mental, spiritual, creative, etc.) activities of man and the physical structure which he possesses as a result of the evolutionary process is so close in the scientific picture that it weighs heavily in favour of the psychosomatic unity of man and so of the 'Hebraic' rather than the 'Hellenistic' anthropology, if we may so roughly epitomize these views. Unfortunately much Christian theology, both learned and popular, has been based on the latter, where the designation 'Hellenistic' refers to the concept of man as possessing an immortal entity ('soul') which naturally survives death. The scientific perspective is more consonant with the 'Hebraic' emphasis of the 'Biblical theology' of recent decades.

The evolutionary account of man's origins and such evidence as we have for his development likewise makes it impossible to assert that there was a point in time when man was in some sense innocent and perfect and after which he 'fell'. For all the evidence shows rather a creature gradually emerging out of consciousness into self-consciousness so that the first self-conscious thought was *ipso facto* the first possibility of free choice and of putting a consciousness at the centre of the universe as a rival centre to God. Thus the possibility of man not realizing the fullest potentialities of his nature (his 'sin') was an inevitable part of his personalness. Equally, however, the lack of realization of his potentialities was universal and the experience of every man. It is this interpretation of the traditional 'Fall' narratives to which our awareness of the evolutionary sequence now points. Here, as in many other instances, a discovery emanating from the scientific enterprise by showing some ways of speaking to be misleading and in parts false has opened the way to a deeper understanding of the Biblical stories. Science by eliminating a naïve literalism has restored the credibility of the early Genesis stories as dramatic accounts, not so much of history, but of the way things are.

The understanding of Jesus as God Incarnate also acquires a new relevance when he is seen as the consummation of a process of cosmic evolution which occurred as an expression of God's creative will. The meaning of the incarnation of God in the man Jesus and the realization of all that men might be, all that God intended men should be, in the person of Jesus of Nazareth is illuminated in various ways by the scientific account of man's origins. For God-becoming-man, the Incarnation, as an event in human history, can now be seen as the consummation of that evolutionary process in which the rise of man succeeded the general biological sequence. The sequence observed and inferred scientifically implies for Christians that both the processes of cosmic evolution and the Incarnation are alike expressions of the creative, self-limiting love of God. The expression of the being of God in Christ was particular, and explicit, whereas in the processes of creation it was general, and implicit, but it was the same God who was operative in both. Both involved self-limitation on behalf of an end in which, if judgement is based on its culmination in the risen and ascended Christ and God's indwelling man as 'Holy Spirit', derived and transcendent personalness enter into a new diversity-in-unity. Since God willed it so, we must presume that, in some sense, this consummation intensifies and enhances the inner life of God whose only name is Love.

The life, death, resurrection and ascension of Christ can now be seen, in the light of the scientific perspective, not so much as the sudden return of a God withdrawn from a rebellious empire, but as the culminating expression of a process through which God had hitherto been working. Why then and there, and in Jesus of Nazareth? The familiar arguments for a *preparatio evangelii*[1] still apply, but the particularity of the event of the Incarnation is not thereby reduced and this particularity must be grounded in the human individuality of Jesus and in his own willingness, *qua* man, to go on being the vehicle of expression of the divine life even when it meant turning his face back towards Jerusalem and the bitter death which awaited him there.

The affinity between the costliness of the evolutionary process and the individual self-sacrifice of Christ has already been discussed. The continuity of this process which culminates in Christ also alters the terms of reference of the framework for thinking about the 'redemptive' and 'reconciling' work of Christ. These are the descriptions classically given to describe the release of men from 'sin' once for all by virtue of Christ's death and resurrection and his restoration to a right relationship with God. It is closely linked with the idea of 'sanctification', the continued action in men of God the Holy Spirit[2] who, as it were, re-creates each man and so prepares him for the vision of God and that life in his presence which is 'eternal', beyond space and time. Traditionally, this work of Christ has been interpreted as something that occurred once in history and is effective in us here and now by virtue both of our solidarity as men with the humanity of Christ and our own act of will to be incorporated into that restored human nature which was Christ's. E. L. Mascall, for example, states it thus:

. . . the esssence of redemption lies in the fact that the Son of God has hypostatically united to himself the nature of the species that he has come to redeem and, by offering himself to God the Father in their nature, has offered them to God the Father in him; and, although of course it would not be maintained that this redemption operates, as it were, automatically in all the members of the human

[1] The events and circumstances which surrounded and preceded the life, death and resurrection of Jesus which are thought to have made it possible for a gospel to be proclaimed and to have helped its eventual spread.

[2] Chapter 5 (2) and later this section.

race by the mere fact that the Son of God has lived and died as man, it would be maintained that it operates in them by their incorporation into that human nature in its risen and ascended glory and by their co-operation with the grace that this incorporation brings.[1]

There is much to be said for this way of putting it but, apart from the direct biological connection, it is hard to see what sort of solidarity we might have with Christ (and even more so with the hypothetical Adam). Indeed the concept of solidarity seems too vacuous in any sense other than the biological, for it to be the foundation of a theory of the work of Christ. Moreover, although in this respect Mascall's statement is more attractive than some other classical images,[2] it relies on a static imagery in terms of which to describe what Christ did, and such imagery fails to make clear how what he did then is actually effective here and now to enable men to act in accord with the divine purposes. The very continuity of the evolutionary process culminating in Christ now necessitates an interpretation of the 'work of Christ' which will employ a dynamic imagery[3] and will make it clear how the *process* of re-creating the individual person-in-community is effected here and now by the Christ-event. This event must be seen as initiating a process which still continues and in which men are free to participate. To the expression of the total mystery which constitutes the Incarnation, and the work Christ accomplished, the classical images have made an extremely important contribution. However, the dynamic character of the cosmos which science has revealed, now renders these images archaic and necessitates a new understanding of the action of God in Christ. Our previous interpretation, in the light of the scientific perspective, was that the essence of human 'sin' was the reiterated and universal negativity of response of men to the call of their Creator to place him at the centre of their personal life and so fulfil their human potentialities, by becoming what he intended they should be, the culmination of his creation of derived personalness. Thus our picture of the work of Christ must make clear how the

---

[1] E. L. Mascall, *Christian Theology and Natural Science* (London, 1956), p. 38.

[2] I am thinking of the images of Christus Victor (the defeat of the powers of evil); of satisfaction for sins; of substitutionary atonement (whereby the Son's loving sacrificial death is accepted by a 'just' God in lieu of the death of sinners); of redemption (like a slave) from the bondage of sin.

[3] Cf. Chapter 1 (3) (d).

incarnate life of God-in-Christ renders that response positive, while remaining free, and thereby opens up for the individual and society a way forward to realize all that they have it in them to be according to the divine purpose.

The scientific perspective has led us to a point at which it becomes imperative to take seriously 'God the Holy Spirit', for he is the vital, processive link between God acting personally in Christ there and then in history and God acting personally in us here and now and indeed throughout created time and space. For God as Holy Spirit represents that mode[1] of God's being who is immanent in creation and who re-creates the inner life of man according to the pattern of Christ. He directs men to Christ and nurtures in men, through prayer, sacrament and obedience, the 'new creation' of man in Christ. He was also, according to the New Testament, as mentioned earlier,[2] operative in the crucial events of Jesus's own personal life: his power and presence at the Incarnation in the Virgin Mary and at the baptism of Jesus, where Jesus as man adopts his assigned role, are specifically mentioned; the Fourth Gospel stresses especially the close relation between the Incarnation and the subsequent possession of Jesus's followers by the Holy Spirit, and St. Paul describes the Holy Spirit as the agent of the resurrection and the source of Christian love.[3] In the light of the scientific perspective, a wider significance can now be assigned to God as Holy Spirit. For His action and presence in the Incarnate life, just described, cannot be discontinuous with his activity in the earlier stages of evolution culminating in man.

Cannot we therefore now think of God the Holy Spirit as the personal mode[1] of God's being who is immanent in the created world in an action which culminates in Christ and in what he can effect through Christ in Christian man, but who is also active at all the preceding levels? God the Holy Spirit would then be conceived of as the power and presence of God as he fulfils the potentialities of matter at each level and stage of the cosmic process through the laws it obeys. At every level the created order reflects in its own measure something of the quality of deity.

[1] See p. 125, n. 1.
[2] Chapter 5 (2) (cf. Luke 1:35, Mark 1:10, Rom. 1:4).
[3] Rom. 5:5.

From atom and molecule to mammal and man, each by its appropriate order and function expressed the design inherent in it, and
contributes, so far as it can by failure or success, to the fulfilment of
the common purpose.[1]

The continuing creative power which is manifest as a *nisus* at
all levels of existence to attain its intended form is the Holy
Spirit Himself. This process culminates in the Incarnation
where the 'form' intended is that of the Son, the Logos, the
'second Person' of God as Trinity,[2] and in men who participate
in this new life God the Holy Spirit is the agent of realization
of their human potentialities.

(c) *Christian humanism*

The scientific perspective therefore impels us to take a more
dynamic view of the creative working of God the Holy Spirit
and a view of his action in Christ and in Christians as continuous with his action in cosmic evolution. But this has further
implications, as the quotation from the late Dr. Raven's Gifford
Lectures hints. For if this continuous dynamic view be correct,
then when men transcend themselves in realizing their peculiarly
human excellences and capabilities they are doing so by virtue
of being possessed by God the Holy Spirit who is the creative
nisus of the whole cosmos, including individual men. We have
seen that the cosmos is one in which personalness, creativity in
picture, word and sound, mutual love, intellectual excellence,
simple goodness, and so on emerge only in man and are his
peculiar glory. It is a corollary of this understanding of the
creative process that these specifically human excellences should
be attributed to God the Holy Spirit working at a new level of
intensity in the matter from which, by natural law, he had
elicited man. Hence all human activities in which men are truly
and fully human and are acting in accord with the divine will
are to be seen as expressions of the creative immanent personalness of God—and *not* just those activities we restrictedly label
as 'religious', indeed perhaps these least of all, under many
circumstances today.

This vision of the continuity of the creative action of God as

[1] C. E. Raven, Gifford Lectures, *Natural Religion and Christian Theology*, vol. ii,
Experience and Interpretation (Cambridge, 1953), p. 157.
[2] See below for a discussion of Trinitarian doctrine.

Holy Spirit and the realization that human excellence, *for its own sake*, is the outcome of God the Holy Spirit's activity in man restores to its rightful place in the whole Christian scheme what can only be called 'Christian humanism'. This might have been protected by the realization that God was incarnate in a complete human nature, in the very stuff of the world, which therefore must have undergone the development he intended. So man with his variegated possibilities of individuality, relationships, social organization and creativity was what one can only presume God intended should evolve from insentient matter. Thus the exercise of any specifically human excellence, provided it is not directed contrarily to the divine purpose, is a realization of the potentialities God intended for man. To be fully human, to develop our special abilities and possibilities separately and together, is what God intended men should be and do. Christ himself represented human perfection not in its particular but in its most universal form. His is a human life which is itself a perfect creation expressing the fundamental elements of all perfected humanity. Christ was not the perfect artist, or composer, or scientist, or statesman. This would have been a restriction and limitation. His humanity is universal because it is potentially what all men have it in their nature to be. His life is a perfect life in the society of other men and the perfection of his humanity is all in his life, death, resurrection and ascension—the creation of a perfect human existence, not of a perfect sonnet, or theory, or sonata. Christ is the universal man because he is the fulfilment of those potentialities which all men have in common. Correspondingly, when individual men can fulfil their own individual perfections they are expressing God's intentions for them and God as Holy Spirit acts in their efforts. It is this correspondence, which has been too often neglected in Christian thinking, to which the scope and width of vista of the scientific perspective should re-direct the attention of Christians. The whole life of man is what God intended should reach perfection, and nothing human need be outside the operation of God's Holy Spirit. The secular and sacred can be one because it is all God's world and he made it so. A genuinely Christian humanism so based has immense implications for the Church and its attitude to natural resources, society, work, the arts, science and education. If Christians acquired an openness of this kind, it would restore the universality of the Christian faith which has recently been in danger of becoming the subjective belief of a private coterie.

(d) God as Triune

We have several times now[1] not found it possible to speak about the understanding of God on the basis of the Christian experience without referring to the being of God Himself. Because God was experienced as transcendent ground of all being ('God the Father'), as incarnate in Jesus ('God the Son'), and as possessing the disciples of Jesus ('God the Holy Spirit'), a threefold diversity within the never-doubted unity of the divine life was inferred. God is one and acts fully, completely, in all his manifestations (he is 'coinherent') yet the postulate of three modes within his being seems unavoidable and since the whole is suprapersonal and the individual modes cannot be less than personal, personal pronouns have been thought to be the least we can use in designating each.

Our argument so far has led us to see the one God as transcendent, incarnate, and immanent in one creative process, which is nevertheless distinguishable in three forms. As transcendent, God (the Father) initiates by his will the whole cosmic development; as incarnate, God (the Son) focuses and reduces his being into the confines of a human personality; as immanent, God (the Holy Spirit) works through the whole cosmic development, which culminates in the life 'in Christ' now available to his creature, man. These three modes of activity have been variously designated (*persona*, in Latin; *hypostasis*, in Greek; 'person', least satisfactorily, in English) and the terms express the difficulty of asserting the unity and the diversity-in-unity simultaneously.[2] The diversity implies a mutual relationship which most writers have taken as a new intensity of God's essential being as self-offering Love (*agapē*) which Christ manifested at the human level. Oneness does not imply simplicity[3] and in the being of God implies a new intensity of

---

[1] *Inter alia*, Chapter 5 (2); Chapter 6 (2) (b); Chapter 6 (3) (b).

[2] A geometrical analogy could be the three cross-sectional planes of a three-dimensional solid?

[3] Cf., for example, L. Hodgson, *The Doctrine of the Trinity* (London, 1943) and C. Welch, *The Trinity in Contemporary Theology* (London, 1953).

integration of diversity which is beyond human experience. This intensity of unification with no loss of individuality is of the essence of the divine life, for God holds the whole cosmos in being, and transcends space, time and all the events of space-time without destroying the individuality of these components. The doctrine of three persons in one Godhead can easily be reduced to what appears to be arithmetical nonsense.[1] Nevertheless, its affirmation remains the over-arching keystone of the Christian insight and its very difficulty serves to remind us that a complete harmonization of all our understanding of God lies beyond human language and imaginings and beyond life itself —and Dante, as he expresses so sublimely in the last Canto[2] of *Il Paradiso*, experienced no less.

[1] It must be noted that those who are Three are not completely identical with him who is One.

[2] q.v. the end of Chapter 8.

CHAPTER 7

Matter in the theological and
scientific perspectives

I. THE EXISTENCE OF A CHRISTIAN VIEW OF MATTER

There was a tendency amongst Christian thinkers in response to the controversies with T. H. Huxley, which followed the publication of Darwin's and Wallace's ideas, to find their way out of the impasse then created by reverting to a naïve dualism in which the physical and biological world was assigned to science and that of 'mind' and 'spirit' to religion in general and Christianity in particular. This saved Christians from thinking too hard about the developing sciences and salved the consciences of the scientists who were thereby freed to get on with their job. As discussed in the Introduction, this they unfortunately did and the scientific and Christian communities continued, and still continue, to go their separate ways. Yet the Christian faith should not have delegated to science all the responsibility for formulating ideas concerning the stuff, the matter, of the cosmos. For its teaching about the 'two natures' in the one 'person' of Jesus had, as we have seen, profound implications about what was possible in the material universe which includes men's bodies and personalities (Chapter 6). Moreover, by their character some of the central practices of the Christian faith predispose and point to, even if they do not logically compel, a certain way of regarding the material aspects of the cosmos. I refer to its sacramental use of bread, wine and water. Technically, these have been denoted as the 'matter' which constitutes the appropriate sacrament along with its particular 'form'. In these sacramental communal acts of worship a particular significance is being attributed to these very material objects in a Christian context. Coherent with and, to some extent, implicit in this usage there is a teaching concerning the meaning to be attached to matter, the stuff of the cosmos. For it is a generally recognized feature of a sacrament that it is something singled out and set apart, yet of a universal character. Hence we might reasonably hope that from an understanding of the significance of the Christian use of the matter of bread and wine in the eucharist, in particular, further insight into the meaning of the material cosmos might be derived. *Mutatis mutandis*, we might hope that light will be thrown on the meaning of the sacraments by our scientific understanding of the behaviour and potentialities of matter. It must be stressed that these hopes are not certain of fulfilment, but nevertheless it seems worth exploring possible answers to the two questions that have been implicitly posed.

2. WHAT IS THE ROLE OF THE MATTER IN A SACRAMENT, IN GENERAL, AND IN THE EUCHARIST IN PARTICULAR?

The answer to this question is the subject of many of the standard works on the Christian sacraments. It is worth recalling briefly, though inadequately, the treatment of Quick,[1] who distinguishes between two functions of the matter of a sacrament: the *symbolic function* whereby the outward expresses what is inward, so that the inward is known; and the *instrumental function* whereby the outward takes its character from what the inward reality is effecting by it. (Here, by 'outward', Quick means everything occupying both space and time and, in principle, perceptible by the bodily senses;[2] and by 'inward' everything not so occupying space and time nor perceptible by the senses.) These two functions, the symbolic and instrumental, constitute the special character of the use of matter in a particular sacrament. Since there is a universal reference in each particular sacrament, the whole material order may be regarded as having this dual sacramental character in relation to its Creator. From this viewpoint, created matter has both the symbolic function of expressing God and the instrumental function of being the means whereby God effects His purpose.

The created world is valued by Christians as a symbol because it is a mode of God's revelation, an expression of his truth

---

[1] O. C. Quick, *The Christian Sacraments* (London, 1932), 4th ed.

[2] And, it must be added, scientific instruments regarded as extensions of the senses.

and beauty which are the 'spiritual' reality of the outward.[1] It is also valued by them for what is effected instrumentally through it, what God does for us in and through it, and through particular sacraments. Thus some meaning can be attached to speaking of the created world as a sacrament. However, it has to be admitted that this sacramental character is only implicit, and that it is obscure and partial both because of man's limited perception and sensitivity and because of evil. The significance of the Incarnation of God in a man within the created world is that in the Incarnate Christ the sacramental character of that world is made explicit and is perfected. In this sense, it seems legitimate to regard the Incarnate life of Christ as the supreme sacrament. For in this outward historical life, there is both uniquely expressed and uniquely operative that purpose of goodness which is the purpose of God himself that all life and all nature should fulfil.

In the sacraments of the Church, these two ultimate sacraments, the created order and Christ as God Incarnate, regularly come together and are brought into one focus in time and place. At the Last Supper, which developed into the church's eucharist, Jesus indentified the mode of his incarnation and atonement (his 'Body and Blood') with the very stuff of the universe, when he took the bread, blessed, broke and gave it to his disciples saying[2] 'This: my flesh for you' and similarly the wine, saying 'This, my blood of the (new) covenant', or, in parallel to the other saying, and more simply, 'This: my blood for you (and for many)'. It seems to me that it is a legitimate extension and development of the ideas and symbolic references which are implicit in these features of this original historical act to affirm that, in this act, a new value was set upon the bread and wine, obstinately molecular as they are, an intimate part of the natural world (corn and grapes) and a product of men's co-operation with nature (bread and wine). His words and these

---

[1] Cf. W. Temple, *Nature, Man and God* (London, 1934), Chapter IV.

[2] There has been much investigation of what is the most authentic account of what Jesus actually said over the bread and the cup. Those quoted represent a common convergence of several such studies; all agree that, as there is no Aramaic word for 'is', it is justifiable to insert the break indicated by the colon (for further discussion see, for example, J. Jeremias, *The Eucharistic Words of Jesus* (Eng. translation, London, 1966) and *The Foolishness of God*, by J. A. Baker (London, 1970), pp. 233–4).

acts seem to me to have involved a re-valuation of the things themselves, a new value assigned by God himself in Christ. A further development seems natural in the light of what has been said above about the universal references of sacramental acts: that to which a new value was imputed was not only these particular elements of bread and wine used in *this* way, but the whole created material world. For 'a sacrament has significance only as a part of a whole, of which the true relation to God is being represented and effectively realised'.[1]

This value was implicit, though not available to man's observation, in the act of creation. It remained a potentiality of matter, only partially realized by man. It was the ground of the Incarnation, the root of its possibility, for it was in his own world that God was incarnate in a man, that world of which he was already the formative principle. Even at the historic Last Supper, he was still largely incognito to his disciples, but to Christians he is now no longer unknown. So in Christian thinking the sacraments as a whole, especially the eucharist, manifest continually the ultimate meaning of matter as a symbol of God's being and as an instrument of his purpose.

The participants in the eucharist consciously and humbly offer their own lives in service to God and man in unity with the self-offered life of Christ which is believed to be present in and with the elements of bread and wine in the context of the total communal act. Thus, in this act, Christians believe they are participating in that re-formation and new creation of humanity which the coming of Jesus initiated through his Incarnation and self-offering, cogently represented by the bread and wine offered with sacrificial reference both at the original Last Supper and at every eucharist of the Church since then. This union with the offering of Christ is not self-directed but 'for others' and it is worth noticing that what Christ took and what is used in the Eucharist is the product of man's action on nature, bread not corn, wine not grapes. So the whole life and work of man may be regarded as offered in this act which is so closely associated with the historic initiation of the new humanity 'in Christ'. Many themes interlock and interweave in this central act of Christian worship and all of these themes have immense

[1] Quick, op. cit.

13A

significance for our attitude to the stuff of the cosmos of which we ourselves are part. It is interesting to note that the eucharist of the Christian Church, which, like a parabolic mirror, focuses so many parallel rays into one point of time and space, from the earliest times always contained overt references to God's creative activity, although this insight has been somewhat obscured since then. For the 'words of institution' of Jesus, already referred to, took place within the context of the Jewish mealtime blessings over bread and wine (the 'cup of blessing'). These blessings took the form of a thanksgiving to God for creation[1] and similarly directed thanksgivings appear in the earliest liturgies of the Church's eucharist[2] and are referred to by Irenaeus (*ca.* 130–*ca.* 200) whose words are worth quoting more fully.[3] He speaks of Jesus as

Instructing his disciples to offer to God the first-fruits of His own creation, not as though He had need of them, but, that they themselves might be neither unfruitful nor ungrateful, He took that bread which cometh of the (material) creation and gave thanks saying, This is My Body. And the cup likewise, which is (taken) from created things, like ourselves, he acknowledged for His own Blood, and taught the new oblation of the New Covenant . . . we ought to make oblation to God . . . offering first-fruits of these things which are His creatures.

These prayers of thanksgiving in the eucharist developed naturally into an offertory of other foods, in addition to bread and wine. In the course of a complex history this basic feature has been fragmented and overlaid but still survives in the '. . . these thy *creatures* of bread and wine . . .' in Holy Communion in the Book of Common Prayer of the Church of England and

---

[1] Probably the word over the bread was very close to the form in the present Hebrew prayer-book, 'Blessed art Thou, O Lord our God, King of the Universe, who bringest forth bread from the earth'. This is the pattern followed in the new Roman Catholic *Missa Normativa*.

[2] q.v. G. Dix, *The Shape of the Liturgy* (London, 1945).

[3] From Dix, op. cit., pp. 113–14 (Irenaeus, *Adv. Haer*, IV, xvii–xviii, 6). It is not suggested, of course, that Irenaeus, in using such 'first-fruits' terminology, had adopted the view developed here. No doubt he was much more concerned with parallels between certain biblical texts. However, it is suggested here that this feature of the eucharist of the early church to which he refers, does in fact represent a genuine insight and a growth point for legitimate further development.

in the '. . . *haec dona,* haec munera, haec sancta sacrificia illibata
. . .' of the traditional Latin Mass.

3. HOW DOES THE SCIENTIFIC PERSPECTIVE AFFECT OUR UNDERSTANDING OF MATTER?

The cosmic development from sub-nuclear particles through a hierarchy of levels of complexity to man we have seen (Chapters 2 & 3) to be continuous and creative, to occur by 'laws of nature' and to have a direction which culminates in man, even by the criteria of the biological sciences. But man has characteristics, in particular his personalness as an operative centre of rational action, which cannot be fully described by the language of the sciences and we have to recognize that man is not only a successful biological organism, *the* most successful, but that he also reflects, loves, hates, creates, plays, prays, and so on.

I have already in the discussion of the continuity of the cosmic development (Chapter 3) pointed out the need for us to revise what we mean by 'matter' and its associated adjective 'materialistic'. For, to recapitulate, just as the wetness of water, or the viscosity of a DNA solution, are not properties of their constituent atoms but features of their higher molecular and macromolecular levels of organization, so the properties and behaviour of living organisms can be regarded as manifestations of what matter is capable of if incorporated into certain organized structures. How such incorporation can come about and how the 'boundary conditions' of the structures are established are problems we have mentioned already. However, once they are established each level of organization displays its characteristic features. To be consistent, one would say that matter organized in the way we call man, especially, of course, in the labyrinth which constitutes his brain, is capable of activities which we describe as those of conscious thought, of self-reflection (self-consciousness), of communication with other human beings, and all the interrelations of personal life and ethical behaviour, or creativity in art and science and, indeed, all the activities individual and social which characterize and differentiate man from the rest of the biological world. In one sense, therefore, we can say that the potentialities of matter have been and are being realized in the cosmic development and that the evolution of man demonstrates the ability of matter to display properties which we normally, in talking about this human level of matter, call mental, personal and spiritual. In other words, by starting with the scientific perspective, we have arrived at a view of matter which sees it as manifesting mental, personal and spiritual activities. If we regarded these qualities as pertaining to a different mode of existence we might reasonably describe matter as the vehicle or means of expression of this mental, personal and spiritual mode. Whether or not we adopt this more metaphysical view of mind, persons and spirit, there is a real convergence between the implication of the scientific perspective for the capabilities of matter and the sacramental view of matter which Christians have adopted as the natural consequences of the meaning they attach to Jesus's life and the continued existence of the Church. For, as explained above, Christians have had to understand matter both in the light of their conviction that matter was able in the man Jesus to express the being of God, who is nevertheless regarded as supra-mental, supra-personal and supra-spiritual, so that his mode of being lies beyond any sequence of mental, etc., superlatives we can delineate; and in the light of their understanding of the sacramental acts of Jesus made in the context of his death and resurrection which originate the continuing life of Christian humanity. Briefly, it looks as if Christians starting, as it were, from one end, with their experience of God in Christ through the Holy Spirit acting in the stuff of the world have developed an insight into matter which is consonant with that which is now evoked by the scientific perspective working from matter towards man, and beyond.

This convergence now constitutes one of the major indications that the unity of outlook we seek (Chapter 1) has been rendered more attainable through the new scientific perspective than might have seemed possible a few decades ago. It also gives a new relevance to Christian sacramental worship which is now seen, not to be representing some magical, cabbalistic and esoteric doctrine, but expressing, in a communal context, the basic nature of the cosmic process which has brought man to this point and in which he is now invited by his Creator to participate consciously and willingly.

4. A SACRAMENTAL VIEW OF THE COSMOS

A summary of this sacramental view,[1] which incorporates the Christian understanding of God's trinity of being and which recognizes the new scientific perspective, might be expressed thus.

The world is created and sustained in being by the will of God, the will of perfect Love. The Son, the Logos, is the all-sufficient principle and form of this created order. At every level, this order reflects in its own measure something of the quality of deity. 'From atom and molecule to mammal and man, each by its appropriate order and function expresses the design inherent in it, and contributes, so far as it can by failure or success, to the fulfilment of the common purpose.'[2] The continuing creative power which is manifest as a *nisus* at all levels of existence to attain its intended form is the Holy Spirit himself.

The process of creation has been unfolded by the natural sciences as one in which new qualities and modes of existence continuously emerge out of simpler forms of matter by the operation of natural laws. The newer forms depend for their existence on the regularity of behaviour of the simpler entities out of which they are constructed but manifest properties and activities which are specific to that level of organization of matter. The level of organization which is reached in man represents not only a new summit in this evolutionary process but a new departure in the way in which change is initiated. For the mode of organization which constitutes man is characterized by activities and purposes which are describable only in terms of mind and self-consciousness. What appear to be freely-willed decisions determine how the individual and society develop and how they alter their environment, which then interacts with each succeeding generation. By his intelligent apprehensions of his environment, man has become the controller and arbiter of the

---

[1] The approach outlined in this chapter has, I find *post hoc*, been adumbrated long since in W. Temple's *Nature, Man and God* (London, 1934), Chapter XIX. But that profound book speaks in somewhat Hegelian terms and it is hoped that the approach offered here provides a contemporary elaboration of Temple's penetrating insight into the relevance of the Christian sacraments for providing the basis of a unified view of matter and of 'spirit'.

[2] C. E. Raven, op. cit., vol. ii, p. 157.

future of other forms of matter. He is nevertheless incomplete and unfulfilled and is tragically aware of the lack of fulfilment of his own potentialities. Thus it can be said that in man matter has become aware of itself, of its past, and of its unfulfilled potentialities.

The Christian claim then amounts to the affirmation that this whole process is the outworking of the creative being of God in the world and goes on to assert further that this process has culminated in the manifestation of God as a man within the created world. Only in a perfect man could God express explicitly his character as creative love: all other levels of created being up to this point were inadequate for this purpose and but implicit manifestations of a God still *incognito*. Thus, on the one hand, that which God has brought into existence, the stuff of the cosmos, is seen through the sciences to be the matrix and necessary condition for the appearance of purpose, mind, self-consciousness and values—all that characterizes the human person; and, on the other, the Christian revelation affirms that this character of the stuff of the cosmos is so fundamental that God expressed his being in, and acted through, the perfect culmination of this process in the person of Jesus of Nazareth. Indeed, in Jesus we really see what personalness amounts to. The two enterprises converge in a view of the cosmos which can therefore be properly called 'sacramental'. This technical theological term may be uncongenial to some (and not only to agnostics) but none other seems to be available which expresses so succinctly the simultaneous recognition of both the duality in our experience represented by the familiar body/mind, subjective/objective, etc., dichotomies and the observed fact, in our own experience and in the evolutionary development revealed by the sciences, that all the 'higher' qualities of existence which characterize personal and mental life are qualities of matter organized in particular forms and *only* appear when matter is so organized. The term recognizes bluntly the duality necessary in our talk about ourselves and about the character of the evolutionary process but also recognizes that the mental and spiritual features of existence are always features of, and only of, the organized matter which constitutes the observable cosmos. It is not pretended that description of the cosmos as 'sacramental' represents any real solution of the body-mind and related problems. Nevertheless, the use of this term not only avoids both idealism and the grosser forms of materialism (in the old sense) but also serves to stress the consonance between the scientific understanding of the cosmic process and the Christian understanding of the nature of man and God as thought to be revealed through the life and actions of Jesus, himself the culmination of that historical process which was at work in the Hebraic culture and which has been attested in its literature.

At the historical crisis of the human life of the Jesus, who was God incarnate, at the moment before 'the love which moves the sun and all the stars' culminated in the self-offering of the cross, Jesus himself gave a new significance to that characteristic act of man's creaturehood, his need to imbibe the world of matter in order to live. Eventually, that common meal became the symbolic meal of the new humanity stemming from Christ, one might almost say of a new level of evolution of human potentialities. For the Church believes that in the eucharist God acts to re-create both the individual man and society, to bring to fruition the purpose of his creation, manifest in the Incarnation. In the eucharist, God expresses the significance of the created material order and through it he is achieving his purpose for that order of protons, atoms, molecules, proteins, amoebae, mammals and man.

The eucharist focuses and summarizes the sacramental character of the whole existence and thereby enhances our appreciation of that character: it does not subtract from it. Thus in the eucharist is expressed the Christian understanding of *all* human activity, which is in accordance with God's creative purposes, as the end of man and as man's proper fulfilment. The eucharist is then the concentrated expression of what the whole of life is about, not just the specifically 'religiously' oriented moments. The eucharist stands as a regular expression of the life-affirming character of the Christian faith, of a Christian humanism which, stems from the fact that God has, *per impossibile*, expressed himself in and through an actual, historical human individual whose human nature is itself the outcome of the evolution of matter. While it expresses the sacramental character of the whole of human life as it fulfils God's purposes, the eucharist also links this understanding with the historical life, death and resurrection of the man Jesus and its significance for all men.

The perfect human life with which the Christian identifies himself by participating in the eucharist is the self-offered life of the 'man for others'. The eucharist is therefore not only fully human in its reference but also utterly and uniquely Christ-centred.

POSTSCRIPT

CHAPTER 8

Man in a scientific world

This essay began by describing and comparing the characters of the scientific and of the theological enterprises, primarily as experienced by participants in each. The experimental nature of both enterprises was stressed, not surprisingly with respect to science, but also with respect to theology. In this introduction, we saw the need of an integrated vision which comprehended both enterprises: or, to change the metaphor, we saw the need of a map which would elucidate the relation and aims of both explorations. The scientific perspective from matter to man and the distinctive features of the processes of inorganic and biological evolution were then described in Part I and, in Part II, the results of the theological enterprise, which I have called the Christian experiment, were set within the context of this scientific perspective.

The two enterprises, at first apparently so disparate, converged when, on the one hand, the immanental character of God's creativity and the incarnational–sacramental character of God's relation to the world and man was clearly brought out; and when, on the other hand, the continuity of development of the cosmos, which the sciences depicted, was recognized as culminating in persons, in human personalness. It then became apparent that the two enterprises not only complemented and completed each other, but that both could be taken into that single vision of existence which we have called sacramental. This term was meant to denote the necessity of materiality as the condition and sub-stratum from which that human and derived personalness has emerged with which the transcendent personalness of God can enter into a harmonious and enriching relation. This broad vista, which I have attempted to fill out with more detail in Part II, seems to me to have that unifying power which we set out to seek. It is not that the scientific and theological enterprises, indeed the whole gamut of human explorations, are in agreement in content or outlook, but that they appear to converge in what is implied in the broad sweep of their discoveries and intimations. If this is so, it is important that men should take the results of both enterprises seriously if they are going to live and act in a way which is in accordance with what is actually the case about themselves and their environment and its history.

Adoption of the sacramental view of the cosmos which I have outlined as providing at least the basic elements of a unified vision of nature, man and God, has certain consequences and implications for our present situation which are worth outlining briefly, as a postscript to the large vistas of the essay so far.

I. MAN IN CONTROL

The sciences reveal man as biologically the most successful of all organisms. His power and influence dominate the Earth and are even now penetrating into the space around. He has such control of his environment that practically all biological life is now within his power so that the fate of whole areas of the Earth's surface and of the species that live there depends on his will or whim. The effects of the actions of man on other living organisms and on his physical environment have reached the proportions of a threat to the very existence of a wide range of biological life, including ironically even his own. The writings[1] of Rachel Carson and others, the effects of the *Torrey Canyon* oil disaster, the slaughter of whales, the disappearance of African wild life, the sober assessments of professional biologists of the effects of insecticides and other pollutions, all point *inter alia* to an impact of man on his environment which would be seen to be reaching crisis proportions were it not for their slow insidious character and the predominantly urban and industrialized life so many of us lead. Man is the first creature in evolution who has deliberately shaped his environment and so has altered not only his own evolution but that of other living organisms. He therefore exercises powers over other creatures which are almost those of the Creator himself. Curiously, the mythical poems of Genesis 1

---

[1] R. Carson, *Silent Spring* (New York, 1963); M. Nicholson, *The Environmental Revolution* (London, 1970); H. Montefiore, *The Question Mark* (London, 1969); a short useful survey of the problems and their ethical implications is to be found in *Man in His Living Environment,* a report of the Church Assembly Board for Social Responsibility, Church Information Office, Westminster (London, 1970).

recognized this and affirmed man's role as the exercise of his powers in concordance with the creative purposes of God.

And God created man in his own image, in the image of God created he him; male and female created he them. And God blessed them: and God said unto them, Be fruitful, and multiply, and replenish the earth, and subdue it: and have dominion over the fish of the sea, and over the fowl of the air, and over every living thing that moveth upon the earth.[1]

It is a significant feature of this story, and of the subsequent Christian understanding of man's relation to his environment, that it is man as the image of God who is given this dominion. That is, it is man under God, as God's vicegerent, who is encouraged to exercise his dominion. Man's is a delegated authority in this story, which goes on to tell how man failed to have the right relation to his environment because he lost his right relation to God. 'Ye shall be as gods', said the tempter, and from that moment man is set in opposition to his environment. The story tells of a temporal sequence of events whereby it shrewdly depicts man's perennial situation. It is the exercise of man's powers under God which is the proper destiny of man *vis-à-vis* his environment. Anything else is disaster and leads to the wholesale plunder of natural resources by means of man's enhanced powers for the benefit of a myopic generation. Man has a responsibility under God not only to future generations of men but also to all forms of life. There is a level of destruction of the ecological balance which is not to be permitted. What this level is and how men should properly exercise their powers should be the pressing concern not only of scientists but of all Christian agencies and bodies: it has clearly not been the concern of the politico-military complexes which dominate so many nations, both 'East' and 'West'. The view I have outlined stresses this need for conscious stewardship not only on the grounds of self-preservation but on the grounds that all living forms have their value in the sight of God and are expressions of his creative powers and so are only to be destroyed from sheer necessity for survival. Man should be vicegerent not dictator. The Christian community must be far more active than hitherto

[1] Gen. 1:27, 28.

in consulting with scientists about the application of their work and the work to which individual scientists should devote their lives.[1]

2. MAN'S WORK

At its lowest level the Christian attitude to work has often been only a comforting gloss upon Genesis 3:18: 'cursed is the ground for thy sake; in toil shalt thou eat of it all the days of thy life. . . .' But at its best it has found expression in George Herbert's poem *The Elixir*:

> And what I do in anything,
> To do it as for thee:
>
> . . .
>
> Who sweeps a room as for thy laws
> Makes that and the action fine.

I wonder if a wider, and more Christian understanding of work is not now possible for us in the scientific perspective of evolution and the realization that the complex interactions of the modern technological world are a direct and inevitable outcome of man's intelligence, of his manual skill, and of his power to communicate—all of which have evolved out of the biological world which was his progenitor? For the Christian can affirm that it must have been God's intention that human society should have attained its present economic and technological complexity since he created man, through evolution, with just those abilities which made such complexities inevitable and he, at least, must have known that it would be so. The Christian, taking seriously the scientific perspective, can see his work not as being a kind of sacrificial offering for God, but actually as a genuine *opus Dei* of its own; for in building up human society one is joining in the creative activity of God who made it all possible. Even the humblest job in the complex society created by scientific technology in satisfaction of real and legitimate needs would take on a new point, if seen as part of that creative process which brought man and society into existence. For this creative purpose is seen, in the light of Christ, to be ultimately personal or, to be more accurate, to have the fulfilment of persons as its end and aim. This attitude to work has

[1] q.v., for example, *Biology and Ethics*, ed. F. J. Ebling (London and New York, 1969)—symposium of the Institute of Biology (No. 18).

been expressed in our time both by William Temple, who used to point out that it was the products of nature transformed by the work of man (bread, not wheat, wine, not grapes) which are the sacramental symbols in the eucharist, and by Teilhard de Chardin. The latter's words are addressed to Christians, but they are so apt and express so well the spirit of what I am trying to say that they are worth quoting more fully in the hope that even those who are out of sympathy with his particular, or indeed any, style of Christian devotion might recognize[1] that the provision of such a wider context for human work would, in principle at least, give it a new significance and so counteract the pointlessness and vacuousness which many feel about their day's work:

There was reason to fear, as we have said, that the introduction of Christian perspectives might seriously upset the ordering of human action; that the seeking after, and waiting for, the kingdom of heaven might deflect human activity from its natural tasks, or at least entirely eclipse any interest in them. Now we can see why this cannot and must not be so. The knitting together of God and the world has just taken place under our eyes in the domain of action. No. God does not deflect our gaze prematurely from the work he himself has given us, since he presents himself to us as attainable through that very work. Nor does he blot out, in his intense light, the detail of our earthly aims, since the closeness of our union with him is in fact determined by the exact fulfilment of the least of our tasks. We ought to accustom ourselves to this basic truth till we are steeped in it, until it becomes as familiar to us as the perception of shape or the reading of words. God, in all that is most living and incarnate in him, is not far away from us, altogether apart from the world we see, touch, hear, smell and taste about us. Rather he awaits us every instant in our action, in the work of the moment. There is a sense in which he is at the tip of my pen, my spade, my brush, my needle—of my heart and of my thought. By pressing the stroke, the line, or the stitch, on which I am engaged, to its ultimate natural finish, I shall lay hold of the last end towards which my innermost will tends. Like those formidable physical forces which man contrives to discipline so as to make them perform operations of prodigious delicacy, so the tremendous power of the divine attraction

[1] The claim that it might give this significance to work is not, in itself, an argument for the validity of this Christian approach, which is based, rather, on the wider grounds referred to elsewhere in this essay.

is focused on our frail desires and microscopic intents without breaking their point. . . .

. . .

Within the Church we observe all sorts of groups whose members are vowed to the perfect practice of this or that particular virtue: mercy, detachment, the splendour of the liturgy, the missions, contemplation. Why should there not be men vowed to the task of exemplifying, by their lives, the general sanctification of human endeavour?—men whose common religious ideal would be to give a full and conscious explanation of the divine possibilities or demands which any worldly occupation implies—men, in a word, who would devote themselves, in the fields of thought, art, industry, commerce and politics, etc., to carrying out in the sublime spirit these demands—the basic tasks which form the very bonework of human society? . . .

. . .

May the time come when men, having been awakened to a sense of the close bond linking all the movements of this world in a single, all-embracing work of the Incarnation, shall be unable to give themselves to any one of their tasks without illuminating it with the clear vision that their work—however elementary it may be—is received and put to good use by a Centre of the universe.[1]

Modern man needs the insights of the Christian community to point to the integrating centre of his existence, namely God who was Incarnate and is active Holy Spirit. Equally the Christian community needs the perspective of science to point the relevance of its own message and to sharpen its apprehension of man as a participant in creation and fellow-worker with God in his creative actions. This view has informed my support for Christian humanism which is the understanding that to be fully human, to become potentially what we have it in us to be, is the Christian life. For Christ's life is seen as the fulfilment of the universal possibilities of all men everywhere at all times, of what all men have in common—not only of artistic, scientific or other specific identifiable abilities.

3. MAN'S HOPES

One of the cardinal lost virtues of our age is that of hope, and this loss infects every aspect of our cultural and social life. The *angst* and despair, or the wild search for substitute ends which

---

[1] Teilhard de Chardin, *Le Milieu Divin* (London, Fontana Books, 1964), pp. 64–7.

dominates the affluent West, are sometimes attributed by Christians to a loss of the hope of personal 'salvation', conceived as the restoration of the eternal 'soul' of a man to the presence of God. But 'salvation' has always meant the 'making whole' of the whole man and we have already seen that the Hebraic-Christian view of man allowed no Manichaean dichotomy of an evil body from a spiritual, potentially good, soul. Thus, even on a Christian basis, men must centre their hope on this world in the sense that the arena of their hoping and striving must be the world they know. Any end to be achieved in a sacramental universe must be in and through the medium of the world we are actually in.

In spite of the optimism of scientific and technological endeavour in the short run, in the long term the predictions of science afford no grounds of hope or optimism for man. For example, Hoyle states that '5000 million years hence the oceans will boil because the sun will then have become too hot. No life as we understand it will then survive on the Earth.'[1] In Chapter 3, I reported the reception at Jodrell Bank in May 1968 of a signal which had come from a point 5000 million light years away. On the basis of Hoyle's estimate, we can now say that the light signal is already on its way which will find life extinct on the Earth, just as those now being received began before life here flickered into existence. Some writers, particularly in the popular press and particularly those who are the mouthpieces of the military and political complexes supporting space exploration, speak as if interplanetary space travel will somehow enable man to solve the problem of his future. Yet man has only just achieved a journey to the moon and back and this is, relatively speaking, only an exploration of his own back yard. The nearest star in our own solar system (*Proxima Centauri*) is $4\frac{1}{3}$ light years (25 million million miles) away. It might be possible for man to reach it in the course of a space-journey lasting a single human lifetime, if continuous acceleration were possible ('time-dilation' effects play havoc here with precise estimates). To reach another (hypothetical) planet on which man could live he would need to go to the furthermost reaches of our galaxy and possibly even to others. This would involve the need to transmit not individuals but societies across

[1] Hoyle, op. cit., p. 72.

space for hundreds of generations. No wonder Hoyle continues: 'A final question: Will travel between different planetary systems ever be possible? I am sorry to give an unpopular answer, but I believe this to be an uncompromising, no.'[1]

This judgement of the actual future of the Earth as a planet is more soundly based than the extrapolations based on the Second Law of Thermodynamics. This Law, which in one of its forms affirms that entropy in an *isolated* system always increases with time, has been applied by some to the universe as a whole. There is no knowing if this application is justified and any conclusions on this basis about the universe *as a whole* are unwarranted. The above prediction of the ultimate extinction of all life, including man's, on the planet Earth is based on observations of changes which occur in observable planetary systems in galaxies and can be taken as almost certain on this basis, without asserting what will happen to the whole universe.

Given this scientific background, the questions which are the concern of that aspect of Christian thinking called 'eschatology' (the doctrine of the 'last things') may seem less preposterous than hitherto. 'What is the final destiny of mankind in general?' is the question to which Christian teaching on the 'last things' has directed itself, prompted by the attempts made in the official Hebraic-Christian literature and in the less reputable apocalyptic writings 'between the Testaments'. Practically all scientifically-trained readers would now dismiss most of these writings, exemplified by the Revelation of John, as nonsense. Such a judgement would in fact be based on a failure to understand the poetic and symbolic use of language, and of the use of visual metaphor with a special literary background to express an author's conviction about the basic features of the unknown future in the light of the crisis of his own times, of the revelation in Christ, and of the justice and mercy of God.[2] For the moment I wish to stress not the content of Christian teaching concerning the 'last things' but its addressing itself to a question whose pertinence is now highlighted by the evidence we have that human life on the Earth will not last indefinitely. Five thousand million years is too long for our limited imaginations to grasp,

[1] Ibid., p. 74.
[2] The reader is recommended to read especially pp. 289–301 on the theology of the book of Revelation in the Commentary by G. B. Caird (London, 1966).

but it is the principle which is important. It seems we stand roughly at a point in time midway between the origin of life on this planet and its eventual demise. So the imaginative probings of the apocalyptic writers are at least addressed to a serious and meaningful question, even if their mode of expression is entirely foreign to us. We, in any case, may be able to do no better since symbolism and extrapolation are inevitable tools for prophecy (or 'futurology' as it now tends to be called), as is readily seen in Teilhard de Chardin's attempts to speak of the future goal of cosmic evolution, on which all converges, as 'point Omega'.

Perhaps this much may be said in the light of Christian insights and in the context of the scientific perspective. The cosmos depends for its being on God who is at least personal and has created personalness in man out of non-personal materiality. Man as a person in time can come into relation with the God who is the ground of all being and the Creator of time itself. In coming into such a relation both the individual and the community of such re-formed humanity enter into a mode of existence which, while fully expressible in the temporal, has its origin and being in God's non-temporal mode of existence. The basis of hope is therefore our trust that God will continue this relation and bring his purposes to fruition beyond even the disappearance of that part of the material cosmos, the Earth, in which he has been at work to achieve his ends. The Christian believes that he has and does act in this world to achieve his purposes and it is for man to co-operate in the terms I have already described. On this view, our destiny is in God's hands but our lives here and now are ours to direct, in his way, if we so choose.

Even in writing these few sentences, the power of language to express man's aspirations in accord with God's ultimate purposes scarcely seems available and only the language of symbol and poetry seems at all adequate. I began by expressing a somewhat wistful longing for that vision of unity which was Dante's. Let his be the last words for if it is in the end God who is our end, then it was he of whom Dante spoke in those sublime lines with which he concludes *Il Paradiso*.[1]

[1] From Barbara Reynolds's completion of Dorothy Sayers' translation (Penguin Books, London, 1962), Canto XXXIII, ll. 52–63, 85–93, 100–5, 121–45.

For now my sight, clear and yet clearer grown,
   Pierced through the ray of that exalted light,
   Wherein, as in itself, the truth is known.

Henceforth my vision mounted to a height
   Where speech is vanquished and must lag behind,
   And memory surrenders in such plight.

As from a dream one may awake to find
   Its passion yet imprinted on the heart,
   Although all else is cancelled from the mind,

So of my vision now but little part
   Remains, yet in my inmost soul I know
   The sweet instilling which it did impart.

         . . .

In that abyss I saw how love held bound
   Into one volume all the leaves whose flight
   Is scattered through the universe around;

How substance, accident, and mode unite
   Fused, so to speak, together, in such wise
   That this I tell of is one simple light.

Yea, of this complex I believe mine eyes
   Beheld the universal form—in me,
   Even as I speak, I feel such joy arise.

         . . .

That light doth so transform a man's whole bent
   That never to another sight or thought
   Would he surrender, with his own consent;

For everything the will has ever sought
   Is gathered there, and there is every quest
   Made perfect, which apart from it falls short.

         . . .

How weak are words, and how unfit to frame
   My concept—which lags after what was shown
   So far, 'twould flatter it to call it lame!

Eternal light, that in Thyself alone
   Dwelling, alone dost know Thyself, and smile
   On Thy self-love, so knowing and so known!

The sphering thus begot, perceptible
   In Thee like mirrored light, now to my view—
   When I had looked on it a little while—

Seemed in itself, and in its own self-hue,
   Limned with our image; for which cause mine eyes
   Were altogether drawn and held thereto.

As the geometer his mind applies
   To square the circle, nor for all his wit
   Finds the right formula, howe'er he tries,

So strove I with that wonder—how to fit
   The image to the sphere; so sought to see
   How it maintained the point of rest in it.

Thither my own wings could not carry me,
   But that a flash my understanding clove,
   Whence its desire came to it suddenly.

High phantasy lost power and here broke off;
   Yet, as a wheel moves smoothly, free from jars,
   My will and my desire were turned by love,

The love that moves the sun and the other stars.

APPENDIX A

Magnitudes expressed as powers of ten

One millimetre (mm) is the smallest division shown on ordinary rulers and is readily visible to the naked eye. It is the tenth part of one centimetre (cm), 2·54 of which are equal to one inch. So powers of 10 may be visualized in distances by comparing a millimetre with distances of powers of 10 of millimetres, as follows:

About:

10^1 mm =	10 mm =	1 cm		
10^2 mm =	100 mm =	10 cm		4 inches
10^3 mm =	1000 mm =	100 cm =	1 metre (m)	39 inches
10^4 mm =	10,000 mm =	1000 cm =	10 metres	33 feet
10^5 mm =	(100 thousand mm)	=	100 metres	109 yards
10^6 mm =	(1 million mm)	= 1000 metres =	1 kilometre (km)	$\frac{5}{8}$ mile
10^7 mm		=	10 kilometres	$6\frac{1}{4}$ miles
10^8 mm		=	100 kilometres	$62\frac{1}{2}$ miles
10^9 mm =	(1000 million mm)	=	1000 kilometres	625 miles
10^{10} mm =	(10,000 million mm)	=	10,000 kilometres	6250 miles
10^{11} mm =	(100,000 million mm)	=	100,000 kilometres	62,500 miles

This last magnitude, of 62,500 miles, is already more than twice the circumference of the Earth; even so the relation of one millimetre to this distance is just comprehensible. For higher powers, it is best to think in terms of areas and volumes. For example,

10^6 square mm = area of a square 10^3 mm $\times$ 10^3 mm
= 1 m $\times$ 1 m = 1 square metre   (Just over a square yard)
10^{12} square mm = area of a square 10^6 mm $\times$ 10^6 mm
= 1 km $\times$ 1 km = 1 square km   ($\frac{2}{5}$ of a square mile)
(*N.B.* 10^{12} = 1 'billion' in British usage
= 1000 billion in U.S. usage, in which 1 billion = 10^9).
10^{19} cubic mm is the number of cubic mm in a volume of dimensions
= 10^4 mm $\times$ 10^7 mm $\times$ 10^8 mm
= 10 m deep $\times$ 10 km wide $\times$ 100 km long
33 ft deep $\times$ $6\frac{1}{4}$ miles wide $\times$ $62\frac{1}{2}$ miles long
(roughly the volume of some of the larger waterways of the world, and comparable with the volume of water in, say, the Thames estuary).

202

One cubic millimetre is the volume of a small drop of water, so a chance of 1 in 10^{19} of life appearing on 1 in 10^{19} solar systems (p. 48) is just imaginable.

Negative indices can be visualized from the above figures. Thus 10^{-5} is $1/10^5$ and is the ratio of the length of 1 mm to that of 100 metres (*ca.* 109 yards).

The origin of life

In the early 1960s discussions on the origin of life on the earth centred on the ideas principally of Oparin, as described more fully in his book of that title, and those of Haldane and Bernal (see references below). Up to this point, the main experimental investigations which had been directed specifically towards this problem, as distinct from the whole gamut of 'molecular biology' and 'molecular biophysics' in its study of present living organisms, were those of Miller on the formation of amino acids and other significant small molecules when electric discharges were passed through a re-cycling mixture of gases of a composition similar to that of the primitive atmosphere of the earth before living organisms appeared.

Since then the speculation on the origin of life has been refined and sharpened by new experiments designed to mimic possible primitive chemical processes on the earth in the first million years after its formation 4000 million years ago. The supposed chemical processes must have been initiated by an influx of energy from various sources of which five seem likely to have been significant: sunlight, lightning, radioactive decay of potassium (^{40}K isotope), volcanic activity, and meteoric impact. Laboratory experiments have been made in recent years in which the various mixtures of gases which are thought to have been present at this period of the earth's development have been subjected to ultraviolet light, electric discharges (continuing Miller's earlier work), electron bombardment, heat and shock pressure waves, corresponding respectively to the natural energy sources already listed. In all of these experiments a wide variety of small molecules have been formed, including those which could act as the building blocks of the proteins, nucleic acids, polysaccharides and lipids which characterize living matter. Investigations have been made of the possible processes by which pairs of these small units might, by elimination of water molecules, join together to form the macromolecules needed for life. These processes include dehydration by heat, by polyphosphates and by derivatives of hydrocyanic acid, and the details of possible chemical processes have been elucidated. Presumably the macromolecules which have survived the processes of natural selection at the molecular level and are now present in living organisms have persisted because they were able to catalyse their own formation either directly or indirectly by catalysing the formation of a precursor. Possible processes of 'autocatalysis' and 'reflexive catalysis' have been envisaged and experimental models studied (cf. Calvin, 1969, for example).

Proteins are poorly reproducing but catalytically effective, while nucleic acids are accurately reproducing but poorly catalytic: a system in which both were coupled has distinct competitive advantages and ways in which this could happen have been considered (e.g., Calvin, 1969). The means by which such coupled systems might aggregate into regular larger-scale structures have been examined in the light of current knowledge about the self-aggregation of virus components and of multi-subunit enzymes. Yet other experiments, following the earlier lead of Oparin, have been directed to investigating how a suitable membrane might be formed around such viable systems not only to isolate it sufficiently so that its molecular identity and specificity are maintained but also to allow ingress to and egress from the system of building and waste materials.

In all of these speculations and model experiments, it becomes clear that one is concerned with chemical processes occurring in ordered structures, rather than with the random, statistical kind of reaction which constitutes the normal chemistry of solutions. It is becoming possible to see how such an ordered chemistry might lead to the non-random linear assembly of, for example, amino acids into primitive proteins and how one type of optical asymmetry (around the tetrahedral carbon atom) could become characteristic of living matter.

If these studies on specificity can be made more quantitative, they might provide the answer to the doubts which arise whenever the chances are calculated of forming specific sequences of the component units (amino acids, base-pairs) in proteins or nucleic acids. These chances always turn out to be minute within periods of the order of 10^9 to 10^{12} years, even on 10^{20} planets—let alone on one planet in the 10^9 years available (see, for example, the article by Salisbury (1969)). However, the chemical processes must have had a distinct specificity, as the unique optical asymmetry of biological compounds testifies, so that these processes were not random in the sense the calculations assume. The nature of the growing-points at the ends of a macromolecule may well predispose, even if it does not absolutely determine, the chemical nature of the next unit to be added (Calvin; 1969). Even so, this debate cannot be regarded as concluded and it is frequently conducted in terms of the supposed discrepancy between the 'information' necessary to define a particular living organism and that which could have been imparted to its nucleic acid by natural selection of random mutants (cf. Thorpe, Elsasser, Quastler).

The works listed below provide some suitable starting points for entering these discussions on the origin of life.

(i) *Books*

BERNAL, J. D. *The origin of life.* (London, 1967.)

CALVIN, M. *Chemical evolution.* (Oxford, 1969.)

ELSASSER, W. M. *The physical foundation of biology: an analytical study.* (London and New York, 1958.)

ELSASSER, W. M. *Atom and organism.* (Princeton, 1966.)

FOX, S. W. (ed.). *The origins of prebiological systems and of their molecular matrices.* (New York, 1965.)

HALDANE, J. B. S. (ed.). *Origin of life* (New Biology, No. 16). (London, 1954.)

KEOSIAN, J. *The origin of life,* 2nd ed. (New York and London, 1965.)

OPARIN, A. I. *The origin of life on the earth.* (London, 1959.)

QUASTLER, H. (ed.). *Essays on the use of information theory in biology.* (Urbana, 1953.)

RAMSEY, I. T. (ed.). *Biology and personality.* (Oxford, 1965.)

RUTTEN, M. G. *The geological aspects of the origin of life on earth.* (Amsterdam, 1962.)

THORPE, W. H. *Science, man and morals.* (London, 1965.)

(ii) *Reviews and Articles*

BARGHOORN, E. S. and SCHOPF, J. W. Microorganisms 3 billion years old from the Precambrian of South Africa (Fig Tree). *Science* (1965) **148,** 461.

CAIRNS-SMITH, A. G. The origin of life and the nature of the primitive gene. *J. Theoret. Biol.,* 1966, **10,** 53.

CALVIN, M. Chemical evolution and the origin of life. *Am. Scient.* (1956) **44,** 248.

CRICK, F. H. C. The origin of the genetic code; *J. Mol. Biol.* (1968) **38,** 367.

FOX, S. W. Prebiological formation of biochemical substances, in *Organic Geochemistry* (ed. Breger, I. A.) (New York, 1963), pp. 36–49.

GILVARRY, J. J. and HOCHSTIM, A. R. Possible role of meteorites in the origin of life. *Nature (Lond.)* (1963) **197,** 624.

MILLER, S. L. Production of amino acids under possible primitive earth conditions. *Science* (1953) **117,** 528.

MILLER, S. L. and UREY, H. C. Organic compound synthesis on the primitive earth. *Science* (1959) **130,** 245.

ORGEL, L. E. Evolution of the genetic apparatus. *J. Mol. Biol.* (1968) **38,** 381.

PONNAMPERUMA, C. and GABEL, N. W. Current status of chemical studies on the origin of life. *Space Life Sci.* (1968) **1,** 64.

SALISBURY, F. B. Natural selection and the complexity of the gene. *Nature (Lond.)* (1969) **224,** 342.

WALD, G. The origin of life (possibility of life based on elements other than carbon). *Proc. Nat. Acad. Sci. U.S.A.* (1964) **52,** 595.

WALD, G. The origin of optical activity. *Ann. N.Y. Acad. Sci.,* (1967), **69,** 352.

A discussion on anomalous aspects of biochemistry of possible significance in discussing the origins and distribution of life, November 1967. *Proc. Roy. Soc* (1968) **B171,** pp. 2–89.

Index

Twayne's United States Authors Series

Sylvia E. Bowman, *Editor*

INDIANA UNIVERSITY

Stephen Crane